Kahnawa:ke

THE IROQUOIANS AND THEIR WORLD

Editors
José António Brandão
Mary Druke Becker
William Starna

Kahnawà:ke

Factionalism, Traditionalism, and
Nationalism in a Mohawk Community

GERALD F. REID

UNIVERSITY OF NEBRASKA PRESS • LINCOLN AND LONDON

Library of Congress Cataloging-in-Publication Data
Reid, Gerald F., 1953–
Kahnawà:ke : factionalism, traditionalism, and
nationalism in a Mohawk community /
Gerald F. Reid.
p. cm.—(Iroquoians and their world)
Includes bibliographical references and index.
ISBN 0-8032-3946-7 (cloth : alk. paper)
ISBN 978-0-8032-2255-7 (paper : alk. paper)
1. Mohawk Indians—Quâbec (Province)—
Kahnawake Indian Reserve—History.   2. Mo-
hawk Indians—Quâbec (Province)—Kahnawake
Indian Reserve—Social conditions.   3. Mohawk
Indians—Quâbec (Province)—Kahnawake Indian
Reserve—Politics and government.   4. Kahnawake
Indian Reserve (Quâbec)—History.   5. Kahnawake
Indian Reserve (Quâbec)—Politics and government.
6. Kahnawake Indian Reserve (Quâbec)—Social life
and customs.
I. Title: Factionalism, traditionalism, and national-
ism in a Mohawk community.   II. Title.   III. Series.
E99.M8R45 2004
305.897'5542071434–dc22
2004048045

Contents

Illustrations

Tables

Acknowledgments

I must, first of all, thank the many people in Kahnawà:ke who have been so generous with their time in helping me understand the events and issues that are the focus of this book. A number of people deserve special mention. They include Presida Stacey, Satekenhatie, June Delisle, Joe Deer, Charlotte Bush Provencher, Sandra Beauvais, Annie Phillips Lahache, Stewart Beauvais, Hazel Norton, Christine Zachary Diome, Marvin Zachary, Mary Two-Axe, Frank "Casey" Nolan, Joe McGregor, Mike Woodrow, Tiorahkwathe, Rosie Beauvais, Mel Diabo, and the Elders Advisory Group of the Kanien'kehá:ka Onkwawen:na Raotitiohkwa in Kahnawà:ke.

I am especially grateful to the staff of the Kanien'kehaka Onkwawen:na Raotitiohkwa, whose assistance has been important at every stage of this project. In particular I acknowledge Martin Loft, Shirley Scott, and Alexis Shackelton. I owe special thanks to Kanatakta, the executive director. At an early stage in my research his questions helped bring focus to this project, and on many occasions he took time out of his very busy schedule to listen to my ideas and to read and offer critical comments on drafts of several papers that eventually made their way into this book. I also acknowledge the staff at the National Archives of Canada, in particular Bill Russell. Their cooperation and assistance were invaluable, especially in the early stages of my research.

I must also thank Larry Hauptman and Dean Snow for their support. At the start of this project I was a relative newcomer to the field of Iroquois studies, and both offered encouragement and helped me gain funding for the research. I also am grateful to Brian Deer and Audra Simpson. At several stages during this course of this project each took time to offer support, insight, and constructive criticism.

The Phillips Fund for Native American Research of the American Philosophical Society helped support the initial stages of my research, and its assistance is gratefully acknowledged. I received support from Sacred Heart University, especially the University Research and Creativity Grants Committee and Claire Paolini, the dean of the College of Arts and Sciences.

I must acknowledge Rosie Beauvais and the many members of her family. Since well before this project began they have welcomed me into their home, and during its course they provided me with support, comfort, and friendship. Nia:wen kowa.

Finally, and most important, I thank my wife, Mary, and my children, Emily and John, for their love and patience. They have helped to sustain me throughout this project, and I am profoundly grateful to them.

Introduction

The Focus of This Book

In broad terms, this book is a social, political, and cultural history of the Kanien'kehá:ka community of Kahnawà:ke in the late nineteenth and early twentieth centuries.[1] Situated just a few miles from Montreal, Quebec, Kahnawà:ke was established in the late seventeenth century and today has a population of about 7,200. My connection with Kahnawà:ke began in 1980, when I was hired by the education committee in the community to work for the Kahnawà:ke Survival School. The community had established the Survival School two years before in response, generally, to dissatisfaction with the off-reserve public secondary school attended by many young Kahnawakehró:non and, in particular, to Bill 101, the French-language law passed in Quebec in 1976 that refused to recognize the political sovereignty and cultural interests and autonomy of native people in the province. The Survival School was an experiment in native-run education that emphasized Kanien'kehá:ka culture, history, and identity, and I was hired to research and write social studies curriculum materials. At the time I was a graduate student at the University of Massachusetts. My research interests focused on the economic and social history of nineteenth-century New England and had little to do with the native people of North America; however, I did have experience as a researcher and writer and, through a colleague from the University of Chicago who was doing fieldwork in Kahnawà:ke, I was approached and eventually hired by the education committee to work with the curriculum development team. My work for the Survival School initially involved five months of intensive work, during which I produced *Mohawk Territory: A Cultural Geography*, a social studies and geog-

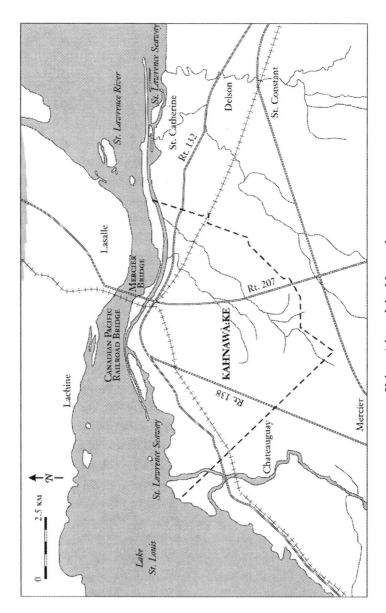

1. Kahnawà:ke and the Montreal area

1. The main village at Kahnawà:ke today. Photograph courtesy of Kanien'kehaka Onkwawen:na Raotitiohkwa.

raphy text that would be used in the lower grades at the school.[2] During this time I worked primarily in Kahnawà:ke and lived in nearby Montreal. Subsequently I returned to my graduate work at the University of Massachusetts, but I continued to research and write curriculum materials for the Survival School until 1983.

During the time I worked for the Survival School I developed a number of relationships and a few friendships with people in Kahnawà:ke. Inevitably, I also developed an interest in the community and its history. After my work for the Survival School ended, I continued to visit the community regularly. In 1989 I began teaching at Sacred Heart University, and I soon began taking small groups of students on brief field trips to Kahnawà:ke as part of a course I taught on North American Indians. The first of those field trips took place in the spring of 1991 after an invitation from one of the families I had come to know during my work with the Survival School. Since that time the field trips have continued, essentially annually. The present book grew out of an experience on one such field trip in 1995.

The 1995 field trip focused on schooling and educational issues in Kahnawà:ke. With this in mind, my students and I visited the Survival School and one of the local elementary schools and met with officials from Kahnawà:ke's Education Center. The students were impressed with what they saw and heard, but among other things they wanted to know more about the history of formal schooling on the reserve. They had become familiar with the development of the Indian boarding school system in the United States and asked some pointed questions about the development of schools in Kahnawà:ke, the connection to Canadian Indian policy, and the impact of the schools and formal education on the local society and culture. They had learned that early in the twentieth century Kahnawà:ke's schools had been taken over by an order of nuns, the Sisters of St. Anne, and they were particularly interested in the circumstances in which that development had taken place and how the people of Kahnawà:ke responded to it. I had few answers for their questions and realized that I knew very little about the history of education in the community or about the nineteenth- and early twentieth-century history of Kahnawà:ke in general. I resolved to learn more.

Initially I focused on the Sisters of St. Anne and the circumstances in which they assumed control of Roman Catholic schools in Kahnawà:ke in 1915. In the course of my research, two points quickly became clear. First, this period of Kahnawà:ke's history had received little scholarly attention. While there were some studies of Kahnawà:ke's seventeenth- and eighteenth-century history and its more recent development in the mid- and late twentieth century, little had been written about the history of the community during the nineteenth and early twentieth centuries. Consequently I found I would have to turn to archival sources and the people of the community themselves to learn anything substantive about this period of the community's history. Second, I learned that in the few secondary sources that did exist, the picture painted of Kahnawà:ke in the late nineteenth century was one in which the community had passively accepted acculturation and gradual assimilation into the larger Euro-Canadian society.

My initial research into some of the archival sources, especially the files of Canada's Department of Indian Affairs, proved enlightening. Not only did these sources provide a wealth of information on Kahnawà:ke's history, they often did so from multiple points of view. Within the files were the reports of Indian agents and religious officials, memoranda of Indian Department officials in Ottawa, newspaper accounts, photographs, maps, minutes of band council meetings, and, most important, letters, petitions, and other documents written by Kahnawakehró:non themselves. Further, these documents depicted a dynamic community, actively responding to the issues and circumstances of the time and making an effort to control and shape its future. Most especially, there was considerable evidence that people in Kahnawà:ke had not passively accepted acculturation and assimilation. While some Kahnawakehró:non actively cooperated with government officials and policies, others actively resisted; they sometimes worked together and at other times were in opposition to one another. One example comes from a petition sent to the governor general of Canada by 121 Kahnawakehró:non in 1890, soon after the band council system had been established on the reserve. The petitioners wrote, in part, as follows:

> The Franchise Act aims [at] the wiping out of our Nationality as Ro-di-no-shion-ni or Confederacy, and your Excellency may further understand concerning our wishes, that we like to retain and preserve our nationality as Ro-di-no-shion-ni . . . to reform and renew our national rites, and ceremonies, which it is the only remedy to preserve our nationality. . . . [W]e do not approve of the republic form of government, as we are not fully British subjects, but merely allies to the British Government. . . . We also find the republic form of government of electing person or persons that it is injurious to our national rights, therefore we wish to have the Hereditary chiefs to take the reins and conduct our welfare.[3]

As I would come to learn, the fight to restore the traditional government and maintain identity as "Ro-di-no-shion-ni" divided the community, a situation that persisted through the 1890s and into the early twentieth century.

A decade and a half after the 1890 petition many Kahnawakehró:non were fighting a decision by the Indian Department to establish the Sisters of St. Anne on the reserve and place them in charge of the community's Roman Catholic schools. One who was actively involved in this opposition was Peter J. Delisle. In

1914 Delisle traveled to Ottawa carrying a petition that had been signed by seventy-one Kahnawakehró:non. In part, the petition read as follows:

> We have been apprised that the schools in the village are to be placed into the hands of the nuns; with all respect due to them as a religious community, we vigorously protest their admission or permission to reside upon the Reserve conceded for our own special use. Our forefathers have always rigorously barred their entry and now we must persist to refuse to allow their coming on the reserve for manifest and obvious reasons. . . . Under a recent enactment we were compelled to submit to compulsory attendance at schools by our children, now, we are to be impugned in our rights of selection as to who should teach our children; must we resign ourselves to such injustice, or can it be said that we have no legal or moral interest in the matter?[4]

Despite these protests, the Indian Department went ahead with its plans to establish the Sisters of St. Anne in Kahnawà:ke. But Delisle and others persisted in their opposition. In 1917 the sister superior in Kahnawà:ke wrote to the deputy superintendent general of Indian affairs to complain about the "man at the bottom of the trouble":

> I beg to inform you that a certain Peter Delisle is influencing the Indians against our Sisters and their schools. He has been antagonistic to them from the very beginning and has taken every opportunity to undermine their authority. . . . He went so far as to say he would not allow the government to erect the sisters' dwelling house because he did not want any white people in the village. . . . If you desire the sisters remain in Caughnawaga I know you will find means to silence this Iroquois because it is a constant strain for them to cope with these inconstant and ignorant people.[5]

In short, my initial research in the archival sources revealed a picture of Kahnawà:ke that was quite different from that presented in published studies.

My initial research also suggested a different view of important political and cultural developments within the Kahnawà:ke community in the late 1920s. These developments, which include the reestablishment of the Longhouse within the community and of formal ties to the Confederacy, have been understood as the beginning point of a cultural and political revitalization that persisted through the twentieth century and continues to reverberate within the community today.[6] The evidence contained in the petitions, letters, and other sources suggested to me that Kahnawà:ke's cultural and political revitalization was rooted in conditions, events, and actions of the late nineteenth and early twentieth centuries and that the developments of the second quarter of the twentieth century were better viewed as the outcome of processes initiated decades earlier.

As a result, this book came to focus on the roots of political and cultural revitalization in Kahnawà:ke. The core of this revitalization involved, first, attempts to revive and refashion the community's indigenous political and cultural institutions and practices, an undertaking I refer to as "traditionalism." The central themes of this traditionalism were, initially, restoration of the community's traditional council of chiefs and, later, reestablishment of a Longhouse following within the community. Second, this revitalization involved reforging ties to and identification with the Rotinonhsiónni (Iroquois) Confederacy and engaging in the struggle for Rotinonhsiónni political and cultural autonomy.[7] I use the term "nationalism" for this movement involving organized efforts to identify with and develop ties to the Confederacy.

In attempting to understand traditionalism and nationalism in Kahnawà:ke in the late nineteenth and early twentieth centuries, I am especially interested in local dynamics. I attempt to trace how the interests and actions of individuals and groups within Kahnawà:ke moved the community toward political and cultural revitalization as they sought, sometimes in competition with one another, to respond to and shape the external forces impinging on their lives, their community, and their culture.

In the effort to grasp the local dynamics of Kahnawà:ke's cultural and political revitalization, I employ a framework centered on factions and factionalism. "Factions" are defined here as informal groups based on differential political interests, and "factionalism" is defined as a political process within a community that involves the interaction between such informal political groups.[8] The analysis of factions and factionalism has been an important theme in Iroquoian studies, and the seminal work in this regard is Fenton's "Factionalism in American Indian Society."[9] Reflecting the structural-functional paradigm of the time, Fenton approached the study of native political systems in general and factionalism in particular from a perspective that emphasized social equilibrium as the normal state of society. In his view, as noncorporate, ad hoc groups in society that formed around the rivalries of ambitious leaders and competed for political ends, factions were considered dysfunctional in that they undermined political stability and social unity. While the destabilizing effects might be held in check by effective leadership, averted by the formalization and ritualization of political division (as, he contended, was the case with the Rotinonhsiónni), or defused and redirected through out-group hostility and warfare (again, he suggested, as was the case with the Rotinonhsiónni), in his view it was a disorganizing form of political behavior that explained the fragility of Iroquois society at the local level and impeded the development of more complex forms of political organization.

According to Fenton, factionalism understood in this way was a central feature of Rotinonhsiónni and of Native American societies in general. He held that factionalism was so deep-seated in native societies that it persisted after European contact and

acculturation and modified whatever form of political organization was imposed on it. In his view, the colonial and postcolonial
settings provided new conditions for the development of factionalism and exacerbated this political tendency by inhibiting or
abolishing indigenous cultural practices that had served to check,
regulate, redirect, or defuse in-group political division, opposition, and hostility. Among the many works that followed Fenton's
lead in the analysis of factionalism among the Rotinonhsiónni
were Berkhofer's study of religion and political division among
the Senecas during the late eighteenth and early nineteenth centuries, Nicholas's analysis of factional politics at the Six Nations
Reserve in the mid-twentieth century, and Frisch's examination
of pan-Indianism and tribalism at St. Regis in the late 1960s.[10]
A common theme in these works was a view of factions and factionalism as symptoms of social disorganization and as disruptive
of political stability and social unity.

The view in Iroquoian studies of factionalism as dysfunctional
and factions as an undesirable social form mirrored studies of
factionalism in anthropology in general.[11] In the 1970s, however, a new perspective emerged within the field that emphasized
change and human agency and viewed factionalism as a dynamic
and adaptive means through which individuals and groups within
society mobilized resources and competed with one another to
adjust to, cope with, or alter changing environmental, technolog-
ical, social, and political circumstances. From this point of view,
factionalism is a legitimate political process that is common to all
societies—one that, over time, influences the direction of social
and cultural change. As Silverman and Salisbury have written,

> [Factionalism] is that part of the political process within a
> community which is characterized by the interaction and
> confrontation of multiple non-corporate sub-groupings—
> groupings that generally satisfy the criteria for being de-
> fined as factions. . . . [F]actionalism has an inherent dy-

namism. Factional confrontations are rarely balanced; one side gains and the other loses ground on every occasion. Each confrontation changes the terms on which the next confrontation will take place. In any confrontation the strategy of one side, or a particular combination of individuals in one faction, does not produce an exact mirror-image or collection of individuals on the other side. Reactions are, in fact, oblique and groupings are systematically unlike. Factionalism, in short, produces actions and reactions that do not simply balance out, but by opposing groups obliquely, it gives a net movement to the whole society, even if this is in a direction no faction intended it to go.[12]

For the most part, studies of factionalism among the Rotinonhsiónni did not reflect this new perspective and continued to emphasize the view of factions as dysfunctional and factionalism as disruptive and disorganizing. For example, in his studies of Oneida factionalism, Campisi examined the role of missionization in intensifying the split that developed between young warriors and older traditional chiefs as a result of warfare and ecological change during the fur trade period. He looked at how this set in motion a trajectory toward further political and religious division among the Oneidas during the late 1700s and early 1800s. He argued that the depth of these divisions compromised the Oneidas' ability to fend off Euro-American depredations and greed and led ultimately to the loss of their lands and the diaspora to Wisconsin and Ontario.[13] Richter also focused on the disruptive and disorganizing consequences of factionalism. He suggested that first the adoption of Christian and non-Christian war captives and then direct Jesuit missionization created a religious split within mid-seventeenth century Rotinonhsiónni communities that disrupted traditional ceremonies and political procedures, undermined community cohesiveness and collective identity, and set in place a pattern that would soon lead to the rupture of the Confederacy.[14] Shimony's analysis of a "conservative" revolt at the Six Nations reserve in 1959 represented a departure from the trend in studies of Rotinonhsiónni factionalism. She argued that the development of factions among Six Nations conservatives after the failure of their uprising gave rise to hostility, accusations of witchcraft, and illness, but that these events in turn led to a resurgence of traditional medical practices and a revitalization of the traditional culture as a whole.[15]

This book draws on the perspective of factionalism that emphasizes human agency and understands factionalism as dynamic and adaptive. It attempts to understand the internal and external ecological, economic, social, political, and cultural circumstances that confronted Kahnawà:ke in the late nineteenth and early twentieth centuries and to explain how the efforts of Kahnawakehró:non to respond to and shape those circumstances moved their community toward a political and cultural revitalization that was traditionalist and nationalist in character.

Note on Sources

To a significant extent, this examination of community division, traditionalism, and nationalism in Kahnawà:ke is based on primary sources, particularly the files of Canada's Department of Indian Affairs. Of course, as a source of historical insight, the files of the Indian Department must be approached with a critical eye. The Indian Department, which became independent of the Department of the Interior and was renamed the Department of Indian Affairs in 1880, was the main agent of the state in its efforts to acculturate and assimilate the native people within its borders. The kinds of records it maintained (and did not maintain), the content of those records, and even their organization can be expected to reflect the bias stemming from the fundamental mission of the Indian Department. This should be expected, especially in the case of reports, memoranda, and other documents written by Indian agents and other Indian Department personnel. Other limitations on the ability of Indian Department officials to report on and interpret events and issues in Kahnawà:ke also suggest the need for caution. For example, as outsiders who often did not speak the native language, it is likely that they did not always understand the nature of the events and issues on which they reported and acted. Also, by virtue of their position within the state apparatus and as its representatives within the Kahnawà:ke community, the agents and other Department officials would have had access to some arenas of the community's life, but not others. It is probably safe to assume that this was most true with regard to those individuals and segments of the Kahnawà:ke community that opposed and resisted Department officials and policies or that were engaged in patterns of activity that were not permitted or were contrary to those policies.

However, the files of the Indian Department are not limited to reports and other documents written by Indian agents and other Department officials. Also included are letters, petitions, affidavits, and a variety of other documents initiated and written by Kahnawakehró:non themselves, both those supportive of and sympathetic to the Department's policies and objectives and those who opposed and resisted them and sought alternative cultural and political ends. The number and variety of native-written documents relating to Kahnawà:ke that are contained in Indian Department files and that I consulted for this book is considerable, and they help to remedy the biases and limitations of the documents written by Indian Department personnel. In my use of these documents I have made an attempt to let the Kahnawakehró:non (and others) speak for themselves by often drawing directly on their written observations, arguments, testimonies, and pleas. Taken as a whole and used with a critical eye, the files of the Indian Department provide a valuable source of insight into Kahnawà:ke's history and the problems that are the concern of this book.

Oral histories provided another major source of insight, particularly for the events and developments surrounding the re-establishment of the Longhouse in the community during the 1920s and 1930s. These oral histories, recorded between 1997 and 2002, came from Kahnawakehró:non who through personal and family experience have an intimate knowledge of these developments. For this time and together with other primary source materials, the oral histories provide a rich and detailed view of this dynamic and complex period of the community's development.

Note on Orthography

In my use of Kanien'kéha terms in this book I have followed the orthographic system suggested by the Elders Advisory Group of the Kanien'kehá:ka Onkwawen:na Raotitiohkwa in Kahnawà:ke.

Kahnawà:ke

1. *"At the Rapids"*

Historical Overview of Kahnawà:ke to the Late Nineteenth Century

Rotinonhsiónni and Kanien'kehá:ka in the Seventeenth Century

In the sixteenth century the territories of the Rotinonhsiónni stretched across present-day upper New York State from the Hudson River west to the Genesee River. Protecting the eastern flank of the Longhouse nations were the Kanien'kehá:ka, or Mohawks, the Keepers of the Eastern Door. To their west were the Oneidas, Onondagas, Cayugas, and Senecas, the Keepers of the Western Door. The organization of these five nations into a confederacy with its Central Fire at Onondaga predates European contact and influence. Based on the clan system of the five nations and the principle of decision making by consensus, the Confederacy was a segmentary network of relations that joined households into villages, villages into nations, and the five nations into a potentially strong but potentially fragile political alliance.[1] According to Rotinonhsiónni tradition, the Confederacy was organized through the efforts of Deganawida, "the Peacemaker," to bring an end to the feuding and strife that had long characterized relations between the five nations. Dennis has argued that the Confederacy was created to bring peace not only to the five nations but to other native nations in the region as well.[2] On the other hand, Brandão has suggested that the alliance was the product of efforts by the five nations to defend themselves and wage war against their common enemies and thus was related as much to war as to peace.[3] Though the date of the founding of the Confederacy has been the subject of much debate, archaeological and historical evidence suggests that the Confederacy of the five nations was completely consolidated by the late fifteenth or early sixteenth century.[4] The population of the Rotinonhsiónni at this time is difficult to estimate, but by the 1630s their numbers exceeded 20,000.[5]

The largest of the five nations was the Kanien'kehá:ka, which numbered about 1,700 in 1580 and grew to nearly twice that size in the early seventeenth century. Owing to natural increase and the integration of large numbers of other native peoples through adoption, by 1634 they totaled more than 7,700 people living in four villages.[6] Early in the sixteenth century the Kanien'kehá:ka controlled and used a large territory extending from the Mohawk River in the south and the Hudson River, Lake George, and Lake Champlain in the east through the Adirondack region north to the St. Lawrence River and west to Lake Oneida. The villages of the Kanien'kehá:ka were along the Mohawk River west of present-day Albany, between Schoharie Creek and East Canada Creek. In the mid-seventeenth century the principal villages were Tionnontoguen, Kanagaro, and Ossernenon, which later became known as Kahnawà:ke.[7]

The first Kanien'kehá:ka contact with Europeans was in 1609 when a small contingent of their number encountered and was defeated by a French-Algonquian force under Samuel de Champlain at Ticonderoga. The confrontation defined Kanien'kehá:ka–French relations for the next half century. The Dutch, and later the English, sought to exploit the Kanien'kehá:ka's enmity for the French to curry their favor, establish trade relations, and forge alliances against the French. Trade with the Dutch was sporadic until 1624, when they expanded upriver from New Amsterdam and established an outpost, Fort Orange, on the doorstep of Kanien'kehá:ka territory at the junction of the Hudson and Mohawk rivers.[8] In 1634 a smallpox epidemic swept through the Kanien'kehá:ka villages and in a just a few months wiped out more than half the total population.[9]

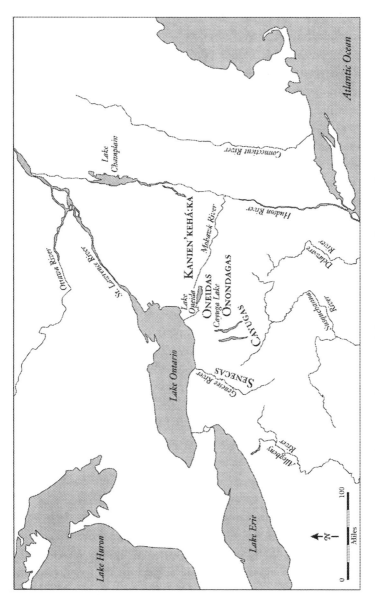

2. The Rotinonhsiónni and their territories in the sixteenth century

During the 1640s continued hostility toward the French and concern about French efforts to establish trading and military ties with their traditional enemies to the north and west led the Kanien'kehá:ka and the Rotinonhsiónni in general into a series of campaigns against French settlements and against the Hurons and other native nations of the Great Lakes region. It has been popular to attribute this pattern of Rotinonhsiónni aggression to economic motives, in particular to an effort to secure, protect, and expand their control over the European fur trade.[10] According to this view, Rotinonhsiónni success in realizing military and economic objectives also provided large numbers of war captives who were adopted and thereby offset the significant and devastating losses of population resulting from epidemics. Brandão, however, casts doubt on this view, which he sees as positing an assimilation of European economic values, and he offers an alternative interpretation that emphasizes the centrality of established Rotinonhsiónni cultural patterns and motives.[11] In essence, he turns the popular view on its head and argues that war against the Hurons and others was both a continuation of a pattern of rivalry and aggression that predates European contact and trade and an effort to deal with the death and loss of population resulting from epidemics and ongoing warfare. Specifically, he suggests that for the Rotinonhsiónni, warfare was a means to obtain captives for adoption to replace recently deceased family members or for use in the torture that was part of the grieving process for those who had experienced such losses. During this period the numbers involved in population loss, capture of prisoners in raids, and adoptions were significant. In his view, Rotinonhsiónni interest in trade and efforts to control trade were motivated less by economic gain and the desire for European trade goods than by the desire to obtain European firearms, keep them from their rivals, and thereby achieve their goals. For the Mohawks, as well as for the other nations, these adoptions had a significant cultural impact. Many of those adopted, the Hurons in particular, had been introduced to Christianity, and their presence opened the door to Catholicism and missionization among the Kanien'kehá:ka.[12] In time this would contribute to division and factionalism within the nation.

In the 1660s the English replaced the Dutch as the main trading partners and military allies of the Kanien'kehá:ka.[13] At the same time, the other nations of the Confederacy initiated peaceful relations and trade ties with the French. A number of factors encouraged the Confederacy to seek a more peaceful and cooperative relationship with France, including political and military setbacks in their relationship with other native nations allied with the English, the uncertainty of political relationships with the English as a result of their conflict with the Dutch, and their desire for increased and more stable access to firearms, ammunition, and other European trade goods. Famine, disease, and Jesuit influence also played a role in the development of a closer alliance with the French.[14] In 1665, over Kanien'kehá:ka objections and despite their continued state of war with the French, the Oneidas, Onondagas, Cayugas, and Senecas formally allowed the French into Rotinonhsiónni territory. The Confederacy was now split. With the Kanien'kehá:ka politically isolated, the French no longer feared the threat of the combined force of the Confederacy and attacked and destroyed the Kanien'kehá:ka villages on the Mohawk River. As a result, in 1667 the Kanien'kehá:ka sued for peace.[15] At this point they found themselves at the center of a struggle between the French (based in Montreal) and the English (based in Albany, formerly Fort Orange) for their loyalty and support. Gradually they found themselves realigning with the French.[16]

The Migration to Kentake

In 1667, with peaceful relations with the Rotinonhsiónni finally at hand, a few French *habitant* families took up residence on the south shore of the St. Lawrence River opposite the island and fortified village of Montreal, then a key transfer point in the growing French fur trade. The land they settled on was known to the Kanien'kehá:ka as Kahentá:ke, or Kentake, meaning "at the meadow," and to the French as La Prairie de la Magdelaine. It had been granted to the Jesuits by the king of France two decades earlier and was part of a broad, fertile valley extending from the St. Lawrence south to the Adirondacks and the Green Mountains. In the same year a small number of Christian Oneidas visited the area and were persuaded by the Jesuits priests to remain in the small farming-mission settlement.[17]

From this modest beginning the native community at Kentake grew rapidly. With only a half dozen families in 1667, it grew to nearly 500 people a little more than a decade later as Oneidas, Onondagas, Hurons, and, increasingly, Kanien'kehá:ka joined the new community. In 1673–74 alone there were 180 newcomers. That many of those who came were adopted war captives only contributed to its diversity and dynamism. Among those who came to settle at Kentake during these first years, many were Christian converts who were encouraged to migrate by the Jesuit missionaries and by the anti-Christian hostility and persecution they faced in their home villages. Increasingly, however, they came for other reasons, and many were non-Christian. The new community's position at a communications and transportation crossroads, the strategic location of the area relative to Montreal and Albany, and access to rich hunting and trapping grounds provided powerful economic incentives to resettle. So too did Jesuit offers of food, land, and houses. Others came to escape the violence and other social problems that alcohol fueled in their home communities. As Richter has suggested, Kentake offered a haven from the factionalism and strife in the home villages and a place where the traditional values of reciprocity and hospitality were still honored and practiced.[18]

Just two years after its establishment, the native and French communities at Kentake separated. This separation was soon reflected in a pattern of settlement in which the two groups constructed their dwellings on opposite sides of the Jesuit chapel, which was built in 1670. In 1676 the native community relocated about a mile upriver to more productive lands at a site near the Lachine Rapids (called the Sault St. Louis by the French), and renamed itself Kahnawà:ke, meaning "at the rapids." The Jesuit mission connected with the community relocated as well and was renamed Saint François Xavier du Sault. Before the move to the new site some Onondagas had left the community, and later many of its Huron members left. As a result, Kanien'kehá:ka increasingly dominated the Kahnawà:ke community. By the early 1680s the community included 120 to 150 families and numbered about 600 people.[19]

The depth of religious conversion and Catholic practice at Kahnawà:ke has been a matter of some debate. Indigenous spiritual belief and practice among the Kanien'kehá:ka emphasized giving thanks for the earth and its bounty, which had been created by spiritual beings and forces. Giving thanks was the central theme of a ceremonial calendar that included a series of festivals, each associated with an important transition in the environmental or subsistence cycle or important spiritual beings and forces.[20] Dreaming, too, was a central element of Kanien'kehá:ka spiritual belief and practice. Dreams were understood as an expression of the desire of one's soul or a supernaturally inspired message that, if not acted on, would lead to sickness and misfortune. To this end, ritual practice emphasized dream interpretation and, if necessary, dream inducement. Dream interpretation was an important individual activity, but it was a communal one as well, as in the Midwinter Festival, which initiated each new cycle of thanksgiving ceremonies. Dreams could be experienced naturally, but dreamlike states could also be induced by means of the sweat lodge, fasting, self-mutilation, and other methods.[21]

Blanchard argues that there was a significant persistence of native belief and practice in early Kahnawà:ke.[22] In his view, most

Kanien'kehá:ka who settled in Kahnawà:ke did so primarily from economic and political motives and engaged in Catholic practice only to the extent necessary to achieve a peaceful coexistence with the resident Jesuit missionaries. In addition, he argues, religious practices acceptable to (and sometimes even celebrated by) the missionaries, such as fasting and self-flagellation, were adopted to achieve traditional spiritual ends, such as dreaming. Thus, in Blanchard's view, Catholic practice at Kahnawà:ke was a thin veneer calculated to enable traditional belief and practice and the pursuit of more secular interests. Axtell takes a quite different view of Catholicism in early Kahnawà:ke.[23] He points to the relatively large size of the Catholic congregation in the community and the many examples of Catholic piety and devotion and argues that the religious conversion among the Kanien'kehá:ka in Kahnawà:ke was sincere, deep, and widespread.

Other scholars have taken a position between the views offered by Blanchard and by Axtell. In her political history of early Kahnawà:ke, Green describes the early community at Kentake as especially devout and zealous in its Catholic religious practice.[24] She also notes, however, that many of the newcomers who swelled the population in the mid-1670s came not to live in a Christian community but for a variety of other reasons, including the economic opportunities offered by the settlement's strategic location. Richter makes a similar observation and points to the emphasis on temperance and the stability of the community in comparison with the high level of drunkenness and related violence in the home communities.[25] In fact, he argues that native Catholic communities like Kahnawà:ke provided not only a haven from the problems of the home communities but an environment more conducive to the traditional values of peace, hospitality, and reciprocity.

Jocks gives some weight to all of these arguments and suggests that Kahnawà:ke saw the development of a more syncretistic spiritual life:

Many early residents of Kentake and Kahnawà:ke, though not all, seem indeed to have embraced Catholic doctrine as well as ritual and moral practice sincerely and enthusiastically. On the other hand, it is possible that most in the community continued concurrently to cultivate key traditional Longhouse values and practices, and to act independently of the Jesuit pastors as well as the French civil authorities. . . . [T]he predominant response was neither complete conversion nor calculated posturing, but sincere selective acceptance and retention of elements of both Catholic and Longhouse complexes.[26]

Alfred agrees with this view and suggests that the synthesis of native and Christian beliefs and rituals resulted in a unique form of Catholicism that contributed to Kahnawà:ke's unique history, identity, and place within the Kanien'kehá:ka nation and the Confederacy.[27]

In most other ways, life in Kahnawà:ke in the 1670s and 1680s followed the traditional Rotinonhsiónni pattern. As Green has described it, this included the native pattern of village settlement and land use, agricultural production and techniques, sexual division of labor, housing style and materials, and extended family longhouses. The native languages also persisted. By the late 1680s the community numbered almost 700 men, women, and children.[28]

The Development of Kahnawà:ke's Distinct Political and Cultural Identity

During the 1680s relations between the Rotinonhsiónni and the French were strained by competition for political and economic influence in the Ohio and Upper Mississippi river valleys. At the same time, ties between the Confederacy and the British were strengthened. For many Rotinonhshiónni, the British were attractive political and economic partners because of the competition with the French in the west and because they represented an alternative source of trade goods without the unwanted pressure and disruption of missionary activity. These circumstances, in turn, increased tension within the Confederacy between non-Christian communities and mission communities, like Kahnawà:ke, that maintained a close relationship with the French and Jesuit missionaries. While there were some in Kahnawà:ke who supported the Confederacy, others assisted the French and saw their own and the community's interests best served by an alliance with the French. In 1684 the Confederacy indicated it no longer recognized Kahnawà:ke as part of the League, and thereafter the community increasingly became a distinct group charting its own course and relations with the European powers. Though cultural and kin ties to other Kanien'kehá:ka and Rotinonhsiónni communities persisted, politically and economically this course emphasized ties to the French.[29]

In 1687 a large contingent of Kahnawakehró:non formed part of the native force in Denonville's expedition against the Senecas. In retaliation, in 1689 the Rotinonhsiónni struck the French community at Lachine, near Montreal and on the north shore of the St. Lawrence a short distance upriver from Kahnawà:ke. The attack and the siege laid to the region in the following months forced the community at Kahnawà:ke to take refuge in Montreal along with many of the French settlers from the surrounding area. This experience served to solidify their political and military ties with the French. In the following year Kahnawakehró:non joined the French and other native allies in attacks on British settlements in New York, and in 1693 they helped guide French forces in a devastating campaign against Kanien'kehá:ka villages in the Mohawk River Valley. Three years later Kahnawakehró:non assisted Frontenac's expedition that laid waste to Onondaga and Oneida villages.[30]

Following the yearlong refuge in Montreal in the wake of the attack on Lachine in 1689, the Kahnawà:ke community established a new village a short distance west and upriver of its former site and renamed itself Kahnawakon. It relocated again six years later, when it was renamed Kanatakwente, and remained there until 1716, when the village was moved to its present location and again became known as Kahnawà:ke. During this time the community continued to grow, owing in large measure to migrations from the Mohawk River Valley after the French campaign against the Kanien'kehá:ka villages there in 1693. By 1716 it numbered between 800 and 1,000 inhabitants.[31]

Though Kahnawà:ke and the Confederacy found their political loyalties divided during the 1680s and 1690s, the relationship between them was complicated. Kahnawakehró:non appear to have been reluctant participants in the Denonville expedition in 1687, and after the fighting was over they sought to assure the Confederacy that they were at war only with the Senecas. For the next two years each side worked to avoid large-scale confrontations with the other and sometimes sought to avoid bloodshed altogether. Though they were part of the French expeditions into Rotinonhsiónni country in 1693 and 1696, Kahnawakehró:non did not make a major contribution to the success of either effort, and during this period they even sought to broker a peace between the Confederacy and the French. During the late 1690s Rotinonhsiónni visits and migrations to Kahnawà:ke and exchanges of war captives served to build trust and more cooperative relations. Both sides, it appears, sought to avoid a permanent rupture of the Confederacy.[32]

In 1697 the French and British agreed to peace, but hostilities between the Confederacy and the French and their native allies persisted for another four years, with the Confederacy continuing to lose ground. In 1701, one year before the French and the British resumed fighting, the Confederacy signed a peace treaty with the French in which it agreed to remain neutral in any future wars between the two European powers. This was a position it for the most part succeeded in maintaining for much of the next fifty years. Kahnawà:ke followed a different course. As major allies of the French during Queen Anne's War (1702–13), Kahnawakehró:non participated in a number of raids on English settlements in New England. When British and French fighting was renewed in King George's War (1744–48), Kahnawà:ke continued to ally itself with the French.[33]

During the late 1740s or early 1750s a number of families left Kahnawà:ke and established a new community some sixty miles upriver near where the St. Regis River flows into the St. Lawrence. The new community was named St. Regis by the French and called Ahkwesáhsne ("where the partridge drums") by the native people who settled there. Factionalism and soil exhaustion at Kahnawà:ke may have been factors in the migration and establishment of the new community. Geopolitics and the encouragement of the French may also have played a role. The establishment of the new community, which was predominantly pro-French, strengthened French control over the St. Lawrence region. Further, it extended the line of Rotinonhsiónni mission settlements that formed a barrier between the French and the Rotinonhsiónni to the south, who by the mid-1750s had begun to abandon their policy of neutrality and support the British.[34]

The independence of Kahnawà:ke's political course was nowhere more evident than in the establishment of the Seven Indian Nations of Canada, a confederacy of native Christian communities allied with the French. Also known as the Seven Fires, the Seven Nations confederacy was headquartered in Kahnawà:ke and included Kanesatake, or Lake of Two Mountains (also known as Oka), which was divided into Kanien'kehá:ka, Algonquian, and Nipissing delegations; the Onondagas and Cayugas of Oswegatchie; the Hurons of Lorette; and the Abenakis of Odanak (St. Francis). After the Oswegatchie community was dispersed to other communities following the American Revolution, Ahkwesáhsne replaced it within the Seven Nations confederacy. The Seven Nations alliance was established in the 1750s and remained active into the early nineteenth century. Snow argues that the

French induced the formation of the Seven Nations confederacy as part of its own colonialist strategy, but other scholars have taken a different view.[35] Alfred and Blanchard, for example, understand the formation of the confederacy more as the outcome of native interests and action, particularly those of Kahnawà:ke. In their view, Kahnawà:ke, which now operated politically outside the Rotinonhsiónni Confederacy and recognized the weakening position of the French vis-à-vis the British in the 1750s, sought to build a new power base for itself by forming an alliance between Christian Indians that had been allied with the French.[36]

When the Kanien'kehá:ka supported the British during King George's War (1744–48), the Rotinonhsiónni Confederacy saw the first signs of the unraveling of its policy of neutrality. In the last phase of the colonial wars between England and France from 1755 to 1763, this trend continued. The Confederacy initially sided with the British, then split in its support, with the Senecas, Onondagas, and Cayugas shifting their allegiance to the French and only the Oneidas and some Kanien'kehá:ka remaining allied with the British. Kahnawà:ke entered this period of conflict with the aim of maintaining a neutral position but soon found itself again aligned with the French. Pressure from the pro-French, native Christian communities with which it had become allied in the Seven Nations confederacy was an important factor in this alignment. Nevertheless, during the war Kahnawà:ke was less active than it had been during previous conflicts. In particular, when Kahnawakehró:non came face to face in battle with their Kanien'kehá:ka brethren at Crown Point on Lake Champlain in 1755, both sides refused to fight and sat out the engagement.[37]

In 1760 the British took Montreal, and for all intents and purposes the war with the French and their contest for control of northeastern North America was over, though the treaty recognizing British victory and ascendancy was not concluded for another three years. After the fall of Montreal, the British Crown recognized Indian title to the land at Kahnawà:ke. The Society of Jesus, however, which had been granted the land by the French Crown in 1680, saw itself as the rightful owner and refused to recognize native title. Kahnawà:ke appealed to the military governor of Lower Canada, General Thomas Gage, and in 1762 he ruled in its favor, stating that the land at "Le Sault" was granted for the settlement of the Indians and was retained by the British Crown for their use.[38]

The distinctive course followed by Kahnawà:ke during the late seventeenth century and much of the eighteenth was cultural and economic as well as political. According to Green, during this period Kahnawakehró:non successfully integrated Rotinonhsiónni and European cultural patterns and interacted with Euro-Canadian society in ways that avoided assimilation and created a unique culture. The community had a definite Catholic character, but traditional spiritual practices persisted and some Kahnawakehró:non were indifferent to Christian belief and practice. Many attended Catholic mass, but the Jesuit priests had to learn Kanien'kéha to function in the community. Catholic ceremonies marked many of the important passages in life but also expressed the Kanien'kehá:ka-Catholic nature of the community. For example, many Kahnawakehró:non took both Christian and native names at baptism. Clans continued to function; every community member belonged to a clan, and French men who married women from Kahnawà:ke were adopted into families and clans. Marriage ceremonies took place in the Catholic Church, but the traditional practices of marriage arrangement and courtship persisted. Men still joined their wives in their households, which continued to emphasize extended family longhouses.[39]

Economically, the community had important ties with the surrounding French Canadian communities, but many Kahnawakehró:non were still engaged in traditional subsistence endeavors and an economy in which subsistence goods, rather

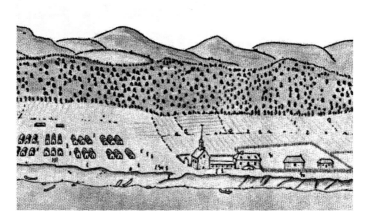

2. The village of Kahnawà:ke in the mid-eighteenth century.
Photograph courtesy of Kanien'kehaka Onkwawen:na Raotitiohkwa.

than cash or trade goods, circulated as payment. Hunting had diminished in importance, but many men continued in the fur trade. Farming persisted and continued to be the responsibility of women, but it had been modified to include the raising of livestock and poultry.[40] In particular, it was Kahnawà:ke's strategic position in the Montreal-Albany trade nexus that came to distinguish it economically. Profits for the French and British on both ends of this route were high, but the trade was illegal; Kahnawakehró:non served as the vital link between the two, a role that not only benefited the community economically but also gave it political leverage in its relations with both European powers. In addition, because this economic role sometimes brought them into close cooperation with their kin and brethren in the Mohawk River Valley, during the periods of French and British conflict the maintenance and protection of this economic role was an important factor in limiting confrontations with the Confederacy nations, the Kanien'kehá:ka in particular.[41]

Kahnawà:ke's Development from the
Mid-Eighteenth to the Early Nineteenth Century

Unlike the Rotinonhsiónni in New York, the people of Kah-nawà:ke survived the American Revolution relatively unscathed. Officially the community maintained a policy of neutrality in the war, but some Kahnawakehró:non, in particular those who were descended from or were themselves captive-adoptees from the British colonies, supported the Americans in their cause and fought alongside them. During the War of 1812, understanding that their own land and community were threatened by American aggression, Kahnawà:ke supported the British and played a key role in a number of military engagements.[42]

In contrast to Kahnawà:ke, the Rotinonhsiónni in general suffered considerably during and after the American Revolution. Though also intending to remain neutral in the conflict, most Rotinonhsiónni were soon pushed by events to the side of the British. In 1777 the Americans and some Oneida allies attacked and plundered the Kanien'kehá:ka villages in the Mohawk River Valley, forcing the inhabitants to take refuge with the British near Montreal. The following year American forces laid waste nearly every other Rotinonhsiónni community in New York and forced many of the inhabitants to seek protection with the British at Fort Niagara in western New York. Unwilling to return to the United States, the Kanien'kehá:ka who had taken refuge near Montreal resettled on land granted to them by the British Crown at the Bay of Quinté (eventually to become the Tynedinaga reserve) and Grand River (eventually to become the Six Nations Reserve). Rotinonhsiónni who did return to the United States soon ceded so much of their lands that by 1797 there remained only a series of small reservations in central and western New York State. Further, even though the land cessions were often realized through American force and fraud, these developments engendered distrust of Rotinonhsiónni leaders and undermined faith in the traditional political institutions. Within a short time, poverty, despair, alcoholism, and family instability plagued life on the reservations.[43]

It was in this context that a revitalization movement developed under the leadership of the Seneca chief Skaniatariio. Skaniatariio, or Handsome Lake, was a member of the Allegheny band of Senecas who in the spring of 1799 experienced the first of a series of visions that foreshadowed an apocalyptic end of the world unless people reformed their behavior. The visions and the cultural response to them gradually evolved into a code of moral and social conduct that was in many ways assimilationist, emphasizing formal schooling, the nuclear family, Euro-American methods of farming, and important changes in gender roles. Spiritually, however, the code was conservative. It stressed maintaining traditional beliefs and practices, especially the traditional cycle of thanksgiving ceremonies, but grafted onto this pattern were various aspects of Christian theology, such as the precepts of heaven and hell and the insistence on confession. Skaniatariio's following was centered on the Allegheny reservation and later on the Tonawanda reservation, to which he moved a few years before his death in 1815. In the years following Skaniatariio's death, his teachings were codified, and gradually the *karihwí:io*, or "good message," spread to other reserves, including Cattaragus, Buffalo Creek, and Onondaga in New York and Six Nations in Ontario. Kahnawà:ke, being predominantly Catholic and not experiencing the social and cultural disruption of other Rotinonhsiónni communities, did not provide ground for the spread of the Handsome Lake movement.[44]

During the course of the nineteenth century Kahnawà:ke moved increasingly toward an economy based on wage labor. After the War of 1812 the center of Canadian fur trapping and trading moved farther west, resulting in a decline in a key component of the community's economic base. Though some men continued to find work with American and Canadian fur trading companies in the west, by the middle of the nineteenth century its economic importance was negligible. Men found work in logging, freighting, and piloting along the St. Lawrence and Ottawa rivers, and during the winters the manufacture and sale of moccasins, snowshoes, beadwork, and other crafts provided additional income. Farming was an economic option, but few pursued it in an important way. According to Devine, in 1843 less than 20 percent of the reserve's 12,400 acres was under cultivation, and few families tilled more than thirty or forty acres. At this time Kahnawà:ke's population numbered about 1,100.[45]

During the middle decades of the nineteenth century the Canadian economy was undergoing an important transition. Before this time a "pioneer" pattern predominated in which lands were colonized and settled by Euro-Canadians and brought within the forces of a market economy. By midcentury this pattern was being replaced by a mature agricultural and commercial economy based on the production and export of natural resources and agricultural commodities. The development of transportation and transportation-related industries was an important part of this economic transition. Railway development in particular was integral to this shift and served to nationalize the economy by tying together Canada's different regional economies and placing emphasis on the role of the state in planning, promoting, and subsidizing economic growth. Railways were also crucial to the growth of urban centers such as Montreal and laid the groundwork for the industrialization that was well under way by the turn of the century.[46]

The mid-nineteenth-century transformation of the Canadian economy had important consequences for the relative isolation of the Kahnawà:ke community. In the early 1850s reserve land was expropriated for the construction of part of the Lake St. Louis and Province Railway, which was to run from Malone, New York, to its terminus at the east end of the village in Kahnawà:ke. Additional reserve land was taken along the riverfront for the construction of wharves and other transportation- and freight-related facilities. From this point ferry services connected the rail line to another on the north side of the St. Lawrence River at Lachine, which ran to the city of Montreal. The entire network was designed to improve transportation of passengers and freight to and from the United States. Many Kahnawakehró:non opposed the rail line and the taking of their land, but it mattered little to the federal government, bent as it was on economic development.[47]

In the late 1850s work was begun on the Victoria Bridge, which was to link Montreal to the south shore of the St. Lawrence River, a few miles downriver of Kahnawà:ke. The construction project provided a new source of employment for men from Kahnawà:ke and was a forerunner to their involvement in high steel construction. After working on the Victoria Bridge, Kahnawà:ke men found similar employment with the Grand Trunk and Canadian Pacific railways. This experience introduced them to metalwork, riveting, and welding, which by the late 1880s were becoming a major source of employment for Kahnawà:ke men. The booming and industrializing Canadian and American economies at the turn of the century provided for a further expansion of steel construction work. In 1912 Kahnawà:ke ironworkers began traveling to work in New York City for the first time, and over the next several decades a growing Kanien'kehá:ka community established itself in Brooklyn. At the turn of the century Kahnawà:ke's population stood at about 1,700.[48]

Another important source of employment and income for Kahnawakehró:non during the second half of the nineteenth century was the entertainment industry. This began with exhibitions of traditional crafts, lacrosse, and paddling at the Universal Exposition in Paris in 1867 and similar exhibitions in London and other cities the following year. In the 1880s Kahnawà:ke entertainers became involved in Wild West shows that toured the United States and Europe, often playing the parts of Plains

Indians and reenacting scenes of Plains Indian life that were of such great interest to white audiences. The popularity of these shows declined in the early twentieth century, but some Kahnawakehró:non continued to work in stage shows and exhibitions.[49] For Kahnawà:ke, the second half of the nineteenth century was a time not only of significant economic transformation, but also of important social, political, and cultural change. White encroachment and settlement on the reserve drove some of these changes, as did growing scarcity of land and resources and inequalities in landownership. At the same time, Kahnawakehró:non faced intensified pressure for assimilation that accompanied the modernizing of the Canadian economy and state. In particular, they were confronted with federal Indian policies aimed at transforming native political institutions, policies that struck at the very heart of their community's distinct history, society, and culture. The Kahnawà:ke community found itself divided as it sought to deal with these issues and pressures and chart a course for itself as it entered the modern era.

2. *"Serious Troubles"*

The Ecology, Economy, and Politics of
Community Division in the 1870s and 1880s

Land, Resource Scarcity, and Landownership

The Kahnawà:ke reserve originated from the Seigneury of Sault St. Louis, which derived from two French Crown grants to the Society of Jesus in 1680 for the purpose of missionizing and ministering to the Rotinonhsiónni. The original grants totaled more than 40,000 acres. Indian title to this land was established after Montreal fell to the British in 1760 and was reaffirmed in 1762 by the military governor, General Thomas Gage. From that time until the end of the nineteenth century the land area of the reserve gradually diminished as a result of mismanagement and white encroachment. First under Jesuit overseers and later under the authority of government agents, white farmers came to control much of the land in the eastern part of the reserve through illegal land sales, renting of reserve lands without the consent of the Kahnawà:ke community, and illegal occupations of reserve land long after rents had ceased to be paid. The government's refusal to recognize the boundary of Indian lands within the seigneury during the eighteenth and nineteenth centuries contributed to this pattern of illegal white encroachment.[1] As Prime Minister Wilfred Laurier observed when the issue was brought before Parliament in 1890, "We know how it is in the vicinity of reserves; the white settlers are very apt to encroach a little every year, and the process goes on so long that the Indians may be deprived very materially of the reserve they originally possessed."[2] Indeed, by 1890 the Kahnawà:ke reserve had been reduced to just 12,328 acres, less than a third of its original size.

Aside from the obvious loss of land, the reduction in the size of the reserve contributed to an increasingly serious scarcity of resources for the growing Kahnawà:ke population, which numbered 951 in 1835, 1,100 in 1843, and 1,700 by the turn of the century. Though relatively few Kahnawakehró:non made their livelihood solely as farmers in the 1870s, nearly all still relied on access to the land in some degree for subsistence, income, firewood, and timber. Land and resource scarcity had become so severe that the community considered selling the entire reserve in 1862, 1870, and again in June 1875, when four of the chiefs petitioned the superintendent general of Indian affairs to sell the entire reserve for $25 an acre.[3] The principal reason the chiefs cited for such drastic action was a decades-old problem of illegal cutting of firewood and timber on common land by private individuals. The chiefs argued that overuse of these resources had caused a serious problem for the band as a whole. A government report on the cutting of wood on the reserve two years earlier indicates that the chiefs were not overstating their case: "Some mode of protection should be arrived at to save the wood for in a very few years, if things go on this way, the Indians of the Seigneury of Sault St. Louis will have none."[4] In their 1875 petition the chiefs noted that in a referendum the previous year a majority of the band had favored selling the reserve and that the revenue produced should be used to enable Kahnawakehró:non to buy land or farms on the former reserve or migrate elsewhere in Canada or the United States.[5] The Indian Department gave serious consideration to the chiefs' proposal, but in the end it never moved forward on their petition.

The growing scarcity of resources such as firewood was especially hard on those in the community who owned no land. Two events in 1878 suggest the seriousness of this problem. After a referendum in February of that year on the council of chiefs system, some sixty or so Kahnawakehró:non notified the Indian agent, Georges Cherrier, that they wanted to separate from the band.[6] According to Cherrier, this group included "those who have not preserved wood nor who have any land; and who now, finding that they cannot take wood from their neighbors without their permission, are determined to force a division."[7] The second event occurred later in that same year when Martin Sakoriatakwa, a former chief, was reported by Cherrier to have illegally fenced land on the reserve not belonging to him.[8] According to the agent, Sakoriatakwa already owned a considerable amount of land, and his action posed a significant hardship for "the poor people who go [to the illegally fenced land] to look for wood to warm their houses." After his report, Cherrier was directed by Indian Affairs to remove Sakoriatakwa from the land in question.

The scarcity of land and resources on the reserve was exacerbated by inequalities in landownership. According to an Indian Department survey, in 1884 the land area of the reserve totaled 12,328 acres, nearly all privately owned.[9] Specifically, 89 percent (10,936 acres) of the reserve was privately owned, and this did not include the village area, which contained 729 acres (6 percent of the total area of the reserve) of mostly small, privately owned house lots. The landowners were mostly native residents of the reserve, but also included were some non-native residents and a few non-natives living in nearby communities. Common land owned by the "tribe" accounted for only 5 percent (581 acres) of the total area of the reserve. Information on land sales collected as part of the Walbank survey in 1884 indicates that private landownership on the reserve was well established and had developed over many years as individuals and families occupied, improved, and eventually claimed ownership of various plots of land. Typically, the claimed plots had irregular and ill-defined boundaries and over the years had been bought, sold, traded, and inherited among the residents of the reserve, all without any system of legal titles.[10]

By the 1880s not only had most of the reserve become privately owned, but much of it was in the hands of a few individuals and families. In its survey of the reserve in 1884 the Indian Department identified 610 heads of families who submitted claims to share in a planned subdivision and allotment of the reserve. Of this number, 56 percent (344) owned some land, while 44 percent (266) owned no land at all.[11] Among the 344 landowners, the average holding was 31.9 acres and the average value of their holdings was $512.51, but there was wide variation in both the amount and the value of land owned. The largest landowner held 261 acres, while the smallest held less than an acre and the most common size was only about 4 acres. The most highly valued landholding was assessed at $5,019, while the most common assessment was $78 and the lowest assessment was just $3. Standard deviations for the amount and value of land owned were 38.21 and 754.09, respectively.

In 1884 the top 5 percent of landowners by acreage owned 24 percent of all privately owned land, and the top 10 percent owned 38 percent. In terms of the value of land owned, the top 5 percent held 31 percent of the value of all privately held land, and the top 10 percent held 45 percent. The largest individual landowner was Thomas Jocks (Atonwa Karatoton), with 261 acres valued at $4,748. Jocks was described as a "merchant" at this time and had been chief of the Rotiskeréwaká:ion (Old Bear) clan since 1878.[12] In terms of the value of land owned, the wealthiest landowner was Baptiste Jocks (Sawatis Karonhiaktatis), whose 255 acres was valued at $5,019; Thomas Jocks was the second wealthiest landowner. The most important family of landowners was the DeLorimiers, consisting of Louisa, the wife of the late George DeLorimier, and her five sons. When George DeLorimier died in 1863, Louisa inherited his land and then passed it to her sons; in 1884 the land they owned totaled 393 acres and was valued at $9,639.[13] In short, in the mid-1880s landownership in Kahnawà:ke was far from equally distributed, and many in the band owned little or no land.

Natives, Whites, and Métis on the Kahnawà:ke Reserve
During the 1870s there was considerable antagonism toward whites and métis living at Kahnawà:ke, a problem that had deep historical roots but that took on particular urgency with the growing scarcity of land and resources on the reserve. Whites living on the reserve in the 1870s and 1880s consisted primarily of white men married to native women. Some of these men were born on the reserve, while others settled there before or after their marriages. Many, but not all, of these couples had children who were raised on the reserve, and there appears to have been a relatively high incidence of intermarriage among métis children. Some specific examples illustrate this pattern.

Edouard Deblois was a French Canadian who was born in 1833 and took up residence on the reserve about 1850. In 1860 he married Kateri Tsawennoseriio, whose mother was native and whose father was white. In the 1880s he served as Kahnawà:ke's postmaster and owned land on the reserve and in neighboring Chateauguay. David Lafleur, also French Canadian, was born in Chambly in 1824 and moved to Kahnawà:ke in 1849. In 1851 he married Henriette Niiokwenniaha in Chateauguay. Niiokwenniaha was a Huron from Lorette and was of mixed native-white parentage. Olivier Vignaut was a French Canadian who was born in St. Pierre, moved to Kahnawà:ke in 1854, and married Caroline Osennenhawi there in 1867. Osennenhawi also was a Huron from Lorette and was of mixed parentage. Alexander Therrien was another French Canadian who married a native woman of mixed native-white parentage. He wed Teres Atewenniiostha in 1857 and they had two daughters. Therrien's wife died in 1876, but he was still living in a house on the reserve in 1885.[14]

Charles Gideon Giasson (Saro Raksatiio), another French Canadian, was born in Kahnawà:ke in 1808 and lived his entire life on the reserve. He married Akat Konwaronhiotakwen in 1832, and they had at least four children who were still living on the reserve in 1885. Giasson owned land on the reserve and a lot in the village that contained his home, a shop and stable, and an orchard. The land, which by 1885 had been inherited by his four children, totaled 155 acres and was valued at $2,133.[15] Giasson's son Napoleon married a daughter of David Lafleur in 1875, and in 1860 his daughter Charlotte married Osias Meloche, a French Canadian who was a long-time resident of Kahnawà:ke. After marrying, Meloche and Charlotte Giasson raised at least six children on the reserve, including three sons. Meloche appears to have been a farmer, owning about thirty-eight acres of land on the reserve and three lots in the village, where he lived and maintained several outbuildings for his livestock and farm implements. He died in 1878, and his wife and sons inherited his property.[16]

Onesime Plante (Resine Kanenaroton), born in Kahnawà:ke in 1855, was the son of a French Canadian father and a mother of mixed native-white parentage. He married a daughter of David Lafleur in Kahnawà:ke in 1875, and after his father's death in 1876 he cared for his mother in her home in the village until her death in 1885. Narcisse Desparois (Narsis Karatoton) also was the son a French Canadian father and a mother of mixed parentage. He was born in Kahnawà:ke in 1836 and lived on the reserve for about seventeen years before moving to Chateauguay, where he lived for the rest of his life. Though no longer living in Kahnawà:ke in 1885, at that time he owned approximately five acres of land on the reserve.[17]

Other whites living on the reserve in the 1870s and 1880s had somewhat unusual personal histories and circumstances. Herbert Antoine (Tewen Tawennaronkwas) appears to have been adopted in infancy by a native couple from Kahnawà:ke sometime around 1810. He lived his entire life on the reserve, married three times, and was widowed twice. In 1885 he owned two pieces of land, but in that same year he deeded it to two other residents of the reserve. At that time he reported to the government officials that he spoke only the Iroquois language and considered himself a member of the band because he had been adopted and raised on the reserve. Michael Nolan was an Englishman who was born in Malta in 1832. As a young man he served in the British army and had settled in the Montreal area by 1867, when he married Wensiek Kanaiesshon. After their marriage, Nolan and his wife settled in Kahnawà:ke, where they raised two sons and two daughters. At least two white women lived on the reserve during the 1870s. Little is known about them except that both were widows whose husbands were Hurons from Lorette. In addition, at various times there appear to have been several white men living on the reserve who owned no property but worked as hired farmhands. Perhaps the most unusual case was Jane Lefort (Kaniatarotsientha). Identified in Indian Department files as a "Negress," Lefort was born in New York and adopted in infancy by a native couple from Kahnawà:ke. She was baptized in Kahnawà:ke in 1834, was raised on the reserve, married a French Canadian man, and gave birth to a son, Moise (Mais Kaienwire), in 1851. Lefort's husband died about 1866, but she continued to live on the reserve supported by her son, who served for many years as the local constable.[18]

Finally, there was the family of George DeLorimier. Born in Kahnawà:ke in 1809, DeLorimier was the son of a French Canadian father from Lachine who served with the British army during the American Revolution and became the Indian agent for Kahnawà:ke in 1783; his mother was a native woman and his father's third wife. DeLorimier married Louisa McComber, who was born in Kahnawà:ke in 1817 and was of Scottish descent, and between 1841 and 1859 they had five sons: Alexander (Areksent Tekanonnowehon), John B. S. (Sawatis Tahahenta), Joseph (Sose Aontiakare), Stephen A., and Albert (Arpet Oronhiataka). In 1834 DeLorimier was granted legal "Indian" status by the

Supreme Court of Montreal, and it is as "Indians" that he and his family lived on the reserve after that time. DeLorimier died in 1863, and in 1884 his sons who inherited his land were the largest and wealthiest family of landowners on the reserve.[19]

In 1868 Edouard Deblois, David Lafleur, Charles Gideon Giasson, Osias Meloche, Onesime Plante, and probably other unidentified white men as well were ordered by the Indian Department to leave the reserve. Several of the men protested their removal on the grounds that they were married to Indian women and thereby had a right to live there. In 1869 the order was rescinded. Giasson, Plante, and Meloche were permitted to remain on the reserve rent free, Giasson permanently and Plante and Meloche "until further order." Deblois and Lafleur were allowed to stay on condition that they pay an annual rent of $25, which they did in 1870 but failed to do in 1871 and 1872. In 1873 the Indian Department investigated their failure to pay the rent, but later accepted their petitions to live on the reserve rent-free because they had married their wives before the Indian Act of 1869. The 1869 act revoked a native woman's "Indian" status (and thus her band membership and right to live on the band's reserve) if she married a non-Indian man, but the policy was not applied retroactively.[20] In 1869 Narcisse Desparois was issued a permit to live on the reserve and be regarded as an "Indian." In 1873 the Kahnawà:ke chiefs protested his permit; nevertheless, the Indian Department allowed Desparois to continue living on the reserve.[21]

The relationship between natives and whites on the reserve was marked by antagonism that dated to at least the late eighteenth century. This antagonism was rooted in the objections of Kahnawakehró:non to the means by which whites had acquired land and the right to live on the reserve and was intensified by the growing scarcity of land and resources. In the 1870s this antagonism turned violent. In 1873 the Kahnawà:ke chiefs complained about the presence of whites and their impact on the supplies of firewood and timber. The chiefs argued that these men had no right to live on the reserve, and they wanted them expelled. As an Indian Department report stated, "[The] Indians are opposed to these white people remaining on the reserve, especially on account of wood, which is now very scarce in the Seigneury, and which the white people use in common with the Indians, thus diminishing their future supply."[22]

The following year, 1874, J. E. R. Pinsonneault, the Indian agent for Kahnawà:ke, reported to the interior minister on what he described as "serious trouble" between Indians and "Metis"— "the whites of this place who are married to women of Indian blood." The "serious trouble" involved Edouard Deblois and David Lafleur. According to Pinsonneault's report, Deblois had permitted Lafleur to cut wood on land he owned through his wife, and a "number of Indians" confiscated the wood from Lafleur. He stated that the view of many of the Indians was that the whites living among them had no right to the wood on reserve land and that they "wish to take it forcibly from all persons in this category of Lafleur." Pinsonneault asked the Indian Department for instructions on dealing with the matter and was informed, unhelpfully, that neither Deblois nor Lafleur had a right to wood on the reserve, but that their wives did.[23] It was at this time, following a communitywide referendum, that the four Kahnawà:ke chiefs petitioned the superintendent general of Indian affairs to sell the entire reserve.

Thus, during the early 1870s native concern about the presence of whites on the reserve increased as a result of resource pressures. At the same time, the Indian Department affirmed or reaffirmed their right to continue living on the reserve and to make use of the land and its resources. The native community and its leaders protested this situation and sought the removal of the whites and their families. By the mid-1870s the situation had become so serious that many agreed the only solution was to sell their entire reserve. However, in none of these instances—protesting the right of whites to live on the reserve and use its resources, seeking the removal of whites, or attempting to sell the reserve—did the native community receive any sort of satisfaction from the Indian Department. As a result, native antagonism toward whites intensified and eventually erupted in a series of violent incidents.

In April 1878 Georges Cherrier, the Indian agent, reported the following to the interior minister:

> I think it my duty to inform you of a placard that has been affixed to the fence at the church door here. It is in these words:
>
>> To the half breed Canadians of the village. We wish to have a final decision to know if DeLorimier, Giasson, Deblois, Meloche & others are masters in our Reserve. There are eight of us who write (Indians) and if you do not leave the village look out for your heads, yr buildings, your cattle & take warning of what we now tell you.
>
> I was not in the village on Sunday or I would have seized the placard. As far as I remember the Indians here have never killed anyone, but as to fires there have been many in the village. The DeLorimiers have passed thro. them twice—Giasson was also burned out, and had an animal killed. Chas. Giasson's horses were cut with axes. Mr. Desparois had a fine cow killed. Many other misfortunes have come to the half breeds without the guilty being discovered except one who made a deathbed confession.
>
> Since the placard was put up they have gone about in a way that may cause serious trouble.
>
> It is desired by some to communicate this circumstance to the public thro. the newspapers but I have opposed it in the interest of the Tribe.
>
> I regret having to trouble you with such things, but I hope you will instruct how to appease this bad spirit.[24]

Later the same month, another "notice" was posted on the door of the mission church:

> We again say, do you doubt what we said in the first notice put up? You appear not to be disquieted. Very well! The day and hour will come to you Canadians residing in the Village. If any Indians take your part they will be treated the same as yourselves. Take care then you Indians, as well as you Canadians, we will bring down vengeance on those who have given trouble—on those Canadians who are making themselves masters here. We do not deceive you; we are 8 picked courageous men, who are working in your interest; we are not Iroquois. The matter has been well looked into—be brave to aid the Indians. Means will be found to cut the neck of this individual. The same thing will happen to the Indians who are for the Canadians. We shall eventually know the Indians who support the Canadians & Cherrier. We will bide our time, if God does not hinder us—death alone can stop us. "It's ready for you every hour every minute."[25]

The hostility directed at the "Canadians," or whites, is clear, and while the notice states that its authors were not "Iroquois," subsequent events and an investigation by Cherrier proved otherwise. Further, in his report on the incident Cherrier stated that he feared "incendiarism" and that after the posting of the notice five sheep belonging to one of the sons of Charles Gideon Giasson had been killed.[26]

On 12 May, about two weeks after the second notice was posted at the mission church, arsonists set fire to the barn and outbuildings of Osias Meloche in the village. The fire also destroyed many of Meloche's horses, sheep, poultry, and farm implements. Even more serious, Meloche himself was killed. As Indian agent Cherrier reported, "The unfortunate Meloche was suffocated in the midst of the fire without it being possible to help him—only a part of the body was recovered." He went on to state, "A large part of the band do not seem much affected by the catastrophe. On Sunday a great number of them amused themselves playing lacrosse and other games. . . . I regret to tell you that the Village is becoming more degraded, and it is absolutely necessary the Government should take the matter in hand, because in consequence of this accident all the inhabitants around the seigniory are indignant and demand vengeance for the odious act."[27] In a subsequent related memorandum, Cherrier continued with his concerns and the reports of violence:

> I fear fresh trouble, it is possible the next may fall on me. . . .
> The Whites outside of the Seigniory are very indignant. At
> Lachine, yesterday, they thrashed two Indians, and seven
> others had to hide in a cellar near the Depot. I much fear
> some will be killed during the summer. I think many of
> the halfbreeds would leave the Village if the Government
> would pay for their properties. . . . They talk of petitioning
> the Govt. to give the widow Meloche a pension. . . . It is
> suggested that as it was members of the Band who reduced
> her to her present condition the funds of the Tribe should
> contribute to her support. She has six children.[28]

A year later the trouble continued. In March 1879 the house of one of the sons of Charles Gideon Giasson was burned, and a month later so too was Giasson's own barn "and a considerable quantity of hay." Writing to a member of Parliament, Giasson pleaded for the protection of "Whites and halfbreeds" on the reserve.[29] After this, Georges Cherrier wrote to the interior minister to recount the most recent fires and the past threats and to reiterate his conclusion that it was "unknown Indians" who were responsible. He also stated the following:

> I have already had occasion to speak about these incendi-
> aries with some of the Chiefs of this tribe & with many of

the Indians & they have confessed that they had no doubt and that it is certain that it was some Indians who placed the fire to satisfy their hatred & vengeance or jealousy. Chief Thomas Jocks was not afraid to write in the columns of the [Montreal] Star of the 23 May 1878 that the event of the 11th May [the burning of Meloche's property and his death in the fire] was owing to a conspiracy of some persons not of the whole tribe.[30]

In late May 1879 the blacksmith shop of one of the DeLorimier brothers was burned, and in mid-June a cabin and sugarbush belonging to Giasson were set afire.[31] By this time Giasson had become so concerned about his own safety that he wrote to the prime minister, John MacDonald. In his letter Giasson stated that "for the past year it would be impossible to enumerate all the cruelties to which myself and my family have been the object on the part of the Indians" and asked that the prime minister look "into the position of halfbreeds and people who are entitled to reside upon the Res[erve]."[32] Giasson's letter was received by one of McDonald's subordinates, who later reported to the prime minister. "The Indians of Caughnawaga," he wrote, "have burnt some houses and feel disposed to do so again, because, as they say, they want to get rid of all the mitis [métis]. It is a real shame to see such a thing near Montreal."[33]

In mid-September 1879 another of Giasson's barns was burned. A few days later the council of chiefs resolved to offer a reward of $100 for the discovery of those guilty of setting the various fires and to ask for the appointment of a constable.[34] The Indian Department approved the request for a constable and one was appointed, but within six months he had resigned. According to Georges Cherrier, the newly appointed constable resigned after a notice was posted on the reserve that stated that "if by the 1st May next halfbreeds do not leave the reserve and Village blood will be spilled." "It is for fear of these troubles," the agent reported, "which induces [the constable] to resign."[35]

Early the next year Cherrier wrote to the minister of the interior on the situation of the families who had been the focus of so much hostility. His letter stressed the determination of the "Indians" to force "whites" and "metis" to leave the reserve and also suggested that the antagonism and this determination had deep roots in the community's history:

> Sir,
>
> I take the liberty of drawing your attention to the critical position of the Giasson family of Sault St. Louis. This family received a permit of occupation from the Govt. giving them the right to stay in the Village and to enjoy the privileges of the Tribe.
>
> But the Indians have never wished to recognize this right nor the right confirmed by the judgment of the court in favor of the DeLorimier family who are in the same position. This judgment seems to give the right of residence to all families descended on one or other side from Indians, [illegible] on the woman's side. This recognized and acquired right has not been done away with by the laws of 1868 or 1876. Nonetheless the Indians seem decided to take every means to expel these families from the Village.
>
> For the past two years many of their barns and buildings have been set on fire on several occasions. Altho I have received instructions from the Department not to notify them to leave the Indians still claim the right to make them go & many have gone so far as to say that if they do not go there will be bloodshed. It is a fact that we are in fear here at the present of great trouble as they have become so excited over this quest which dates back over 200 years but which seems at the present to have reached its sharpest point.[36]

In response to this letter, the deputy superintendent general of Indian affairs, Lawrence Vankoughnet, reported to the interior minister that "while it has been frequently alleged that judgments by courts of law have been given in favor of certain families to live in Caughnawaga, none of the said judgments have been filed in his office." Subsequently, Georges Cherrier was directed to have the individuals and families in question produce copies of the their judgments and file them in his office. Cherrier later reported that the DeLorimier brothers refused to provide a copy of their judgment on the basis that had already done so in 1868 and that "the other persons who claim to have judgments in their favor also refuse to give copies stating that they are too poor to afford the cost of obtaining copies of their judgments."[37]

While the antagonism and hostility toward whites are evident, it also appears that the native community was divided in its view of the whites living on the reserve. Clearly there were many who were opposed to the whites and at least some who were actively hostile toward them. But whites and their families do appear to have had their supporters and sympathizers. The second warning "notice" posted on the door of the mission church in late April 1878 threatened not only "Canadians" but also their "Indian" sympathizers. As agent Cherrier noted in one of his reports to the interior minister after the death of Osias Meloche, Chief Thomas Jocks wrote to the *Montreal Star* to state that the incident "was owing to a conspiracy of some persons not of the whole Tribe."[38] Later, Cherrier reported that Kahnawakehró:non who had been well disposed toward the "halfbreeds" were feeling the pressure of public threats against them.[39] While this division between opponents and supporters of the whites and their families existed, the two sides were nonetheless united in their lack of cooperation with government's efforts to identify those responsible for the various acts of violence. As a report to the prime minister on the "troubles at Caughnawaga" stated, "We cannot get hold of the guilty man as they all support one another."[40]

In addition to the antagonism and hostility directed toward them, whites and métis in Kahnawà:ke were distinct in a number of other ways. Although there is no evidence that any whites held a position of political leadership on the reserve, they do appear to have held government jobs such as postmaster or constable. Further, direct involvement by them in the important political issues or developments in Kahnawà:ke during the 1870s, such as the controversy over the council of chiefs and the Indian Act system, is virtually nonexistent.[41] Their separation from the "native" community was emphasized by their effort in the 1870s to establish a school for their children separate from the school for native children run by the Indian Department. In 1878 they succeeded in doing so, at least for a short time. The school was run by a "Miss Desparois," who was described by Georges Cherrier as a "Méti" and who was probably the daughter of Narcisse Desparois. Thirty children were attending. The Indian Department did not fund the school and forced it to close when it became aware of its existence through a report from Cherrier.[42] Thus, in many respects, by the late 1870s two communities existed in Kahnawà:ke, one native and the other white and métis.

The Walbank Survey

In the early 1880s the Indian Department initiated a plan to survey and subdivide land and allot it to each family with a right to reside and hold land on the Kahnawà:ke reserve.[43] The circumstances of land and resource scarcity, inequalities of landownership, and antagonism between the whites and natives were all important factors in this decision. Another important factor was the goal of federal Indian policy to promote cultural transformation and assimilation by privatizing Indian lands. It was assumed that private landownership would encourage hard work, individual initiative, self-reliance, competition, profit, and economic efficiency. A form of private landownership was widespread in Kahnawà:ke by the 1880s, but it was not based on legal titles or well-defined property boundaries. The result was that disputes over land and property boundaries were commonplace.

To deal with the problems stemming from the unusual circumstances of landownership in Kahnawà:ke, the Indian Department employed James Dawes of Lachine, Quebec, to arbitrate disputes related to property boundaries on the reserve. In June 1880 Dawes wrote to the deputy superintendent general of Indian affairs, Lawrence Vankoughnet, with regard to the problem of "frequent disputes among the Indians," which according to him often involved the theft of firewood. He reported that he had dealt with many such cases in the past and that new cases were constantly arising. He pointed out that the problem was exacerbated by the absence of division lines demarcating one owner's property from another's:

> One steals from his neighbor and he has him arrested and when brought before me he claims the land and wood as his and as there is no lines of division drawn between them it is impossible to come to any proper decision as each side has his witnesses in his favor. This matter of division lines is becoming a serious matter as the number of Indians cultivating the lands is increasing every year and most of the respectable would like to go into it more extensively but are deterred from doing so from the facts above stated.[44]

Dawes's letter to Vankoughnet also noted that the government had been contemplating a survey of the reserve. He urged that it do so, suggesting that it would be "doing the Indians a real service and be the means to putting an end to those endless disputes between them." He added that "quite a number of the better class of Indians" had asked him to write the Department on this matter. Vankoughnet responded that the Department would survey boundary lines on the reserve at "an early date" and then divide the "Indian landholdings." In addition, he anticipated that such a survey and division was likely to cause "dissatisfaction" when some of the land was taken from its present owners and given to "others desirous of cultivating land but not having any to cultivate." Thus, from the Indian Department's perspective, the unusual circumstances of landownership in Kahnawà:ke inhibited the beneficial, assimilative effects of privatization. The Indian Department's objective in deciding to survey, subdivide, and allot the land of the reserve was not so much to privatize as to clarify property lines, establish a system of legal titles, and expand private landownership to other members of the band.[45]

The Indian Department initiated its survey and subdivision of the reserve in 1884. The first stage in this process was a survey of the reserve and of individual and band landholdings.[46] Next the Indian Department, in consultation with the council of chiefs, determined who was entitled to share in the subdivision and own land on the reserve. Only recognized members of the band were entitled to own land on the reserve; thus the central question the Department and the council had to deal with was band membership. Who was and who was not a member of the band? Following the guidelines of the Indian Act of 1880, this stage involved several steps. First, individuals who claimed band membership and a right to share in the subdivision submitted their claims to a review by the council of chiefs. Following this, the Indian Department considered each of the claims contested by one or more of the chiefs and issued a report on the contested claims for further consideration by the chiefs. In its report the Department frequently asked for clarification of the basis for contesting a claim or advised the chiefs on the relevance of Indian Act guidelines to a particular claim. In other cases the Department noted its agreement or disagreement with the chiefs' responses. The council of chiefs considered the Department's report and then issued its own report on the contested claims. As the last step in the claims process, the Indian Department made a final determination on the contested claims based on the chiefs' conclusions and Indian Act guidelines.

In September 1884 the Indian Department directed the local Indian agent, Alexander Brosseau, to convene Kahnawà:ke's council of chiefs "with a view to making their allotments with various Indian heads of families." Mindful of the division and conflict already existing within Kahnawà:ke over land use and land tenure and between the native and white communities, Deputy Superintendent General Vankoughnet suggested in his directions to Brosseau that "the apportionment of the land will require much tact and judgment on the part of yourself and the Chiefs."[47] His point was emphasized some time later when William McLea Walbank, the surveyor contracted by the Indian Department to subdivide the reserve and assist in the allotment, suggested that he and the Indian agent meet with Vankoughnet "previous to broaching the subject in Caughnawaga, as it is one of great importance and will require to be carefully dealt with."[48]

To begin determining who was qualified to share in the subdivision of the reserve, an interview schedule was developed by Walbank and DIA officials. The interview schedule was designed to collect information concerning an individual's ancestry and vital statistics, length of residence on the reserve, landownership, and claim to share in the subdivision.[49] In essence, the information collected, along with the chiefs' personal knowledge about specific individuals, was the basis for evaluating the legitimacy of each claim to membership in the band and right to share in the subdivision of the reserve.

In January 1885 the community was given public notice by the Indian Department of the impending subdivision and notified that those claiming a right to share in the allotment were required to complete the schedule in an interview with DIA officials. All males "of sufficient age to work their farms" and widowed females were eligible to submit a claim and were given sixty days from 16 February to respond to the questions prepared by the Department. Those who failed or refused to comply with the Department's directions were not considered eligible for a share in the subdivision of the reserve. For the most part, the

Table 1. Claims considered by the Council of Chiefs in the Walbank Survey, 1885

	Not Contested	Contested	Unanimously contested	Not unanimously contested	Total
Male	361	152	100	52	513
Female	74	23	22	1	97
Total	435	175	122	53	610

Source: National Archives of Canada, *Records relating to Indian Affairs*, Record Group 10, vols. 8969–72, Walbank Reference Books—Caughnawaga.

claims and interview process devised by the Indian Department was completed by early April 1885.[50]

According to Walbank's report on the claims process, 611 individuals submitted or were eligible to submit a claim to share in the subdivision. One person submitted claims under two names; thus there were 610 actual or potential claimants. Of this number, 84 percent (513) were male and 16 percent (97) were female. Of the total, 80 percent (490) actually submitted claims. Those who were eligible but did not submit claims (120) included individuals who were absent from the reserve or who refused to comply with the Department's directions for submitting their claims (see table 1).[51]

The council of chiefs began its consideration of the individual claims in April 1885. Though the council formally consisted of seven chiefs, only four were active at this time: Louis Beauvais (Rowi Shatekaienton) of the Rotineniothró:non (Rock clan), Thomas Jocks (Atonwa Karatoton) of the Rotiskeré:wakaká:ion (Old Bear clan), Michael Montour (Wishe Sakoientineta) of the Rotiskeré:wakekó:wa (Great Bear clan), and Thomas Deer (Atonwa Asennase). Each chief had the opportunity to review and approve or contest each claim to membership in the band and right to share in the subdivision of the reserve. In all, the chiefs contested 175 (27 percent) of the 610 claims (table 2). Of the contested claims, 152 (87 percent) were male and 23 (13 percent) were female.[52] Analysis of the claims contested by the chiefs indicates that the claims process and the issue of subdivision and allotment were influenced in significant ways by the pressures of land and resource scarcity and the split between the native and white communities.

To begin with, because of the shortage of land on the reserve, the chiefs limited claims to widowed females and to males twenty-one years of age and older. Despite this, a number of claims that did not meet these criteria were submitted and were contested by the chiefs. Specifically, the chiefs unanimously contested the claims of twelve males because they were "underage" and six females because they were unmarried or married but not widowed (see table 2). The chiefs' opposition to these claims was an issue not of band membership but of limiting the number of band members who could legitimately claim a share in the subdivision of the reserve and thereby increasing the size of the holdings that would be allotted. In its review of these claims the Indian Department determined that, based on Indian Act policy, such individuals could not be denied a claim in the subdivision of the reserve. Nevertheless, the chiefs insisted on their position in these cases, and in the end the Indian Department agreed that the claims would not be recognized.

Concern about the shortage of land may also have been reflected in the chiefs' response to cases involving those they considered members of other bands. Typically, these were native people who had lived on the reserve for some period. Some were born on other reserves, while others were born in Kahnawà:ke but had parents who were members of other bands. In all, fifty-eight claims were contested for these reasons, twenty-five unanimously. Generally the chiefs were unanimous in contesting claims in which neither parent was a recognized band member, and in the end the Department agreed with the chiefs on the majority (eighteen) of these cases. Some of the chiefs, Thomas Deer (Atonwa Asennase) in particular, contested a large

Table 2. Claims contested by the Council of Chiefs in the Walbank Survey, 1885

Reason contested	Unanimous (male/female)	Not unanimous (male/female)	Total (male/female)
White/ non-Indian	17 (15/2)	0	17 (15/2)
Father white/ non-Indian	11 (11/0)	8 (8/0)	19 (19/0)
Father white/mother not band member	2 (2/0)	0	2 (2/0)
Belongs to another band	16 (13/3)	5 (5/0)	21 (18/3)
Father belongs to another band	9 (9/0)	20 (20/0)	29 (29/0)
Grandfather belongs to another band	0	8 (8/0)	8 (8/0)
Long absence from reserve	22 (19/3)	0	22 (19/3)
Illegitimate	8 (8/0)	7 (7/0)	15 (15/0)
Underage	12 (12/0)	0	12 (12/0)
Not widow	6 (0/6)	0	6 (0/6)
Husband white	3 (0/3)	0	3 (0/3)
Husband not band member	3 (0/3)	1 (0/1)	4 (0/4)
Not band member	8 (8/0)	1 (1/0)	9 (9/0)
Other	5 (3/2)	3 (3/0)	8 (6/2)
Total	(100/22)	(52/1)	(152/23)

Source: National Archives of Canada, *Records relating to Indian Affairs*, Record Group 10, vols. 8969–72, Walbank Reference Books—Caughnawaga.

number of other cases because the claimant's father or grandfather was a member of another band. According to Indian Act policies, the Indian Department determined, and the council eventually agreed, that those who had at least one parent who was a member of the Kahnawà:ke band were to be recognized as band members as well and thus had a right to share in the subdivision of the reserve. This was the case in thirty-six of the fifty-eight claims contested because of membership in another band.

Finally, the chiefs' concern over limiting the number of rightful claims to share in the subdivision of the reserve may have been reflected in their decisions to contest the claims of individuals who had been absent from the reserve for a prolonged time and those who were of illegitimate birth. Twenty-two claims were contested on the basis of long absence, and for the most part these involved people who had been living and working in the United States. The chiefs unanimously contested these claims, a position that was consistent with the Indian Act of 1876, which revoked the legal Indian status (and thus band membership) of any native person who was absent in a foreign country for more than five years without the permission of the superintendent general of Indian affairs. Not surprisingly, with one exception the Indian Department agreed with the chiefs' objections in these cases. Fifteen claims were contested because of illegitimacy, eight unanimously and the remaining seven by at least two and sometimes three of the four chiefs. Since illegitimacy was not grounds for refusing to recognize band membership, the Indian Department disagreed, and the chiefs' objections were overturned.

As these results suggest, the chiefs' objections to claims sometimes were consistent with Indian Act policy and at other times were not. For example, in contesting claims on the basis of age, marital status, or illegitimacy the chiefs' decisions contradicted Indian Act policy, while in contesting claims because of long absence from the reserve or membership in another band, their position was in line with Indian Act policy. While the Indian Department's determination was based on Indian Act policies and generally overruled the chiefs' objections where they were not consistent with Indian Act policies, the initial intent of at least some of the chiefs was not so much to follow Indian Act policy as to limit the number of potential claims in the subdivision and allotment of the reserve. This is most evident in the decisions not to recognize the claims of those who were underage and not widowed and to persuade the Indian Department to accept their position. With respect to other types of contested claims, the chiefs succeeded only where their objections were consistent with Indian Act policies.

The chiefs were unanimous in contesting the claims of those who were considered white or non-Indian, a total of fifteen males and two females. This group included the widow of George DeLorimier and her five sons, Charles Gideon Giasson, David Lafleur, Edouard Deblois, and others whom the chiefs and the native community had sought to expel from the reserve during the late 1870s.[53] Generally speaking, the Indian Department concurred with the council in contesting the claims of whites and non-Indians. One important exception to this was the case of the DeLorimier family. The Indian Department continued to recognize the 1834 court judgment that granted Indian status to George DeLorimier and his heirs, even after the chiefs protested this decision. Also, while the Department agreed with the council that white men married to native women were not band members and therefore could not claim a share in the subdivision of the reserve, it determined that their wives did have a legitimate claim to a share in the subdivision if they were recognized members of the band. The Department made a similar determination in two cases that the chiefs unanimously contested, which involved widows whose deceased husbands were white. This determination was based on the fact that their marriages took place before the Indian Act of 1869, which revoked the "Indian" status (and thus band membership) of native women who married non-native men. In the end, with the exception of the DeLorimier case, the chiefs accepted the Department's determination in these cases.

Reflecting the antagonism toward "half-breeds" and métis, the chiefs frequently agreed in contesting the claims of individuals who were the offspring of a white father and a native mother. In all, there were nineteen claims of this type. The chiefs unanimously contested eleven of these claims, and three of the four chiefs agreed in contesting the remaining eight. The Indian Department overruled the chiefs' objections in eleven of these cases, since the claimants' mothers were band members and the claimants themselves were born before the Indian Act of 1876. Only in those cases where the mother was not a band member (eight) were the chiefs' objections upheld. Thus, the chiefs were only partially successful in trying to use the land claims process to expel whites and métis from the reserve. Some of the whites and métis were denied the right to claim land and band membership, while others had that right or the right to live on the reserve affirmed by the Indian Department.

There was thus substantial agreement among the four chiefs in contesting claims to band membership and the right to share in the subdivision of the reserve. Nevertheless, they did frequently disagree. The analysis of the chiefs' decisions in cases where they disagreed is complicated by the fact that, for reasons that are not clear, Chief Jocks did not review all the submitted claims. In fact, he may have reviewed of only 103 of the 176 cases contested by one of more of the chiefs. With this in mind, it is still evident that some important distinctions emerge from a comparison of the chiefs' responses in the 53 cases where there was no consensus. These cases primarily involved claims in which the individual belonged to another band or was considered illegitimate, in which the individual's father was considered white or non-Indian, and in which the father or grandfather belonged to another band.

The clearest differences among the chiefs were between Deer, one of the older and longer sitting chiefs on the council, and Jocks, a much younger and more recently elected chief (see table 3). Of all the chiefs, Deer represented a position most inconsistent with Indian Act policies, while Jocks represented a position most consistent with them regarding Indian and band status. Deer contested all but two of the claims in the categories above, while Jocks contested only those two that were not contested by Deer. These two cases involved individuals who were considered members of another band. Deer contested all the claimants whose father was considered white, while Jocks contested none of them. In these cases the two other chiefs, Montour and Beauvais, agreed with Deer and disagreed with Jocks. On the other hand, they consistently agreed with Jocks and disagreed with Deer in not contesting the claims of individuals whose fathers or grandfathers were considered members of another band. Finally, in the matter of claims involving illegitimacy, Beauvais consistently agreed with Deer in contesting such claims, and Montour consistently agreed with Jocks in not contesting them. Overall, in these disputed cases where consensus was not reached, Montour and Beauvais represented a middle road between the extremes represented by Deer and Jocks; but Beauvais, who was also one of the older, long-serving chiefs, was more similar to Deer, while Montour, who was younger and recently elected to his position, was more similar to Jocks. As we will see in the next chapter, this pattern may represent one dimension of a split that developed within the Kahnawà:ke during the 1870s and 1880s over the council of chiefs and the Indian Act system.

The land claims process was completed in March 1886. Of the 175 claims that were originally contested by one or more of the chiefs, 55 percent (96) were not recognized by the Department of Indian Affairs; in the remaining 79 cases the chiefs' objections were overruled and the claims were recognized (see table 4).[54] The largest number of claims not recognized by the Indian De-

Table 3. Nonunanimous claims contested by the Council of Chiefs in the Walbank Survey, 1885

Reason contested	Total	Thomas Deer (Atonwa Asennase)	Thomas Jocks (Atonwa Karatoton)	Michael Montour (Wishe Sakoientineta)	Louis Beauvais (Rowi Shatekaienton)
Father white/non-Indian	8	8 (8)	0 (8)	8 (8)	8 (8)
Belongs to another band	5	3 (5)	2 (3)	3 (5)	3 (5)
Father belongs to another band	20	20 (20)	0 (16)	0 (20)	2 (20)
Grandfather belongs to another band	8	8 (8)	0 (7)	0 (8)	0 (8)
Illegitimate	7	7 (7)	0 (7)	1 (7)	7 (7)
Husband not band member	1	1 (1)	—	0 (1)	0 (1)
Not band member	1	1 (1)	0 (1)	1 (1)	1 (1)
Other	3	3 (3)	0 (3)	1 (3)	1 (3)
Total	53	51 (53)	2 (45)	14 (53)	22 (53)

Source: National Archives of Canada, *Records relating to Indian Affairs*, Record Group 10, vols. 8969–72, Walbank Reference Books—Caughnawaga.

Note: Numbers in parentheses refer to the number of claims out of the total for which the chief's position was indicated.

Table 4. Claims not recognized by the Indian Department in the Walbank Survey, 1885

Reason claim not recognized	Male	Female	Total
Long absence in foreign country	17	5	22
Belongs to another band	19	1	20
White/non-Indian	12	1	13
Underage	12	0	12
Father white/ mother not band member	9	1	10
Parents not band members	6	1	7
Not widow	0	2	2
Adopted	1	1	2
Other	5	3	8
Total	81	15	96

Source: National Archives of Canada, *Records relating to Indian Affairs*, Record Group 10, vol. 2693, file 139964, pt. 1, Brosseau to Vankoughnet, 9 February 1886, and Vankoughnet to Brosseau, 4 March 1886.

partment included those in which the claimant was determined to have violated Indian Act policy against prolonged absence in a foreign country (22) or to belong to another band (20). Thirteen claimants were not recognized because they were white or not Indian, and ten were not recognized because their fathers were white and their mothers were not considered members of the band. Of the 122 claims that were unanimously contested by the chiefs, 75 percent (92) were ultimately not recognized by the Indian Department. Of the 53 claims that were not unanimously contested, 94 percent (51) were ultimately recognized by the Indian Department. Not surprisingly, the end result of the claims process reflected Indian Act policy, though not entirely.[55] The council persisted in its determination to limit potential allotments by denying the claims of those it considered to be underage or not widowed, and eventually the Indian Department accepted their position.

After the completion of the land claims process, the Indian Department planned to expel those whose claims were rejected, subdivide the reserve into lots of about thirty acres with regular boundaries, and locate each recognized claimant on one of these allotments.[56] In June 1886 those whose claims were rejected were ordered to vacate the reserve. Those who had occupied land on the reserve were to be compensated for the value of improvements they had made to their land and allowed to remain until their summer crops had been harvested. Not surprisingly, problems developed at the very start. Some objected to the valuation of the improvements on their land and filed grievances with the Indian Department, and the members of one large family whose claims were rejected because they were not considered Indians fought an extended legal battle to have their right to remain on the reserve recognized by the Indian Department. More generally, and more seriously, most of those whose claims were rejected refused to leave the reserve, and the Indian Department failed to force them; in the 1890s most still remained on the reserve. Further, the Walbank survey team began running subdivision lines, but the process was never completed and allotments to those with rightful claims were never made. Thus the inequalities in landownership that exacerbated the problem of land scarcity and generated tension between "haves" and "have-nots" within the native community persisted. In addition, many of those whose claim to band membership and residence on the reserve was opposed by the native community but approved by the Indian Department remained on the reserve and continued to occupy land. The Indian Department was again dealing with these problems a decade later and planning yet another subdivision of the reserve.[57] Finally, during this period the problems of white encroachment, land and resource scarcity, inequality in landownership, and the polarization of the native and white populations in Kahnawà:ke proved to be important factors in the development of a Conservative/Reform split within the native community over the council of chiefs and the Indian Act system.

3. *"For Three Years" or "For Life"*
The Council of Chiefs and
Establishment of the Band Council System

Kahnawà:ke's Council of Chiefs

T he problems of white encroachment, resource scarcity, and inequality of landownership and the polarization that affected Kahnawà:ke in the 1870s and 1880s were important factors in the community's division over the council of chiefs and the Indian Act system. These problems also played a part in the eventual establishment of the band council system on the reserve and, during the 1890s, in rising opposition to the Indian Act and the development of traditionalist and nationalist impulses within the community. Crucial to understanding these social, political, and cultural developments is an understanding of the organization of Kahnawà:ke's council of chiefs.

Before the establishment of the band council system, Kahnawà:ke was governed at the local level by a council of seven chiefs, each of whom represented one of seven clans or clan segments within the community.[1] The organization and composition of this council of chiefs is suggested by a number of sources: the most important is the files of Canada's Department of Indian Affairs concerning the "election" of chiefs in the mid-1870s and the application of the Indian Advancement Act to the reserve in 1889.[2] In February 1875 a number of Kahnawakehró:non petitioned the Indian Department to "elect" new chiefs and limit their terms of office to three years.[3] The petition also stated that the chiefs holding their positions at the time had been elected in 1872 for a three-year term and that it was time to hold new elections. J. E. R. Pinsonneault, the Indian agent for Kahnawà:ke who received the petition and forwarded it to the minister of the interior, stated in his attached letter that he did not know if in fact the chiefs were named for only a limited term of office or "for life." A notation written on Pinsonneault's letter after it had been received in Ottawa indicates that the petitioners were in error in their understanding of the 1872 election and that the agent was directed to inform them of this fact. According to this notation, the chiefs in 1872 had held their positions for some seventeen or eighteen years and that the 1872 election had instead been a referendum to determine if the sitting chiefs had a majority of supporters in the band—which it appears they did. The notation also refers to the Kahnawà:ke chiefs as "life chiefs" and directs that they continue to hold their positions until "death, resignation, or . . . their removal by the Governor." A related letter from an Indian agent who served in Kahnawà:ke in 1872 states that the chiefs who composed the council at that time were "appointed" to their positions by the superintendent general of Indian affairs.[4]

In addition to seeking new elections and a limit to a chiefs' term of office, the authors of the 1875 petition also sought to reduce the number of chiefs on the council from seven to three. The petitioners stated no reason for seeking this change in the organization of the council of chiefs, and for his part Pinsonneault stated that he saw no reason the number of chiefs should be reduced. In the end the Indian Department took no action on the petitioners' requests. However, the petition does provide some crucial pieces of information about the organization of Kahnawà:ke's council of chiefs in 1875: the number of chiefs was seven, chiefs held their position on the council "for life," and the chiefs composing the council had been "appointed" to their positions twenty years earlier by the superintendent general of Indian affairs.

The issues of the election of chiefs and a chief's term of office arose again two years later when one of the chiefs, Sose Taioroniote, resigned from office in June 1877.[5] In the Indian Department file containing documents relating to his resignation, Taioroniote is identified as the chief of the Rotisennaketekowa "band."[6] After the Indian agent, Georges Cherrier, communicated Taioroniote's resignation to the minister of the interior and suggested a candidate to fill the vacant position, the minister informed him that the Kahnawà:ke chiefs were elected and that he should consult the council in the matter of replacing Taioroniote. Specifically, Cherrier was directed to determine if the council preferred an election and, if so, whether it should be conducted according to "their old rules" or under the provisions of the Indian Act of 1876.[7] The election provisions of the act would have called for the election of a chief by the adult male members of the band, for a term of three years. However, the Indian Act also provided that such an election could take place according to the rules of a particular band, but it is not clear from the minister's directions to the Indian agent what he meant by his reference to Kahnawà:ke's "old rules."[8] The Indian Department took no action on Taioroniote's resignation until the following February, when a referendum was held to determine the community's preference for selecting a replacement according to the Indian Act or Kahnawà:ke's old rules. According to Georges Cherrier's report, the meeting at which the referendum was held was well attended by the people of the community, but the number who actually voted was only forty-two. Of this number, twenty-four voted "for life" and eighteen "for three years." The majority, he stated, "would not declare themselves one way or the other."[9] Following his report on the referendum, Cherrier was directed by the minister of the interior to proceed with an election of a chief according to the "old rules of the Caughnawaga Band, such being the wish expressed by the majority."[10] In late February 1878 Cherrier reported to the minister that the Rotisennaketekowa had met to elect a replacement for Taioroniote and that after several hours' discussion "they decided to ask the Dept. to allow them to choose a Chief from some other Band—either the 'Bande du Loup,' or from the 'Bande la Tortue' or some other, alleging that they had no man capable of representing them."[11] The minister answered that if it was "consistent with the wishes of the Caughnawaga band," the Department had no objection to the Rotisennaketekowa's electing a member of another "band" as its chief.[12] Finally, in March 1878 elections were held, but to replace not one but three chiefs. By this time not only had Taioroniote resigned as chief, but so had Joseph Delisle (Sose Kentarontie), chief of the Rotiskerewakakaion band. In addition, Chief Francis Otonharishon of the Rotiskerewakekowa, had recently died. As new chiefs, the Rotisennaketekowa selected Joseph Williams (Sose Skatsienhati), the Rotisherewakakaion selected Thomas Jocks (Atonwa Karatoton), and the Rotiskerewakekowa chose Peter Murray (Tier Kaheroton).[13]

In reporting on the elections, Cherrier, intentionally or in error, indicated that the new chiefs had been elected to terms of three years, as they would have been under the provisions of the Indian Act of 1876. In response, the minister of the interior made a point of reminding Cherrier that, in accordance with the 1878 referendum, the new chiefs had been chosen by Kahnawà:ke's old rules. And, in fact, there is no evidence of general elections of chiefs three years later, as would have been called for under the Indian Act, or at any other subsequent time until the establishment of the band council system in 1889. The only elections held after 1878 were to replace chiefs who had resigned, died, or been deposed.

Thus the Indian Department file for the 1878 elections in Kahnawà:ke also suggests that chiefs on the council held their positions for life. Several other conclusions are supported as well: the council consisted of seven chiefs; only men served as chiefs; each chief represented a band within the community, and each was selected by some part or all of the membership of the band he represented; typically, a chief was a member of the band he represented in the council, but if a band could not find a suitable candidate from within its membership, it could select a man from another band as its chief.[14]

The process by which a chief was elected is unclear. The Indian Department files give no indication whether a chief was selected by consensus, majority vote, or some other process. Further, it is not evident who within the clan—men or women, or both—participated in selecting the chief. Thus, while the Indian Department files typically refer to the chiefs as being elected, this may be misleading. "Elected" suggests that the chiefs were selected by a process involving nominations and majority vote, as would be called for under the Indian Act of 1876, but these same files indicate that the elections in Kahnawà:ke were taking place according to its old rules, not the Indian Act. In addition, the files concerning the elections give no vote tallies, as might be expected if the chiefs were chosen by majority vote. In this regard it is important to note that vote tallies were recorded for various referenda, such as the one in February 1878, and in band council elections after that system was instituted in 1889. Given this, it is possible that chiefs were selected according some other process, perhaps one involving the general consent of each band. Indian Affairs authorities appear to have had no official role in the selection of a chief, but once one had been selected, the government officials confirmed the appointment. According to Doutre, in the early 1850s a chief's confirmation was symbolized by the presentation of a silver medal bearing the likeness of the British sovereign on one side and the English coat of arms on the other. When a chief died this silver medal remained with his mother and her maternal lineage until a new chief was selected.[15]

The 1878 Indian Department file discussed above also identifies five of the seven Kahnawà:ke bands that were represented in the council of chiefs. These five, as their names appeared in the documents, are the Rotisennaketekowa, Rotiskerewakakaion, Rotiskerewakekowa, "Bande du Loup," and "Bande la Tortue."

These five bands as well as two others are also identified in a series of petitions from 1889 related to electing new chiefs and the application of the Indian Advancement Act to the reserve.[16] The series includes a separate petition from each band and identifies the members of the band that supported the petition. As identified and written in these petitions, the seven bands are the Rotinesiioh, Rotisenakete, Ratiniaten, Rotiskerewakekowa, Rotik8ho, Onkwaskerewake, and Rotineniotronon. It is evident that in these contexts the term "band" is not used as it was defined according to the Indian Act of 1876 and subsequent Indian Act legislation, that is, as the entire group of native people occupying a particular reserve. Rather, in these contexts "band," or "bande," refers to descent groups customarily referred to as "clans" or lineages within clans. Four of these seven bands identified refer to the three original Kanien'kehá:ka clans and point to the Kanien'kehá:ka roots of the Kahnawà:ke community: Ratiniaten (and "Bande la Tortue") refers to the Turtle clan; Rotiskere-wakekowa refers to the "Big Bears" or "Great Bears," while Onkwaskerewake (and Rotiskerewakakaion) refers to the "Old Bears" or "Small Bears"; and Rotik8ho (and "Bande du Loup") refers to the Wolf clan.[17] The names of the three remaining bands refer to clans or peoples of other Iroquois nations and perhaps point to the Onondaga and Oneida ancestry of the Kahnawà:ke community. Rotinesiioh refers to Snipe, a clan of the Onondaga Nation, and Rotisenakete (and Rotisennaketekowa) refers to the Deer clan and is a variant of the council name for the Onondaga meaning "name bearers" or "they carry the name." Last, Rotineniotronon, referring to "the people of the erected stone," suggests that this band included Kahnawakehró:non who traced descent from Oneida ancestors of the community.[18] In modernized spelling these seven clans are the Ratiniáhton (Turtle), Rotiskeré:wakeḱó:wa (Great Bear), Rotiskeré:wakaká:ion (Old Bear), Rotikwáho (Wolf), Rotinehsí:io (Snipe), Rotihsennakéhte (Deer), and Rotineniothró:non (Rock).

While a clan-based council of chiefs probably existed in Kahnawà:ke since at least the early eighteenth century, the council of seven chiefs appears to date to only about the early 1840s. This is suggested by the correspondence of an Indian agent in which it is noted that the chiefs constituting the council in 1875 first received official confirmation of their positions sometime in the early or mid-1850s.[19] A somewhat earlier date for the establishment of a council of seven chiefs is suggested by documents relating to an official government inquiry in 1840 into complaints made by some Kahnawakehró:non to the governor general against their chiefs and a local missionary. At the close of the investigation the officials who conducted the inquiry recommended "that all of the Commissions granted to the Chiefs of [Caughnawaga] be Cancelled . . . that the number of Chiefs be reduced to seven . . . one to each band as they are presently Constituted . . . [t]hat each Band shall select their Chief subject to the approval of the Governor General."[20] An inscription deposited in the cornerstone of the St. Francis Xavier Mission church in Kahnawà:ke in 1845 suggests that the change to a council of seven chiefs had take place by this time. The inscription records the names of seven men who are described as "the principal grand chiefs of this village." They were Martin Tekanasontie, Thomas Tiohatekwen, Charles Katsirakeron, Thomas Sakaohetsta, Jean Baptiste Saonwentiowane, Joseph Tenihatie, and Pierre Atawenrate.[21]

Thus, while the process by which a clan chief was chosen is not entirely clear, once he was selected his appointment received an official confirmation from the federal government.[22] Dating from the 1840s, this form of Kahnawà:ke's village council was of relatively recent origin. The council of seven chiefs was based on the clan system but was modified to include all segments of the community, including those whose clan membership derived from its Oneida and Onondaga roots as well as its Kanien'kehá:ka roots. It was not a "traditional" council, yet it was based on two important principles at the heart of Iroquois political organization—equal voice and government and decision making based on the clan system.

This development of a form of village political organization rooted in the clan system and the principle of equal voice, but reflecting Kahnawà:ke's unique history, has parallels in other Kanien'kehá:ka and Rotinonhsiónni communities.[23] In the eighteenth century the Kanien'keha:ka at Tyendinaga developed a council system of eleven chiefs representing the founding lineages of that community. The chiefs were appointed by the senior women of the lineages and held their positions for life. This form of a council of chiefs persisted at Tyendinaga until the band council system was established there in 1870.[24] At Ahkwesáhsne, on the Canadian side of the international border, a council of twelve chiefs developed sometime after the community's establishment in the mid-eighteenth century and persisted until it was forcibly replaced by the band council system in the late nineteenth century. The council consisted of three chiefs from each of the four clans represented in the community—the Bear, Wolf, Turtle, and Snipe. As at Tyendinaga, the chiefs were appointed by clan mothers and held their positions for life.[25] At Six Nations reserve, where Cayugas, Kanien'kehá:ka, Oneidas, Onondagas, Senecas, Tuscaroras, and members of other native nations settled after the American Revolution, the Confederacy Council was reconstituted and was responsible for matters affecting the Six Nations as a whole, while villages within the reserve were governed by the national councils of the individual nations. After 1847 the national councils were abandoned and the Confederacy Council became the sole governing body on the reserve.[26] Clearly, local governments in these Kanien'kehá:ka and Rotinonhsiónni communities were based on "traditional" Iroquois political organization and principles but were modified in ways that reflected their specific local and historical circumstances.

A similar pattern of development in local political organization took place in Kahnawà:ke.

There were a number of changes in the composition of Kahnawà:ke's council of chiefs between 1850 and 1889 (see table 5). In 1878 Joseph Williams replaced Sose Taioroniote as chief of the Rotihsennakéhte, Thomas Jocks replaced Sose Kentarontie as chief of the Rotiskeré:wakaká:ion, and Peter Murray succeeded Francis Otonharishon as chief of the Rotiskeré:wakekó:wa. At the time he was named chief, Williams was thirty-two years old, had been married nine years, and was described as a "rich merchant"; in 1884 he was identified as the owner of 104 acres, placing him among the top 5 percent of landowners on the reserve at that time. Jocks was thirty-seven years old and described as a "contractor" when he was named chief; in 1884 he owned 261 acres and was the largest individual landowner on the reserve. Murray was forty-one and had been married for sixteen years when he was named chief. In contrast to Williams and Jocks, in 1884 he owned only a small garden plot in the village area of the reserve.[27] Williams resigned as chief about 1884 and died in 1885. The position of chief of the Rotihsennakéhte remained vacant until the council of chiefs was abolished in 1889. Jocks continued to serve as chief until 1889 and was among the first councillors elected when the band council system was instituted in that year. Murray was deposed in 1881 and replaced by Michael Montour (Wishe Sakoientineta), who continued as chief of the Rotiskeré:wakekó:wa until 1889. At the time he was named chief, Montour was thirty-two and had been married nine years; in 1884 he owned a modest thirty-five acres of land.

Soon after the selection of the three new chiefs in 1878, Thomas Rice (Atonwa Onharakete) replaced Martin Sakoriatakwa as the chief of an unidentified fourth clan. At that time Sakoriatakwa was fifty-nine and Rice was just twenty-six. Rice may not even have been living on the reserve at the time he was named chief. Evidence indicates that he moved to Michigan

Table 5. The Kahnawà:ke chiefs, 1853–89

Clan	Year			
	1860	1870	1880	1890
Rotiskeré:wakekó:wa (Great Bear)	Francis Oronharishon ca. 1853–78	– – – –	Peter Murray (Tier Kaheroton) 1878–81	– – –	Michael Montour (Wishe Sakoientineta) 1881–89
Rotiskeré:wakakái:ion (Old Bear)	Sose Kentarontie ca. 1853–78	– – – –	Thomas Jocks (Atonwa Karatoton) 1878–89	– – –	– –
Rotihsennakéhte (Deer)	Sose Taioroniote ca. 1853–77	– – – –	Joseph Williams (Sose Skatsienhati) 1878–85	– – –	– –
Rotineniothró:non (Rock)	Louis Beauvais (Rowi Shatekaienton) ca. 1853–89	– – – –	– – – –	– – –	– –
Unidentified clan	Thomas Deer (Atonwa Asennase) ca. 1853–87	– – – –	– – – –	– – –	– –
Unidentified clan	Rowi Tehorakaron ca. 1853–86	– – – –	– – – –	– – –	– –
Unidentified clan	Martin Sakoriatakwa ca. 1853–78	– – – –	Thomas Rice (Atonwa Onharakete) 1878–86	– – –	– –

about 1871, married in Bay City in 1873, and was living in Detroit in 1884. He was investigated by the Indian Department for misconduct in 1885 and resigned or was deposed soon thereafter. From that time until the council of chiefs was abolished in 1889, the position of chief of his clan appears to have remained vacant. Louis Beauvais (Rowi Shatekaienton) was chief of the Rotineniothró:non and in 1884 was identified as having been a "grand chief" for thirty years. At that time he was fifty-one (meaning that he was named chief at just twenty years of age), and continued to serve as chief until the council was abolished in 1889. Rowi Tehorakaron and Thomas Deer (Atonwa Asennase), the chiefs of two other unidentified clans, died within a year of one another in 1886 and 1887. Deer was seventy-three years old and had been chief for some thirty years. After their deaths the positions of chief of their clans appear to have remained vacant until 1889.

Division within Kahnawà:ke over the Council of Chiefs and the Indian Act System

Beginning with the Enfranchisement Act of 1869, the transformation of native political institutions was a principal objective of the Indian Act system and its overall goal of cultural assimilation. Aimed primarily at the Rotinonhsiónni and other native peoples with a long history of European contact, the Enfranchisement Act gave the governor general-in-council the power to impose an elective form of government on Indian bands and to remove from elected office anyone it deemed unfit or unqualified. In addition, under the Enfranchisement Act elected band councils were empowered to pass bylaws, but only on a variety of minor municipal matters and only with the approval of the superintendent general of Indian affairs. It was expected that such experience with Euro-Canadian political ideals and institutions would lead to more complete assimilation to other Euro-Canadian values and practices.[28] The Indian Act of 1876 represented a shift in strategy with regard to native political institutions by providing that the elective band council system would be instituted on a reserve only if the band applied for it. Generally, however, there was widespread native resistance to the Indian Act because most Indian bands did not want to sacrifice their political autonomy or give up their own political institutions. In Kahnawà:ke there was opposition to the Indian Act system, but there was also support for abolishing the traditional council and establishing the elective system, so the community became deeply divided over the issue.

The February 1875 petition in which a number of Kahnawakehró:non sought to elect new chiefs and modify the structure of the traditional council was in essence an effort to apply the Indian Act system to the reserve. Specifically, by reducing the number of chiefs from seven to three, holding periodic elections, and limiting a chief's term of office to three years, the petitioners were seeking to bring Kahnawà:ke's council into conformity with the Enfranchisement Act of 1869. Significantly, the petition carried 134 signatures, all those of men. If we assume these are the signatures of males at least twenty-one years old, the petition represents approximately 37 percent of the adult male population of the reserve at that time.[29] The petitioners did not state their reasons for seeking to elect new chiefs and modify the council system, but related documents in the Indian Department file containing the petition suggest some possible explanations. In March 1875, one month after the petition, three Kahnawakehró:non deposed affidavits against two of the sitting chiefs, Joseph Delisle, chief of the Rotiskeré:wakaká:ion, and Francis Otonharishon, chief of the Rotiskeré:wakekó:wa, accusing them of immoral and drunken behavior.[30] In June 1875 Thomas Jocks wrote to the minister of the interior and stated that the chiefs did not command the confidence and respect of the people. He pointed out that all the chiefs "are accused of receiving money from the Government and refusing to render an account of it . . . of dishonesty, and other things equally incompatible with their position." He referred to the March affidavits in support of his view and claimed that there was "a strong and general desire among the Indians for elections."[31]

His letter in 1875 was not the first time Jocks attempted to bring his opinion of the chiefs' conduct to the attention of government officials. As he also stated in that letter, "I may say that I have written several letters and sent a great number of documents to the Indian Department during the last few years with a view of obtaining an election of new chiefs." Jocks also attempted to make it clear that he had acted in the best interests of the community and that its wishes had been purposely frustrated by the local Indian agent:

> I beg now to say that it would be a mistake [to hold elections for new chiefs] if there was no desire from the tribe for an election. But there is such a desire and it is very strong and very general among the tribes and each time that an attempt was made on the part of our people to express their opinion on the subject openly, the Agent at the time used his influence to prevent the people from acting freely and according to their own judgement. . . . As a reason for the interest I take in the welfare of the tribe, and as an excuse for the trouble I have given you, I may say that I was born at Caughnawaga, have always lived there, my family and relatives live there and my business centered there closely identifies me with the place and its people, and above all [I] am a member of the tribe. What I ask and what all the worthy people and the great majority of the tribe desire, is that the tribe should be allowed to give a free and unbiased opinion on whether there should be new chiefs elected or not and not subjected as heretofore to threats of ill treatment, or pecuniary loss if they attempt to express their own opinions.[32]

It is unusual that the Indian agent would attempt to undermine a desire for a change in the council of chiefs system, given that it would bring the reserve into line with the government's own policy of assimilation. Jocks, however, offered no explanation for why the agent sought to do so.

In December 1875 Chief Otonharishon was again the focus of concern when thirteen members of his clan petitioned the governor general for an investigation of his conduct and asked that they be permitted to elect a replacement. Otonharishon was accused of being a drunkard and "thereby incapable of fulfilling his duties as chief." The local Indian agent was directed to look into the matter, and in February 1876 the minister of the interior did recommend that Otonharishon be removed from office.[33] Eventually he was replaced by one of the petitioners who had sought his removal, Peter Murray.

Complaints similar to those made in 1875 had been lodged against the chiefs three years earlier. These complaints resulted in a community meeting in April 1872 to consider the question of electing new chiefs. According to Indian Department records, the majority of the people attending the meeting supported the sitting chiefs and did not want to appoint replacements. In response to the outcome of the meeting, Thomas Jocks wrote to the secretary of state objecting that E. N. DeLorimier, the Indian agent who conducted the meeting, had "not taken the sense of the Tribes [clans] in regard to their desire of having an election." Referring to the Kahnawà:ke clans as "tribes," he went on to state, "It might be and it is probable that if an election was fairly granted to us some of the old Chiefs would be elected. Section 10 of the Act gives the right to each tribe to elect its Chief. To show you, Sir, what is the sense of one of the Tribes, the members of the Rotiskerewakekowa are almost unanimously willing to proceed to an election. When Mr. de Lorimier pretended to consult the Indians, he should have taken separately the opinions of each Tribe."[34]

In short, within the Kahnawà:ke community there was ongoing dissatisfaction with the conduct and leadership of the chiefs. A factor contributing to the dissatisfaction may have been land and resource scarcity. The year 1875, when a large segment of the community petitioned to elect new chiefs and restructure the council, when a number of official complaints were made against the chiefs, and when the members of the Rotiskeré:wakekó:wa clan sought to replace their chief, was the same year when four of the chiefs sought to sell the entire reserve for $25 an acre.

The dissatisfaction with the chiefs may also have been coupled with the political aspirations of young men within the community who were eager to unseat the long-serving chiefs. According to E. N. DeLorimier, who was the Indian agent for Kahnawà:ke at the time, the complaints against the chiefs in 1872 had been lodged by "young warriors anxious to be made chiefs," and the "young warriors" were greatly disappointed by the support for the sitting chiefs.[35] DeLorimier did not indicate whether Thomas Jocks, who was about thirty-one at this time, was among the young warriors, but given his involvement in these issues up to this point, he almost certainly was. Peter Murray, who was about thirty-five, was probably a member of this group as well. Overall, the signers of the February 1875 petition to abolish the council of chiefs and institute the elective system were in fact relatively young. The average age of the 94 (out of 134) petitioners for whom birth dates could be determined was 36.7 years. Thirty-three percent of this group were under thirty, and 34 percent were between thirty and thirty-nine; 18 percent were between forty and forty-nine; 5.3 percent were between fifty and fifty-nine; and 9.6 percent were sixty or older. Among the petitioners were Thomas Jocks, Peter Murray, and Joseph Williams (age twenty-nine), each of who would become a chief in 1878. The members of the Rotiskeré:wakekó:wa who petitioned the governor general to replace Chief Otonharishon in December 1975 also were relatively young: their average age was 34.8 years. The petitioners included Peter Murray and six other men who also had signed the February 1875 petition to bring Kahnawakà:ke's council into conformity with the Enfranchisement Act of 1869.

Sose Taioroniote resigned as chief of the Rotihsennakéhte in 1877, and his action prompted a referendum on the length of a chief's term of office—"for life" or "for three years." In effect, the referendum was a measure of support for Kahnawà:ke's "old rules" and the traditional council of chiefs as against support for the Indian Act and the elective band council system. The referendum was held in February 1878, and the majority (twenty-four) favored the old rules and chiefs for life. The age pattern evident among the petitioners in the February and December 1875 petitions can also be seen in the 1878 referendum, though perhaps less clearly. The average age of those who supported the change to the Indian Act system was thirty-four, and they were all between twenty-one and forty-six. Among them, again, were Thomas Jocks and Peter Murray. Those who favored maintaining the traditional council of chiefs were generally an older and more diverse group: their average age was forty-two, and they ranged from twenty-two to seventy.[36] After the referendum, the Indian agent informed the minister of the interior that in response to the outcome there was a "party in the Tribe who wish to separate." He was "forced," he stated, "to take down the names of about 60 . . . [who] are determined to force a division."[37]

In addition to age, inequalities in landownership were an important dimension of the split within the community over the Indian Act system. Ninety-eight of the 134 signers of the February 1875 petition to bring Kahnawà:ke's council into conformity with the Enfranchisement Act could be identified in the records of the Walbank land survey of 1884. Of this number, 75 percent (seventy-three) owned some land. Further, the average landholding among them was about fifty-three acres, considerably above the average for all landowners at that time (thirty-two acres).

Nearly three-quarters (70 percent) of those among the top 5 percent of landowners in 1884 signed the February 1875 petition. In the 1878 referendum on the length of a chief's term of office, large landowners composed the majority of those who voted "for three years" and the Indian Act system. Their average landholding was seventy-three acres, and among them were three of Kahnawà:ke's largest landowners, including Thomas Jocks. None of the top landowners supported chiefs for life and Kahnawà:ke's old rules. Those who did support the traditional system were mainly small landholders and those who owned no land at all.[38] Since there is an eight- to ten-year period between the 1875 petition and the 1878 referendum and the records of landownership, conclusions must be drawn cautiously. Nevertheless, this evidence does suggest that those who sought to replace the life chiefs, apply the Indian Act, abolish the council of chiefs, and establish an elected band council system tended to be landowners, and large landowners in particular.

Despite the February referendum expressing support for life chiefs and the old rules, when Joseph Williams, Thomas Jocks, and Peter Murray were selected as chiefs of the Rotihsennakéhte, Rotiskeré:wakaká:ion, and Rotiskeré:wakekó:wa in March 1878, they and the Indian agent, Georges Cherrier, attempted to proceed in their duties as if the three had been elected in accordance with the Indian Act of 1876. Immediately after the elections Cherrier informed the minister of the interior that the three chiefs had been elected to terms of three years.[39] Subsequently he reported that "the Chiefs desire to have special instructions on their duties toward the Tribe, having been elected in conformity with the Indian Act of 1876. They ask to have instructions in accordance therewith that they may be able to act with more facility in following the law, which they have studied since their appointment."[40] In reply, Cherrier was informed that "the Chiefs are under a misapprehension as to their having been selected in conformity with the provisions of the Indian Act of 1876." He was reminded of the February referendum at which the majority supported chiefs "elected in accordance with the usages of the Band" and was directed to "carry the wishes of the Indians into effect."[41]

After the March 1878 elections, Cherrier reported that "the majority of the village desire to have only these three chiefs last elected." Further, in a development he interpreted as an effort by the community to emphasize its preference for the new chiefs and its dissatisfaction with the other sitting chiefs, Cherrier also stated that the band "in council" had decided to ask the Indian Department to provide each of the three newly elected chiefs $50 annually for expenses but that they were "unwilling to give a cent to the other three old chiefs."[42] Notwithstanding Cherrier's comments, there is evidence of rather significant opposition to the three newly selected chiefs. Less than two years after the 1878 elections, 159 Kahnawakehró:non petitioned the governor general to depose Williams, Jocks, and Murray and a fourth chief, Thomas Rice, and hold new elections to replace them. The petitioners were all men and represent approximately 40 percent of the adult male population of the reserve at that time.[43] Murray was accused of intemperance, and a replacement for Rice was sought because he was not living on the reserve. More important, the petitioners argued that Jocks, Williams, and Murray "refuse to act in the interest and at the request of the Band and do not act honestly to the Band." The issue here was the presence of whites on the reserve and the refusal of the three chiefs to remove them as many desired. As the petitioners stated,

> The said [Caughnawaga] Band in a meeting duly called and attended by a large majority of the members entitled to vote thereat almost unanimously resolved that the squatters upon their reserve should be expelled and required that their chiefs to take active measures to carry out their will in the matter.

That the said Joseph Williams, Thomas Jocks, and Peter Murray refuse to carry out the law or to take any steps towards the same, but with a view to making personal profit out of the squatters and at the expense of the Band they encourage and allow them to remain. All of which your Petitioners are ready to prove.

Wherefore your Petitioners pray that Your Excellency in Council will be pleased to depose the said . . . chiefs and to summon a meeting of the Band to elect . . . chiefs in their places, and that the said squatters may be removed from their reserve.[44]

Murray was eventually removed from office (in 1881) and replaced by Michael Montour, but Williams continued as chief until his death in 1885 and Jocks until the council of chiefs was abolished in 1889. Rice was encouraged by the DIA to return to the reserve, but he apparently failed to do so, for in 1883 the Department investigated his right to continue as chief because of his continued absence.[45] Eventually he did return, but in 1885 he was investigated on charges of fraud and theft, and soon thereafter his position on the council became vacant and remained so until 1889.[46]

These developments suggest that the Kahnawà:ke community split into two factions during the 1870s and 1880s over the issue of the Indian Act system. One was a "Reform" faction that supported the Indian Act system and sought to abolish the old rules and the traditional council of chiefs. The Reformers favored the Indian Act system and sought the end of the traditional council at least in part because of dissatisfaction with the perceived conduct, character, and incompetence of the traditional chiefs. In their view, Kahnawà:ke's old rules served to protect the sitting chiefs and perpetuate ineffective leadership, circumstances they sought to change by instituting the Indian Act system. Young men were the core of the Reform faction; they tended to be business owners and large landowners and thus were probably more assimilated than other members of the community. They may also have had a more open attitude toward whites on the reserve and felt closer to them. These young warriors not only were dissatisfied with the leadership of the sitting chiefs but were ambitious men for whom the old rules were an obstacle to their political aspirations. For them the Indian Act system was a means to open the door to political office and leadership. In 1878 some of these young warriors gained access to political office within the existing traditional system and continued to press for the adoption of the Indian Act system. Most prominent within the Reform faction and its core of young warriors was Thomas Jocks.

The second faction was "Conservative." In opposition to the Reformers, the Conservative faction sought to maintain Kahnawà:ke's old rules and its traditional council of chiefs; they opposed the Indian Act and the establishment of the elective band council system. In terms of age, they constituted a more diverse membership than the Reform faction. In addition, they tended to be small landowners or to own no land, and antagonism toward whites residing on the reserve was probably highest among this group. Their numbers were significant, and during the 1870s they successfully countered Reform attempts to abolish the traditional council and institute the Indian Act system. In addition, Conservatives actively pressured the young warriors of the Reform faction after they gained seats on the council of chiefs. It was in these circumstances that in 1889 the Indian Advancement Act was applied to Kahnawà:ke and the band council system replaced the traditional council of chiefs.

The Indian Advancement Act and Establishment of the Band Council System

Government officials viewed native opposition to the 1876 act, such as that in Kahnawà:ke, as evidence that Indian people continued to need government direction and further assimilation.

Consequently, in 1880 the Indian Act was amended to again empower the superintendent general to impose the band council system on those bands he considered prepared to receive it. After this, the Indian Advancement Act of 1884 made establishment of band councils on reserves a principal objective of Indian policy. The central aim of the Advancement Act was more aggressive transformation of native political institutions by replacing traditional governments with an elective band council system modeled on the municipal government system characteristic of Euro-Canadian towns. Band councils established under the Advancement Act involved proportional representation and annual elections (under the 1876 act elections took place every three years) and could be applied to any band by order of the governor general-in-council.[47]

In November 1887 fifty-four Kahnawakehró:non petitioned the minister of the interior to have the Indian Act of 1880 applied to the reserve. The fifty-four petitioners represented approximately 11 percent of the adult male population on the reserve at that time. In addition to abolishing the council of chiefs and replacing it with the band council system, the petitioners also sought to deal with a more immediate problem: an incomplete and ineffectively functioning council. By this time several chiefs had died or been removed from office, and some of the remaining chiefs were considered unfit for their responsibilities. The petitioners stated:

> That in this instance the motive of our urgent prayer is of the most eminent character, which is the alteration in the Council of Chiefs; that is to say, a general election of a suitable number of chiefs, if not for the term of three years, as provided by law hereinafter mentioned, at least temporarily. The actual council is defective on account of its quorum being insufficient. . . . That we deem it unnecessary to state in detail the extent of our grievances towards our chiefs; in a

word, be it given us the humble expectation that the benefit of "section 72 of the Indian Act of 1880" be applied to us.[48]

Section 72 of the Indian Act of 1880 provided for the election of chiefs for terms of three years and limited the number of chiefs on a reserve to six.[49] This petition, like the earlier 1875 petition, sought to reduce the number of chiefs, institute periodic elections of chiefs, and limit a chief's term to three years.

Early the following year, in mid-January 1888, members of the Kahnawà:ke community met to consider the application of the Indian Advancement Act of 1884 to the reserve. As noted, the Advancement Act took a more aggressive approach to the transformation of native political institutions. The means for accomplishing this was the one-year elective band council system. Under this system, an Indian reserve would be governed locally by a council of representatives elected by and from among the adult male members of the band inhabiting the reserve. For the purposes of electing the council, the reserve would be divided into sections, each with an equal proportion of the reserve's population. The adult males twenty-one years of age and older living in each section would elect one or more councillors to represent their section on the reserve's band council. To be eligible for election to the council, an individual had to be a member of the band and own or live in a house on the reserve. The elected councillors would each serve a one-year term and would elect one of their own to serve as "chief" councillor. The Advancement Act also stipulated that chiefs would no longer be officially recognized as such; while they could be elected as councillors according to the provisions of the Advancement Act, they would have no automatic right to a seat on their reserve's band council. In effect, the Advancement Act sought to replace native governments with a municipal system like that of Euro-Canadian towns. Finally, the Advancement Act could be applied to any band in any province by order of the governor general-in-council.[50]

According to the Indian agent, Alexander Brosseau, the January 1888 meeting held to consider application of the Advancement Act was called at the request of a "certain number of the principal Indians of Caughnawaga."[51] Brosseau did not identify these "principal Indians," nor did he report who attended the meeting, stating only that it was a "numerous one" and that those in attendance "unanimously decided" to request application of the Advancement Act to the reserve. Brosseau suggested that there were several reasons to grant this request. First, echoing concerns expressed in the petition of the previous November, he wrote that several of the chiefs had died, only three remained on the council, and there had been difficulty in getting these three together for council meetings. Second, the Walbank survey and subdivision of the reserve was under way, and he considered it an opportune time to divide the reserve into sections for the election of band councillors as required by the Advancement Act. Finally, in evident reference to the division within the community over this issue, Brosseau argued that if the request to apply the act was not granted quickly, there would be pressure "to give satisfaction to a portion of the band to go on with the old system and elect chiefs to replace those who died."

Within a few days of the January meeting at which application of the Advancement Act was requested, another petition was directed to the interior minister. The petitioners sought to "be allowed an election of chiefs while pending the decision of the Government to grant us the Indian Advancement Act."[52] The petition was signed by 160 Kahnawakehró:non, about 32 percent of the adult male population of the reserve. The wording of this petition is curious. On the one hand, it may be understood to be supporting application of the Advancement Act and seeking the election of chief as an interim measure. In support of this interpretation, 59 percent (thirty-two) of those who signed the November 1887 petition for application of the Advancement Act also signed the January 1888 petition, which clearly was intended to seek application of the act.

Another interpretation, however, is possible and more likely. The January 1888 petition appears to have been an effort to reconstitute and continue with a fully functioning council of chiefs and thereby head off the application of the Advancement Act. The lead signatory of the petition was Louis Jackson (Rowi Tawehiakenra). As will be discussed in detail in the next chapter, Tawehiakenra was an active and vocal opponent of the band council system almost from the moment it was instituted, and official complaints about his interference in the implementation of the Advancement Act and band council affairs in the early 1890s identified him as the organizer of the January 1888 petition. In addition, in the weeks following the petition, one of the petitioners, Joseph Foster (Sose Anenharontonkwas), sent a series of telegrams to the interior minister seeking a response to their petition "demanding the election of chiefs." His telegrams made no mention of the application of the Indian Advancement Act.[53] Foster too was a critic of the band council system and the Advancement Act and in the early 1890s was intimately involved with efforts to restore the traditional council of chiefs. In short, the November 1887 and January 1888 petitions probably represent the Conservative/Reform division within the community over the Indian Act system.

Lawrence Vankoughnet, the deputy superintendent general of Indian affairs, denied the petitioners' January 1888 request for the election of chiefs; however, he did inform Alexander Brosseau that the Department looked favorably on the request to apply the Advancement Act to the reserve and directed him to proceed with preparations for the election of a band council. By April 1888 the division of the reserve into six sections and other preparations were completed, but not until early the following year was further action taken on applying the Advancement Act to the reserve.[54]

The delay in the government's response to the petition to apply the Advancement Act and its refusal to allow the elections for the council of chiefs caused concern among many Kahnawakehró:non. In early January 1889 Brosseau reported that the "people of the village are again agitating the question of the election of councilors or chiefs" and expressed to Vankoughnet his hope that the Department would move forward on the matter.[55] In mid-January the seven Kahnawà:ke clans each sent separate but identical petitions to the superintendent general of Indian affairs seeking to elect new chiefs.[56] In all there are 210 names on the seven petitions, representing about 43 percent of the adult male population of the reserve. As with the January 1888 petition, the wording of these petitions is somewhat confusing and subject to other interpretations, but the expressed "desire for the election of chiefs" rather than some further action with regard to the Advancement Act suggests that it represents the Conservative position in support of the traditional council and in opposition to the Indian Act system. A large percentage of those who signed the January 1888 petition (58 percent, or ninety-two) also signed one of the January 1889 "clan" petitions.

No official action was taken on the petitioners' January 1889 request for the election of chiefs, but Lawrence Vankoughnet did direct Alexander Brosseau to recommend a date and location for band council elections. On 31 January 1889 the superintendent general recommended application of the Indian Advancement Act to the "Iroquois Band of Caughnawaga," and finally, on 5 March 1889, the Advancement Act was officially applied to the Kahnawà:ke reserve. Kahnawà:ke's council of chiefs was abolished, and its first band council elections were held three weeks later. However, far from bringing to a close the division within the community over the Indian Act, these developments only intensified the split and, within a very short time, led to an effort to restore the traditional council of chiefs and forge ties with Rotinonhsiónni in other communities faced with similar issues.

4. *"An Ill-Feeling Which Is Yet Burning"*

Indian Act Opposition and the Roots of Kahnawà:ke Traditionalism and Nationalism

Kahnawà:ke's First Band Council Elections

T he Department of Indian Affairs initiated preparations for applying the Indian Advancement Act to Kahnawà:ke in early 1888 when it developed a plan to divide the reserve into election districts. A plan developed by the local Indian agent in consultation with the council of chiefs was eventually scrapped in favor of another recommended by William McLea Walbank, who had recently completed the land survey and subdivision of the reserve. Walbank's plan called for dividing the reserve into six districts, with one councillor elected from each. Thus Kahnawà:ke's band council was to consist of six councillors, one of whom would be elected by the council as its chief councillor. When the Indian agent, Alexander Brosseau, called a meeting of the community in early April 1888 to explain the plan, a number of protestors objected, many of whom had signed the petition to the superintendent general the previous January to elect new chiefs. According to Brosseau's report, the protestors left the meeting when they saw that the majority of those attending did not support them.[1]

According to the Indian Advancement Act, election districts on a reserve were to contain equal proportions of the resident Indian population. In Kahnawà:ke's case, however, this was not possible. The large majority of the population lived in the small, compact village along the St. Lawrence River. The rest of the land east and west of the village along the river and south away from the river consisted of farmland and forest that was only sparsely occupied. According to the Department's plan, the village area constituted one of the election districts, while the other five were spread across the rest of the reserve surrounding the village.[2] Walbank and the Indian Department officials recognized this problem but expected that as a result of the recent subdivision, in time the population would become more evenly distributed as families moved to their selected allotments outside the village.[3] For the time being, at Walbank's suggestion, the Department intended for voters to select a councillor in the same election district as their unoccupied allotment.[4] According to the Indian Advancement Act, only male members of the band twenty-one years of age and older had the right to vote in and stand for band council elections. In addition, candidates for band council seats were required to own and occupy a home on their reserve. In Kahnawà:ke's case, it was also stipulated that a candidate must live on or own land in that district of the reserve that he sought to represent on the band council.

Kahnawà:ke's first band council election was held on 26 March 1889, and it involved considerable controversy. The five councillors elected from the outlying districts included Thomas Jocks (Atonwa Karatoton), Jacques Montour, Louis Delisle (Rowi Ronwarahare), Michel Daillebout, and Michel Bourdeau (Wishe Sotienton).[5] Thomas Jocks was the only chief among the newly elected band councillors, and of course he was a prominent figure in the Reform faction and had frequently led the push for the establishment of the Indian Act system. The candidate receiving the most votes in the village district was Louis Jackson (Rowi Tawehiakenra), who defeated Louis Jocks (Rowi Oroniatakon) by a vote of 131 to 76. Louis Jocks was the son of Kahnawà:ke's wealthiest landowner, Baptiste Jocks (Sawatis Karonhiaktatis).

For understanding Kahnawà:ke politics at this time, the village district is key because it contained most of the community's voters. In this first band council election over two hundred votes were polled in the village district, while there were no more than twelve votes for any of the outlying districts. After the election, Louis Jackson's victory was protested by Thomas Jocks, who claimed that Jackson was not a qualified candidate because he did not own land or occupy his own residence on the reserve. Jackson's election was also protested by several other Kahnawakehró:non, who claimed that he was a "habitual drunkard and . . . generally known to be dishonest." Jackson, in turn, disputed his opponent's qualification for election and sought to annul the votes he had received. Brosseau, the local Indian agent who received the protests, was unable to declare a winner for the village district and sought advice from the superintendent general, Edgar Dewdney.[6] After this, 131 "electors of Jackson" telegraphed Dewdney demanding that Jackson's election be upheld.[7]

Louis Jackson was well known in Kahnawà:ke and had wide experience in the world outside the reserve. He was born in Kahnawà:ke in 1843, his mother being from Kahnawà:ke and his father from St. Regis. In the mid-1880s he earned notoriety as a captain of the Canadian voyageur contingent of the Gordon Relief Expedition in Egypt and as the author of a chronicle of that experience titled *Our Caughnawagas in Egypt.*[8] A number of Kahnawakehró:non served in the voyageur contingent, and some of them nominated Jackson as a band councillor and voted for him. At the time of the Walbank survey in 1885 he owned no land of his own, but his widowed mother owned about seventy-two acres of farmland and sugarbush. After his return from the Nile expedition he married Honorise Lafleur, the daughter of David Lafleur and the widow of Onesime Plante (Resine Kanenaroton). Recall that Lafleur was a French Canadian who had settled in Kahnawà:ke in 1849 and that in the 1870s many Kahnawakehró:non had protested his presence on the reserve. Plante, Honorise Lafleur's first husband, was born in Kahnawà:ke and was the son of a French Canadian father and a mother of mixed parentage. Kahnawakehró:non had protested

3. Louis Jackson (Rowi Tawehiakenra), who led local opposition to the Indian Act system in the early 1890s. Photograph courtesy of Kanien'kehaka Onkwawen:na Raotitiohkwa.

his presence on the reserve as well. In the late 1880s and early 1890s Jackson served as an interpreter in the courts of Montreal through an appointment by the provincial government. In January 1888 he was one of the organizers and the lead signatory of the petition to the superintendent general to elect new chiefs (see fig. 3).[9]

The first meeting of Kahnawà:ke's band council was called on 1 April 1889 but was cancelled because no councillor for the village district had yet been named. A second meeting was called and held on 8 April, and even though the sixth councillor still had not been named, Thomas Jocks was elected chief councillor with the support of Jacques Montour and Louis Delisle. Michel Bourdeau and Michel Daillebout opposed Jocks as the chief councillor, and after the meeting they and 117 others petitioned the superintendent general to investigate the conduct of the Indian agent in the elections of the council members and of Jocks as the chief councillor.[10] In addition, the Indian Department eventually upheld Louis Jackson's victory, determining that he did indeed own and occupy a home on the reserve.[11] Once Jackson took his position on the council he, Bourdeau, and Delisle sought, but failed, to annul the election of Jocks as chief councillor.[12] Predictably, relations among the band councillors were contentious, and the council itself was split into two factions, one led by Jackson and the other by Jocks.

The split is well illustrated by events surrounding a series of council meetings in late 1889 and early 1890. During this period the council enacted a number of resolutions and bylaws; Superintendent General Dewdney approved some, but others he did not approve or did not act on. For example, resolutions for such mundane matters as roads and tollgates were passed by the council, but Department approval was very slow in coming. More sensitive matters were even more of a problem. In a council meeting on 27 September 1889, Jackson proposed and Bourdeau seconded a motion that white children on the reserve not be allowed to attend the school in Kahnawà:ke. The motion apparently was carried unanimously and then forwarded by the Indian agent for Dewdney's approval, which appears never to have come. At another meeting the council resolved to name Louis Beauvais (Rowi Shatekaienton), the hereditary chief of the Rotineniothró:non (Rock clan), as a replacement for the current constable, who was described as being not Indian, but "mulatto." Dewdney refused to approve this resolution even though Beauvais was willing to work at a salary well below that of the man he was to replace. Finally, at a meeting in October 1889, Jackson, Bourdeau, and Daillebout objected to the council's conducting its business before the Indian Department had approved its earlier resolutions. Jackson concluded his objection by stating, reportedly in Kanien'kéha and French: "If the [Government] finds that we are not savage enough to approve the resolutions we have passed, we can paint our faces so as to make us look more so." After Jackson's objection, Jocks, Montour, and Delisle voted with Brosseau, the Indian agent, to proceed with the council's business, whereupon Jackson, Bourdeau, and Daillebout left and the meeting was closed for lack of a quorum. Later Jackson wrote to the deputy superintendent general explaining that the council had yet to hear from him about its resolutions and that he and his supporters were anxious to see the results of the council's work before it met again.[13]

Brosseau and the Indian Department regarded Jackson and his supporters as an obstacle to the implementation of the Indian Act system and sought to remove them from office. As the Department's annual report for 1889 stated, "The Indian Act was . . . applied by Order of Your Excellency to this band [Caughnawaga], but owing to the obstructive conduct of some of the councilors, notoriously one of them who acts as their ringleader, the beneficial effects of the same upon the community, which were so hopefully looked for, have not been as yet experienced."[14] Before a band council meeting in late January 1890, Brosseau warned Jackson that he would be dismissed if he did not attend. Nevertheless, neither Jackson nor the other "recalcitrant" councillors (Bourdeau and Daillebout) attended the meeting, and in early February the superintendent general did indeed recommend that all three be deposed. That did not happen, however, because, as he learned from the Department of Justice, under the Indian Advancement Act the superintendent general did not have the authority to depose councillors simply for disrupting band council business. Stymied in his attempt to remove Jackson and the others from the Kahnawà:ke council, Dewdney sought an amendment to the Advancement Act that would give him such power so that, as he stated in a departmental memorandum, "we shall have that to hold over their heads in the future."[15] The amendment he sought, however, was opposed by the Liberals in Parliament and was not adopted.[16]

Despite these events and their conduct, or perhaps because of them, Jackson and his fellow councillors continued to garner support within the community. In the band council elections of 1890 Jackson, Bourdeau, and Daillebout were returned to their council seats, Jackson by a 124 to 25 margin over his opponent. Jacques Montour was returned to his seat on the council, and two new councillors were added, Michel Montour (Wishe Sakoientineta), the chief of the Rotiskeré:wakekó:wa (Great Bear clan), and François Phillipe. Thomas Jocks does not appear to have sought reelection, and Phillipe appears to have been a Jackson supporter, thus tipping the split within the band council in Jackson's favor. At its first meeting in late March 1890 the new band council elected Jackson as its chief councillor.[17]

Among the issues that divided the Kahnawà:ke band council, and that distinguished Jackson in particular, was the authority of the band council under the Indian Act system. According to the Indian Advancement Act, band councils could pass resolutions and bylaws on a variety of municipal matters, but these became effective only with the approval of the superintendent general of Indian affairs. Jackson and his supporters pressed the Indian Department on this issue and frequently refused to conduct council business until it approved the actions of the council. Recalling Jackson's comments directed toward the superintendent general at the October 1889 council meeting, Jackson mocked the Department and expressed his disapproval of their paternalistic and ethnocentric attitude toward Indians. On the other hand, Thomas Jocks and his supporters on the band council that supported the Indian Act system took a less confrontational approach. They cooperated with Indian Department officials and preferred conducting council business within the constraints of the Advancement Act. The band council elections, especially those of 1890 in which Jackson and the other "recalcitrant" councillors were returned to office, suggest that he and the others had substantial support within the community and that the issue was a divisive one within the community as well as the band council.

Jackson and his supporters pushed the issue of the autonomy of the Kahnawà:ke band council even further. At about the time of the second band council election in early 1890, they sought an amendment to the Indian Advancement Act that would enable the band council of Kahnawà:ke to enact bylaws without the approval of the superintendent general. Though the amendment was never enacted, the development of this issue further exemplifies and elucidates the division within the Kahnawà:ke community over this issue. Jackson and his supporters sought the amendment through the member of Parliament representing the county of Laprairie, where the Kahnawà:ke reserve was located. A move for a second reading of the bill containing the proposed amendment in the House of Commons in March 1890 provoked considerable debate.[18] The debate within the House closely followed party lines, with Liberals supporting the amendment and Conservatives opposing it. The member from Laprairie, a Mr. Doyon, argued in favor of broadening the powers of the Kahnawà:ke council because in his view the native community had shown sufficient cultural assimilation and advancement to be accorded the rights and powers of a regular municipality. They were, he stated, "more advanced than a good many other Indians." As he observed, "There are to be found among the inhabitants of the reserve well-educated people. There are doctors, lawyers, law students, and they generally, a good many of them, speak the French language and the English as fluently as their own language. There are even some who have taken to farming with the implements used by the farmers of the adjacent counties."[19]

Doyon went on to argue for the amendment based on the federal government's own policies. He observed that in 1885 Indians were given the right to vote for a member of the House of Commons and stipulated that if the government considered Indians capable of exercising that right, then it should also recognize their fitness to govern their own local affairs without the interference of the Indian Department. In Doyon's view, the people of Kahnawà:ke recognized their own needs and interests and were qualified to manage them. Other Liberals, including the party leader, Sir Wilfred Laurier, supported Doyon's argument. Laurier, in fact, went even further by suggesting that the expanded powers proposed for Kahnawà:ke be extended to all band councils operating under the Advancement Act.

The minister of the interior, Edgar Dewdney, who served as the superintendent general of Indian affairs, disputed Doyon's observations about Kahnawà:ke and opposed the expansion of its band council's authority. He argued that the divisiveness within the Kahnawà:ke council, and particularly the obstructionist behavior of Jackson and his supporters, demonstrated that the people of Kahnawà:ke were not prepared to exercise full municipal powers. "From what has been reported," Dewdney stated, "if there is one band of Indians who should not get the advantages proposed to be given to them . . . it is the band which [Doyon] has been advocating. The reports we have had in reference to the business which has been transacted by the council of the Caughnawaga tribe has been anything but satisfactory." He went on to suggest that until more "sound and intelligent Indians" took an active part in the affairs of the reserve, it was necessary to retain the superintendent general's authority over the Kahnawà:ke band council.[20] The interior minister also noted that in 1888 Jackson and his supporters had opposed the application of the Advancement Act and that they were among those who had petitioned in January of that year to elect new chiefs to their council. As he stated, "Before this Act was extended to this reserve, a petition was sent to the Department signed by a majority of the band. There was a large minority who were opposed to it, and when the election took place, the leaders of the obstructive party were the ones who returned as members to the council."[21]

Several Conservative members agreed with the interior minister, including the prime minister, Sir John MacDonald. MacDonald observed more broadly that only enfranchised Indians had the right to vote in federal elections, while all Indians, including the "wild and dissolute," were permitted to vote in band council elections and participate in the management of their band's local affairs. Under these conditions, he argued, band councils simply could not be allowed to act without the supervision and sanctioning power of the superintendent general.[22]

The views expressed in this debate by Sam Burdett, a Liberal representing the county that included the Tyendinaga reserve, are particularly noteworthy and foreshadowed a position taken by Kahnawakehró:non and other Rotinonhsiónni dealing with similar problems in their communities. Burdett identified himself as a "full-breed" Indian born on the Tyendinaga reserve. He echoed the arguments of Doyon and Laurier and supported the expansion of band council powers, including those of the Kahnawà:ke council. He added that the sanctioning power of the superintendent general over band councils did not permit Indians to freely exercise their right to vote. He also spoke specifically about the Six Nations. He stated that they rejected the authority of the superintendent general because his was not a legitimate exercise of power. The Six Nations, he said, regarded themselves as allies, not subjects, of the British Crown and therefore, so far as the Six Nations were concerned, the Indian Act system was illegal:

> The Six Nations claim that they came in by treaty, that they are independent nations, that they are allies, and when they address the Governor General or any other superior, they address him as brother, because they claim that they are equals in a national sense, although under the protection of this Government, because the Government gave them that right in our original treaties. But by law and by statute

they are allies of the British Crown, and any liberty that has been taken from them, or any rights that have been taken from them, have been take by Act of Parliament, and they now ask to have some measure of those rights given back to them . . . they ought to be treated as equals and not as wards.[23]

The interior minister's comments before the House of Commons suggest that the division within the Kahnawà:ke council and community was a significant factor in the debate over the proposed amendment to the Indian Act. In the course of the debate it emerged that just before the 1890 band council elections, "ten principal Indians on the reserve and one councillor" had petitioned Dewdney to disqualify Louis Jackson from standing for reelection. As a basis for their petition, they cited Jackson's obstructive behavior and stated that he was a "habitual drunkard." Given the circumstances at the time, it seems likely that the petition with its charge of drunkenness was a calculated response to the inability of the superintendent general to depose Jackson on the grounds of obstructive behavior alone. Under the Indian Advancement Act, habitual drunkenness was sufficient cause for deposing an elected band councillor. Dewdney was unable to investigate the drunkenness charge against Jackson before the March elections, but he did offer it as support for his argument against expanding the powers of the Kahnawà:ke band council.

It also appears that in response to the petition against Jackson, another was sent to the superintendent general in support of Jackson and his followers on the council. Sir Wilfred Laurier referred to this second petition in his arguments and noted that 110 men signed it; he also noted that in the second band council election, Jackson was reelected over his opponent by a wide margin. "How in the name of justice and fair play," argued Laurier, "could the [superintendent general] rely upon a petition of ten men only . . . when the conduct of Mr. Jackson as a member of the council has been approved by his election by a handsome majority over his adversaries."[24] It is worth noting that one of the "adversaries" that Jackson defeated in the band council elections was one of the petitioners seeking his disqualification.

Following the debate in the House of Commons, a petition was sent from Kahnawà:ke to the superintendent general opposing the proposed amendment. The petition carried fifty-two names, including those of two of Jackson's opponents on the band council, Jacques Montour and Michel Montour. The petitioners stated that the proposed amendment was "contrary to the interests of the Indians of the . . . Reserve of Caughnawaga." The amendment, they argued, would give too much power to the band council and provide no means of redress to those whose interests were affected or "attacked" by its decisions.[25] The petition opposing the amendment to the Advancement Act indicates that landownership was an important dimension of the split within the community over the Indian Act system and the autonomy of the Kahnawà:ke band council. The petition opposing the powers that Jackson and his supporters sought by amending the Advancement Act argued that it was an injustice for "landed proprietors" to be governed by "those who have no property," and that this was currently the situation at Kahnawà:ke. "Several of the Councillors," they stated, "have been elected by those who have no property." Further, not only did the petitioners oppose the amendment expanding the powers of the Kahnawà:ke council, they suggested a new amendment that would allow only enfranchised Indians (and thus only those with property or professional training) to vote in band council elections. The petition included fifty-two signatures. Of the forty-six individuals who could be located in the records of the 1885 Walbank survey, 65 percent (thirty) owned some land. The average landholding among these landowners was about fifty-eight acres, and they included Baptiste Jocks, who was Kahnawà:ke's wealthiest and second-largest landowner in 1885 (with 255 acres) and the lead signer in the petition. Thirteen percent of the petitioners were in the top 5 percent of landholders, and 26 percent were in the top 20 percent.

These figures, however, do not give the full picture because a number of the petitioners who owned little or no land were men in the thirties and forties who were the sons of landowning fathers or widowed mothers. In some cases the father or mother was among the top landholders on the reserve. For example, among the petitioners were Thomas B. Jocks (Atonwa Kanenhar-ton), age thirty-two, and Louis Jocks, age twenty-seven; neither owned land in 1885, but they were the sons of leading landowner Baptiste Jocks. In addition, about 1886 Louis Jocks married a widow who owned 104 acres. (He was also Louis Jackson's opponent for a seat on the band council in 1889.) Another petitioner, Baptiste Rice (Sawatis Thaiaiake), owned 106 acres in 1885 and was the son of a widow who owned another 181 acres. When these connections of immediate descent from landowning parents are taken into consideration, the property-owning profile of the petitioners is even more evident. Eighty-five percent (thirty-nine) of the petitioners were landowners or the immediate descendants of landowning parents; 22 percent (ten) were among or directly connected to the top 5 percent of landholders, and 46 percent (twenty-one) were among or directly connected to the top 20 percent. Clearly, the petition opposed to the expansion of band council powers and seeking to restrict voting in band council elections was the initiative of those in the propertied segment of Kahnawà:ke's population. Clearly as well, land and the inequality of landownership continued to be an important dimension of the division within the community over the Indian Act system and the autonomy of the Kahnawà:ke council.

After the elections in Kahnawà:ke and the debate in Parliament in March 1890, relations within the band council continued to be contentious, and the business of the council was carried out only with considerable difficulty. The central issue remained as before: Jackson and others questioned the Indian Department's authority to interfere in the business of the council. Not surprisingly, band council elections in 1891 were again difficult. Jackson was reelected, and the council was again split into two factions. At this time the two factions were identified in DIA correspondence and newspaper accounts with the two major national political parties, the Liberals and Conservatives. Those who were identified with the Liberal Party were led by Jackson, and they held two additional seats on the new band council. Those who were identified with the Conservative Party held three seats on the council, and their choice for chief councillor was Michel Montour, who had been reelected. It is important to note that in his race for a council seat Montour tied with his opponent and was named to his seat only through the tie-breaking vote of the Indian agent. Before the meeting at which the chief councillor was to be selected, Jackson charged Montour with selling liquor to an Indian and had him arrested. Jackson's purpose seems to have been to ensure his own election as chief councillor rather than Montour, but his strategy failed when the other "Conservative" councillors boycotted the meeting and it was canceled. All three "Conservative" councillors attended a subsequent meeting, but Jackson and his supporters did not, knowing that they could not control the outcome of the election of the chief councillor.[26]

Problems persisted in the council elections of 1892. In February of that year the Indian agent, Alexander Brosseau, reported to the superintendent general that a number of Indians within the village on the reserve were moving into sections outside the village with the objective of obtaining majorities to control the composition of the next council. Brosseau was especially concerned about an "obstructionist" majority within the council and went so far as to suggest that "the Indian law in this respect should be amended, at least as far as the Caughnawaga reserve is concerned, so that they may be enabled to elect progressive men as councillors." Brosseau was advised that he had the authority to approve or disapprove any voter's eligibility. This set the stage for an even more complicated and divisive election, in which many votes were contested and the election results were disputed. Louis Jackson was elected yet again, but the composition of the council was tipped against him and his supporters when Brosseau used his authority to name "Conservative" candidates over their "Liberal" opponents as councillors in two of the districts in which the eligibility of various voters had been contested. Louis Jocks, the son of leading landowner Baptiste Jocks and Jackson's defeated opponent in the first band council election, was one of the "Conservative" councillors the agent named. The council was still split, but now unevenly, and Jackson could not secure the position of chief councillor. Dr. Angus Patton, whose election over a "Liberal" candidate was also secured by Brosseau, was named as the new chief councillor.[27]

Thus, Kahnawà:ke's initial experience under the Indian Advancement Act proved to be divisive. The division manifested itself in the band council and represented both continuity with and development of the past factionalism within the community. Reformers who had pressed for the application of the Indian Act system and the establishment a band council composed one faction. They were led by Thomas Jocks and advocated adherence to Indian Act policies and governance within the guidelines of the Indian Advancement Act. The Reform faction continued to draw much of its support from wealthy and landowning individuals and families within the community and, at the national level, was identified with the Conservative Party. The Conservative faction, which had become identified with the Liberal Party, continued to oppose the Indian Act system, and at the core of the members' position was an emphasis on local autonomy. While they had opposed band council system, once it was established they sought to work within that system to secure greater autonomy by pressing for full municipal powers. In effect, the Conservative faction sought to work within the system to terminate the application of the Advancement Act to the reserve at least regarding local governance. Its leader was Louis Jackson, and the position he represented drew much of its support from the village district on the reserve and from individuals and families of lesser means and who owned little or no land. Their objective led them to obstruct the business of the band council, to press for changes in the Indian Advancement Act, and to come into obvious conflict with the Reform faction and the Indian Department. Ultimately, the Conservative faction failed in its objective, but one result of its opposition and resistance was to give impetus to a third political direction that had begun to develop within the community after the application of the Indian Advancement Act.

The Traditionalist Movement
to Restore the Council of Chiefs

In early December 1890, 121 Kahnawakehró:non petitioned the governor general, stating that they did not approve of "the republic form of government of electing persons."[28] They regarded the band council system as "injurious" and argued that it was "not calculated to promote the welfare of the Band." As a remedy, they sought "to have the Hereditary Chiefs . . . take the reins and conduct our welfare." Of the 121 petitioners, at least 64 percent (77) had signed either the January 1888 or the January 1889 petition seeking to elect new chiefs to the council of chiefs. In contrast, only 13 percent had signed the November 1887 petition to apply the Indian Act and establish a band council system.[29] Within days of this first petition being sent to the governor general, a second was sent by seven women of the Bear clan. The women declared in their petition that before the Advancement Act their people "lived in peace and harmony," and that the band council system was the cause of "a great deal of ill feelings between us Indians." They too hoped that their community could return to the "line of Hereditary Chiefs." Both petitions were denied.[30]

The movement within Kahnawà:ke to restore its traditional council was distinguished by a strong identification with the Confederacy and the sovereignty of the Six Nations. In the December 1890 petition in which 121 "Caughnawaga Indians" complained about the band council system and sought to return to their traditional council, they also wrote at some length about the issues of sovereignty, their understanding of their relationship to the British government, and their identity as Rotinonhsiónni. They emphasized that their response to the Indian Advancement Act needed to be understood in the context of these issues. I quote their words at some length so we can fully appreciate their position.

> We the Seven Nations of Caughnawaga Indians desire to reform and renew our national rites, and ceremonies, which it is the only remedy to preserve our nationality, but we do not wish to take a step back of paganism, that it will not hinder us to advance in civilization, but we find it is the only remedy to preserve of the treaties made between the British Government and the Indians.[31]
>
> We the said Caughnawaga Confederate Nation, further declare of our desire that we do not approve the republic form of government, as we are not fully British subjects, but, merely allies to the British Government. . . . We also find the republic form of government of electing person or persons that it is injurious to our national rights, therefore we wish to have the Hereditary Chiefs to take the reins and conduct our welfare. . . .
>
> [O]ur real desire is to have the old form of creating Chiefs to be created to control and frame our welfare which at the present time that we cannot control our rights and properties until first obtained the consent from our agent, we rather control our own rights and properties without asking somebody to control it for us, and moreover, that we never adopted the Indian Act through by our general council and also we are determined not to enter into any elections in

future of any shape or manner, and we further declare it, and cause it to make known of our wishes to your Excellency, 1st The Indian Act aims to abolishment of all the Indian Nations of Canada, 2nd That the Franchise Act aims the wiping out of our Nationality as Ro-di-no-Shiou-ni or Confederacy, and your Excellency may further understand concerning our wishes, that we like to retain and preserve our nationality as Ro-di-no-Shiou-ni until the Lord comes.

Brother, we thought that it is high time to declare our grievances and lay before your Excellency to consider it well. . . . [W]e solicit your Excellency nothing but peace, and to cause it to be restored our system form of creating Chiefs, because it is our custom and manners of our Confederacy.[32]

To emphasize, the petitioners made it clear that in their view they were part of a sovereign nation with the right to control their own affairs and destiny; that they were allies, not subjects, of the British; that because of their sovereign status and relationship to the British government, the application of Canada's Indian policies to them was unjust and detrimental to their claim of sovereignty and identity as "Ro-di-no-Shiou-ni" (Rotinonhsiónni); and that they desired to "retain and preserve" that sovereignty and identity.

The seven women from the Bear clan expressed similar views when they petitioned the governor general for relief from the Advancement Act in December 1890: "We rather retain our nationality. Since every nation throughout the world retains their own customs, rites and ceremonies. . . . It grieves us sorely of the actions of her Majesty's Canadian Government of passing laws to encroach our rights, and therefore the Indian Act aims to curtail our rights, liberties and privileges, and also our works."[33]

Kahnawà:ke was not alone in confronting the troubling and divisive issues of the Indian Act system and local autonomy or in the traditionalist and nationalist impulses it experienced. The band council system had existed at Tyendinaga since 1870, but beginning in 1887 many Kanien'kehá:ka there were seeking a return to a traditional council of hereditary chiefs. Like many Kahnawakehró:non, they believed that the Indian Act system undermined the welfare of their community and had created a great deal of animosity and division within it. They too argued the issues of sovereignty and independence, the illegitimacy of the Indian Act system as it was applied to the Six Nations, and the need to recognize the nation-to-nation status of the relationship between the Confederacy and Great Britain. As part of this movement, in 1887 Tyendinaga renewed its council fire with the Six Nations Confederacy at Grand River.[34] At Ahkwesáhsne the band council system replaced the council of heredity chiefs in 1888, the same year that this community was admitted to the Confederacy. As at Kahnawà:ke, there was both acceptance and opposition to the Indian Act system. Eventually this community too sought to return to its hereditary council.[35]

An important occurrence in the development of traditionalist and nationalist aspirations of Tyendinaga and other Six Nations communities in Canada was a meeting of the Grand Council at Tyendinaga in August 1890. Its purpose was to demonstrate and reaffirm Six Nations sovereignty. According to a newspaper article announcing the plans for the council, it was to be attended by chiefs from Tyendinaga, Six Nations chiefs from Grand River, Oneida chiefs from Muncy, and the "Seven Nations," which presumably included Kahnawà:ke. Representatives from the Grand Council of the Six Nations at Onondaga in New York were also invited. At the meeting the Grand River chiefs were to present wampum belts and "the great silver pipe of peace" that recorded treaties with the British government and demonstrated the independence of the Six Nations.[36]

Unlike the situation at Tyendinaga, Ahkwesáhsne, and Kahnawà:ke, at Grand River the council of hereditary chiefs had persisted, but during the 1880s and 1890s this community too was under considerable pressure to accept the Indian Act. This pressure was both external and internal. With the passage of the Indian Act in 1876 and its numerous amendments in the 1880s, the reserve community and the council of chiefs in particular came under increasing political pressure to accept an elected band council system of government. While the chiefs rejected an elected system, they did have frequent discussions about whether the council should operate autonomously or under the Indian Act system. Although no band council system was instituted until 1924, in its responsibilities and actual practice the traditional council of chiefs gradually began to operate in accordance with the Indian Act.[37] Pressure also came from within from the "Progressive Warriors"—young, educated men who thought the hereditary council system was outmoded and sought to replace it with an elected government. These pressures led to strong traditionalist and nationalist impulses at Six Nations.[38] One manifestation of this was the attempt by Seth Newhouse (Dayodekane) to record the history of the Confederacy and codify its traditions. Though Newhouse's effort was motivated by a number of concerns relating to political issues on the Six Nations reserve, the threat to governance by a council of chiefs was among the most important. Other manifestations included the continued reaffirmation of the traditional system by the hereditary chiefs and the commissioning and approving of John Gibson's version of the League's constitution in 1899–1900.[39] Thus, in the 1880s and early 1890s several Rotinonhsiónni communities in Canada, including Kahnawà:ke, experienced the development of traditionalist and nationalist impulses. Undoubtedly these impulses encouraged and supported one another.

An important moment in this movement was a meeting of the Grand Council of the Six Nations at Ahkwesáhsne in September 1894. Participants came from Ahkwesáhsne, Grand River, Kanehsatà:ke, and Kahnawà:ke and numbered more than twelve hundred. One result of the Grand Council was a statement addressed to the superintendent general of Indian affairs that detailed concerns that by now had become familiar on all the reserves. It stated that "the system of elective councilors . . . [had an] evil effect for it created a bad and ill feeling among our people and previous of this we were in harmony, peace, and on friendly brotherly terms." The council indicated that the Six Nations intended to "hand back" the system of elected councillors and reinstitute their "systematical Iroquois government that is governed by our chiefs." The letter is signed with six names, including that of Joseph Foster (Sose Anenharontonkwas) of "Caughnawaga." Foster had signed the December 1890 petition from Kahnawà:ke seeking a return to the traditional council of chiefs. He had also endorsed the January 1888 petition to elect new chiefs before the band council system was established in Kahnawà:ke, and he was an active advocate for Louis Jackson when the Indian Department delayed in recognizing Jackson's election to the band council in 1890. Seth Newhouse, one of the participants from Grand River, also signed the letter addressed to the superintendent general. Newhouse, of course, had drafted a version of the "constitution" of the Rotinonhsiónni Confederacy (in 1880), but he had also been a supporter of the traditional council system and opposed government interference at the Six Nations reserve in the 1870s. He became active in this cause once again as new threats to the Grand River council emerged in the 1890s.[40] Representatives from Ahkwesáhsne and Kanehsatà:ke also signed the letter to the superintendent general.[41]

Representatives from Kahnawà:ke at the Ahkwesáhsne Grand Council prepared another statement addressed to the superintendent general, T. Mayne Daly. In part, it reads as follows:

> [The Indian Act] only breeds sorrow, contention, hatred, disrespect of family ties, spite against one another and absence of unity among us Indians. Also creates two distinct

parties at the elections. . . . Therefore, Sir, we deliver it to you—free ourselves from it and ask you to accept for it is your whiteman's law and not of the Indians. We are glad that there is one way to recover brotherly feelings it is by substituting the seven lords (chiefs) appointed by each of the seven totems according to the ancient custom which we know gave us peace, prosperity, friendship and brotherly feelings in every cause either for personal good or for the benefit of the whole band. There seemed to be one family only. We desire to adhere to the Iroquois system of government where the source of the power will be in parallel with the whiteman's law. This ancient constitution is called "lordship." We will elect our lords who shall have full power to control the varied affairs that we Indians have.[42]

Accompanying these statements addressed to Daly were three others from Kahnawà:ke, Grand River, and Ahkwesáhsne supporting the position and actions of the Grand Council to return to their "confederate government." The statement from Kahnawà:ke carried the endorsement of 168 "warriors of Caughnawaga," and those from Ahkwesáhsne and Grand River carried 148 and 99 signatures, respectively. The statement from Kahnawà:ke is in poor condition, and many of the names included on it are illegible. Nevertheless, it is clear that many of the Kahnawakehró:non who supported the Grand Council had previously supported the 1888 and 1889 petitions to select new chiefs and the December 1890 petition to revoke the Indian Advancement Act and reestablish the council of chiefs.[43]

Just two months later, in November 1894, 245 Kahnawakehró:non sent a separate petition to the superintendent general: "We, the undersigned Iroquois Indians of Caughnawaga, humbly pray that you will grant the petition of the Iroquois Indians and suspend the operation of the Indian Act insofar as the same provides for the election of Councilors, and allow the said Indians to return to their ancient constitution of government by chiefs."[44] The signatures on the petition represent about 50 percent of the adult male population of the reserve at the time. In reporting on the petition to the deputy superintendent general, the Kahnawà:ke Indian agent reported that it was very similar to the 1888 petition seeking the election of chiefs, and the petitioners were largely the same.[45]

In response to these petitions protesting the Indian Act system and seeking a return to the traditional council of clan chiefs, a Kahnawakehró:non named Peter Stacey wrote to the superintendent general offering a different point of view. At the time Stacey was living in Fargo, North Dakota, but in the early 1890s he was living on the reserve, had been involved in Kahnawà:ke politics, and was associated with the Reform faction led by Thomas Jocks. Stacey had been informed about the September Grand Council at Ahkwesáhsne and Kahnawà:ke's December petition, and he wrote as follows:

> Sir,
>
> I thought I would write to you a few words regarding a letter I received yesterday from Caughnawaga, stating that they are about to receive back the hereditary chiefs. I am sorry that at last your children have the upper hand. . . . If you are a parent no doubt you are aware of the absence of a desire in a child for education and if the parent is persistent the child will be happy some day. So God has appointed you, whites who are wise and called fathers of the Indians, to educate in learning and instruct them in the way of a prosperous livelihood. The Caughnawagas have learned these to a great extent, but if you grant them the old system they will probably fall back to their ancient state as seen when white men first landed on this island.[46]

In February 1895 Superintendent General Daly and his deputy, Hayter Reed, visited Kahnawà:ke and met with some four hundred residents to discuss their concerns relating to the Advancement Act and the band council system.[47] Representatives from Ahkwesáhsne and Kanehsatà:ke also attended the meeting, a detailed record of which was made by an Indian Department official.[48] At the meeting Joseph Foster, who had been active in the September 1894 grand council at Ahkwesáhsne, spoke on behalf of the petitioners who had sought a return to the "old system of Chiefs" and stated that "the introduction of the new Indian laws had brought strife and law suits; that under the old system better feelings prevailed." Foster also explained that the factions within the Kahnawà:ke council and the community at large had become identified with Canada's major political parties. "Council elections," he stated, "were run on Federal party lines and that from the standpoint of Federal politics the Council decided questions coming before it. This was not so under the old system; and hence the greater accord existing of old." Loran Pike of Ahkwesáhsne, who had presented the Grand Council's September 1894 petition to the Indian Department in Ottawa, added that the object of the Grand Council meeting and the resolve to return to the "old system" was to "reunite the old confederacy."

A number of Kahnawakehró:non spoke in favor of abandoning the band council system and returning to the traditional council of clan chiefs. John Standup declared the "the present law was not beneficial." "The old system," he is reported to have said, "ran smoothly and worked for good; the new system causes trouble, and under it bad feeling has spread to the women and divided the band." Joseph Jocks stated that he never voted and that the Advancement Act was only for white men. John Sky "favored the return to the old system because old men were on that side and they had greater experience than others." Michel Bourdeau, who had been a supporter of Louis Jackson and had continued to serve as a band councillor, stated his support for returning to the old system because, among other reasons, "the elections engendered and inflamed ill feeling."

During the course of the meeting Superintendent Daly sought comments from those who favored the band council system. Few had much to say. Thomas Jocks, who supported the Indian Act system and who by this time had been returned to the band council and was its chief councillor, explained that "those of that mind were content to give all the time to the others." Louis Jackson spoke about the problems of the present system but also questioned whether returning to the "old system" would solve the problems that concerned so many. He did not favor the existing band council system, but he did not endorse a revival of the traditional council. He argued that there was discord under the old system as well and questioned whether chiefs under the traditional system would have the power its advocates claimed. Like those who had supported the September Grand Council and the December petition, Jackson sought greater local power and autonomy, but he did not agree that this could be achieved by a return to the traditional council of chiefs. In his view greater autonomy was better achieved by loosening the restrictions of the Advancement Act and expanding band council powers to a level comparable to those of Canadian municipalities.

After the comments of those who wished to speak, Daly stated the federal government's position in the matter. He explained that the government had passed the Indian Advancement Act so that Indian people would have a system of municipal government similar to their white neighbors' once they "had become nearly equal, if not the very equal, of whitemen in advancement." "As to the divisions in the band," he stated, "all cannot think alike—there must be differences of opinion. . . . Do as whitemen do. They differ and take opposite sides, but they shake hands afterwards and do not become enemies because they do not see eye to eye on all questions." He followed with a lecture on the "evils of agitation." Notwithstanding his remark that he "never saw a more intelligent body of Indians," Daly went on to emphasize that the responsibility for the decision in the band council issue was his and that he would "decide the question solely with a view to their best interests." But if Daly's views on the band council were not yet clear, they must have been when he suggested that when those in attendance thought the matter over, "they would conclude . . . that when the Government applied the Indian Advancement Act to them, it was done in their best interest . . . and that it would take a great deal to lead them to revoke its application."

Some days after the meeting with Superintendent Daly, Louis L. Beauvais of Kahnawà:ke published a letter in the *Montreal Daily Witness* in which he expressed his own view of the meeting and the interests of those who, like himself, sought to return to the traditional council of chiefs:

> The Hon. Mr. Daly, Minister of the Interior, in his visit to Caughnawaga on the thirteenth of February last, in his reply to the Indian questions concerning the Indian Advancement act, which we want to abandon and resume to the old system of chiefs, said that we want to go back one hundred and fifty years and be looked upon as minors rather than be made equal to the white race of people; said that it is to our own welfare that we should cherish the new system the Indian Advancement act, that it will promote and enlighten us and in the course of years would be equal to the white race of people. We do not regret to say that it is better to draw back, even as far back as one hundred and fifty years, to save our reserve from ruin, for the new system, the Indian Advancement act, has created nothing but divisions, enmity and separation among us, it has degraded us rather than promoted.[49]

When Daly informed the governor general about the meeting in Kahnawà:ke, he noted that those who wanted to return to the old system believed "that under it the Indians would be left under their own laws and freed from Departmental supervision." Referring to the division within the Kahnawà:ke community and noting with concern the precedent that would be set if the Indian Department were to accede to Kahnawakehró:non demands, he went on:

> The progressive members of the band preferred the system of Municipal government afforded them by the Indian Advancement Act to the old form of government by life Chiefs, and that to assent to the proposal of the others would be regarded by the more advanced Indians as a sanctioning of a retrograde movement. . . . After carefully considering the question, the undersigned [Daly] came to the conclusion that it would not be in the best interest of the Caughnawaga Indians to remove the band from the operation of the Indian Advancement Act and allow a return to the former system: for apart from the detrimental effect of such a movement on the band itself, it would furnish a very undesirable precedent, and would likely be regarded by Indians in other sections of the country as a confession that the Department of Indian Affairs had found that the form of government and the system of law of the Indians themselves were more in their interest than those which had been framed by Parliament.[50]

After submitting his report, Deputy Superintendent Reed directed the Indian agent, Alexander Brosseau, to inform the petitioners that the Department denied their request to reinstitute the traditional council of chiefs.[51] Not surprisingly, in his annual report for 1895 Brosseau highlighted "the agitation of a large number of the Indians for a return to the ancient system of electing chiefs.[52]

Thus, in the years immediately following the establishment of the band council system, a third course of political action emerged that sought to revoke the Advancement Act and restore the traditional council of clan chiefs. Conservatives who previously had opposed the Indian Act system and sought to maintain the traditional council were its main supporters. This course was traditionalist in the sense that it aimed to revive the community's traditional political institutions and practices. The division and antagonism within the band council between Reformers supporting the Indian Act system and Conservatives working within the system to secure greater autonomy for the band council contributed to this traditionalist movement. It also gathered support from and contributed to similar movements in other Rotinonhsiónni communities and thereby strengthened political ties and identification with those communities and the Confederacy itself.

The Late 1890s

During the late 1890s and the first decade of the twentieth century the election system for the band council on the Kahnawà:ke reserve underwent a number of changes. In at least one instance the initiative for the change appears to have been directly related to the problems and difficulties associated with Kahnawà:ke's initial experience under the Advancement Act. In late 1896 the local Indian agent recommended that the six-district system be eliminated and that six councillors be elected at large, and the Indian Department initially agreed. Voters in the village district supported this proposed change, but those in the outlying districts opposed it, probably fearing that representation of their interests within the band council would suffer under the new system. The opponents, 110 of them, registered their protest in a petition to the superintendent general in late January 1897. In the end, no change was made.[53] Changes did come, however, a decade later. In 1906 the six-district system was replaced by the single-district system, and in 1907 secret balloting was introduced for band council elections.[54]

Through the rest of the 1890s and into the early twentieth century band council elections in Kahnawà:ke continued to be a problem, and some Kahnawakehró:non continued to press for a return to the traditional council of chiefs. At a "grand general council" at St. Regis in November 1896 Kahnawakehró:non and representatives from Kanesehtake and Ahkwesáhsne again called for an end to the band council system and a return to their "original laws."[55] As he had done in 1895, in 1897 the Indian agent reported the dissatisfaction of the "Caughnawagas" with the Indian Advancement Act.[56] In that year eighty-eight women from Kahnawà:ke petitioned the superintendent general, Clifford Sifton, to address the situation in their community and allow a return to the council of chiefs:

> Our men have repeatedly tried and without success and it is for that cause that now we women stand appealingly before you. . . . You gave us your law [the Indian Advancement Act], on the statement that if it did not run smoothly after it was tested, it would be retracted at the will of our people, but it seems that is forgotten. . . . Since the change of our chiefs into councillors our sorrows were manifolded, we have lost many advantages, it has caused many family disputes, brother against brother. It has separated them, and it has caused an ill-feeling which is yet burning, we do not specify all, but we are sensible that a great change has been made from good to the worse with us.

They went on to request that "justice be imparted" and that they "have back our just form of election of chiefs."[57]

The women received little satisfaction. Duncan Campbell Scott, the acting deputy superintendent general, sent the Indian Department's response. Scott noted that the superintendent general had considered the subject of their petition on several previous occasions, and that each time it had been decided to continue with the band council system. This had been done, he said, with their best interests in mind. He confirmed that their petition to return to the old system of chiefs would not be entertained and that the Department would give no consideration to any such representations by them or anyone else in the future.

During the following year, 1898, the community refused to elect councillors as the Advancement Act required them to do.[58] On three subsequent occasions—twice in 1901 and again in 1905—Kahnawakehró:non petitioned the DIA to revoke the Advancement Act and allow them to return to their traditional council government. Among the signers of one of the 1901 petitions were several former clan chiefs. In the 1905 "Petition of Chiefs and Warriors of the Iroquois Band of Indians at Caughnawaga," the superintendent general was asked to "relieve" the Kahnawà:ke community from the Indian Advancement Act and permit the people "to return to the ancient system of governing by Chiefs." As before, the petitions were denied, one with the comment that "a return to the old system would be a retrograde step detrimental to the interests of the Indians.[59]

Given that the native community at Kahnawà:ke had become so divided over the issues of the Advancement Act and the band council system and persistently pressed for a return to the traditional council of chiefs, it was inevitable that the tensions and pressures it generated would be manifested in other arenas of community life. One of these arenas was local schooling.

Formal schooling was introduced in Kahnawà:ke by British colonial authorities in 1835 and permanently established under the auspices of the Roman Catholic Church in 1843.[60] During the 1870s school enrollment and attendance rates were low by Indian Department standards and were declining. According to the Indian agent at the time, a major reason was the poor quality of instruction and the language barrier between the Kanien'kéha-speaking students and their French-speaking teachers.[61]

Low enrollment and low daily attendance persisted in the 1890s and continued to concern the Indian Department, but for reasons quite apart from the language barrier or the quality of instruction. In 1893, perhaps in an attempt to reverse the slide in school enrollment and attendance, the teacher in the Roman Catholic boys' school was replaced by a Kahnawakehró:non, Frank McDonald Jacobs. Jacobs remained as teacher in the boys' school until 1897, when he was dismissed, for reasons that are unclear. Jacobs was replaced by another man from Kahnawà:ke, Omer Plante, who had been educated at the Mohawk Institute, had the approval of the Roman Catholic priest in Kahnawà:ke, and was considered by Indian Department officials to be well qualified for his responsibilities. There was considerable controversy within the community over Plante's appointment, however, and it was tied to the tensions and pressures within the community over the Indian Advancement Act and reinstituting the traditional council of clan chiefs. Plante was of mixed native-white parentage and, more important in this instance, he was the stepson of Louis Jackson. Jackson, of course, was an opponent of the Indian Act system, but he was not a proponent of a return to the traditional council. The Indian agent, Alexander Brosseau, described Jackson as "unwilling to join the portion of the band that is agitating for the return to the old system of chiefs." According to Brosseau, the feeling against Jackson because of his position was so strong that many parents refused to send their children to the school taught by his stepson. He recommended transferring Plante and replacing him with another teacher as the only solution to increasing enrollment and attendance. Enforcing attendance while Plante continued as teacher "would cause a revolt among the Indians."[62]

Many Kahnawakehró:non who opposed Plante's appointment supported Peter J. Delisle as Jacobs's replacement. Delisle was from Kahnawà:ke and a graduate of St. Laurent College. His political position at this time with regard to the Advancement Act and the band council system is not evident, though he would in time become a leader in local opposition to the DIA and its policies. A report by the secretary of the Indian Department noted that "as regards compulsory education, the Indians expressed themselves as not being desirous of having the law enforced in this regard unless they were allowed their choice of teachers." In response to their concerns, the secretary stated in his report that "under the law the appointment of teachers does not rest with the band but with the Department." Eventually, however, Indian Department officials relented. After the 1899–1900 school year Plante was transferred, and Delisle replaced him at the beginning of the new school year. DIA officials noted an immediate improvement in school attendance under Delisle and acknowledged the replacement of Plante as the reason. Under Delisle's leadership, school enrollment and attendance continued to improve until he and other native teachers in the Kahnawà:ke schools were replaced by the Sisters of St. Anne in 1915, a change that intensified nationalist impulses within the community and strengthened its ties to other Rotinonhsiónni communities.

5. "Must We Resign Ourselves to Such Injustice?"

The Sisters of St. Anne and the Thunderwater Movement

The Establishment of the Sisters of St. Anne in Kahnawà:ke

During the latter part of the nineteenth century and the early decades of the twentieth, most Kahnawà:ke schoolchildren were enrolled in the Roman Catholic day schools on the reserve. These included separate boys' and girls' schools in the village near the St. Francis Xavier mission and, by the late 1890s, a third school in the southern part of the reserve that served families in the outlying areas. The schools were taught by lay teachers appointed and paid by the Department of Indian Affairs, but the local missionaries had a strong hand in their operation and in the assignment of the men and women responsible for administration and instruction. The curriculum included reading, writing, arithmetic, geography, history, fine arts, English, and the Roman Catholic catechism. In 1890, when the population of the reserve numbered 1,722, there were 78 students enrolled in the Catholic day schools. By 1900 this number had increased to 122 (45 boys and 77 girls) in the village schools and 27 (18 boys and 9 girls) in the outlying school, commonly referred to as the Bush school. By 1910 enrollment in the village school had increased to 175 (98 boys and 77 girls) and in the Bush school to 39 (22 boys and 17 girls).[1]

In addition to the Catholic schools, there was a Protestant day school that had been established in the late 1890s. This school was funded partly by the Indian Department and partly by the Methodist Missionary Society. Except for religious instruction, its curriculum mirrored that of the Catholic schools. In 1890 enrollment in the Protestant school numbered 29, which by 1910 had increased to 54 (20 boys and 34 girls). A number of Kahnawà:ke children also attended the Roman Catholic Wikwemikong Industrial School at Manitoulin Island in Ontario and the Anglican Mt. Elgin Industrial School in Muncy, Ontario. In 1910, there were 37 Kahnawà:ke children (22 boys and 15 girls) attending Wikwemikong and 15 attending Mt. Elgin. Later, children from Kahnawà:ke were also sent to the Jesuit-run St. Peter Claver's Indian Residential School in Spanish, Ontario.[2]

Throughout the 1880s and 1890s the Indian Department had been disappointed by the low school enrollments and attendance in Kahnawà:ke. In 1890 average daily attendance in the Roman Catholic day schools was only about 50 percent of those enrolled. In 1900 the average daily attendance was even lower, with only about one-third of the school-age children actually enrolled in school. Indian Department officials attributed this pattern to the poor quality of instruction and to the language barrier between the teachers, who spoke French, and their students, most of who spoke only their native language. By the late 1890s, with new teachers, the language barrier was no longer an issue, yet low enrollment and attendance persisted. At this time the political divisions within the community over the Indian Act system and a desire to return to the traditional council of clan chiefs were central to the problem. These circumstances had resulted in considerable opposition to the head teacher at the time and generated support for Peter J. Delisle as his replacement.

Born in Kahnawà:ke about 1877, Delisle had been serving as secretary and interpreter for the band council, had completed commercial coursework with honors at St. Laurent College, and was qualified to secure teaching credentials.[3] Indicating his interest in the position as head teacher in Kahnawà:ke's Catholic schools, Delisle wrote to the secretary of the Indian Department in 1900 about the situation in Kahnawà:ke and his own qualifications as a teacher: "Indian children knowing only their own language teach faster with a teacher of their own race who has passed the necessary examinations and who can explain things in their own tongue."[4] Following his appointment at the beginning of the school year in 1900, Indian Department officials reported an immediate improvement in school enrollment and attendance and acknowledged that Delisle's replacement of the previous teacher was the main reason. In fact, the upturn was so dramatic that in 1901 the head of the Schools Branch of the Department recommended that another male teacher be hired to assist the overburdened Delisle. One was, but not until 1903. The new teacher, Peter Williams, was also from Kahnawà:ke, and his appointment was supported by one of the local missionaries, who wrote to Indian Department officials stating that Williams filled the continuing need for instructors who could teach in the native language. In addition to Delisle and Williams, some of the female teachers also appear to have been Kahnawakehró:non.

Under the leadership of Delisle and Williams, school enrollment and attendance continued to improve. By 1910, 71 percent of the school-age children were enrolled in schools, and average daily attendance had risen above 50 percent.[5] The Indian Department cited Delisle's skill as a teacher and the ability of Delisle and Williams (who were trilingual) to teach in their native language as crucial to the success of schooling at this time. In fact, Indian Department officials were so impressed with Delisle's performance and the improvement in the Kahnawà:ke schools that his periodic requests for salary increases were usually granted, and by the fall term of 1912 he had become the highest-paid native teacher in Quebec.[6]

Given the improvements in local schooling that had taken shape under Delisle's leadership, it is surprising that in 1913 the Indian Department decided to replace him and the entire teaching staff in the village schools with an order of teaching nuns. The Indian Department had made a similar attempt to place an order of nuns in charge of Kahnawà:ke's schools in 1902, but it failed, primarily because of widespread community opposition. This time the result was different. In early 1914 Delisle, Williams, and the other teachers were informed of the Department's decision and the impending change. In January 1915 they were dismissed and replaced by nuns from the order of the Sisters of St. Anne, which had been active in Indian education in British Columbia since the 1850s and which maintained a provincial house in Lachine, on the north shore of the St. Lawrence River directly opposite Kahnawà:ke. In addition to giving the Sisters of St. Anne control of instruction and administration in Kahnawà:ke's Catholic schools, the Indian Department also promised a permanent residence on the reserve for the nuns who came to teach and work.[7]

The change in the administration of Kahnawà:ke's Catholic schools at this time may have been related to recent developments in Indian education policy. Beginning in the late 1890s, there had been a growing trend within the Indian Department toward greater cost efficiency. This trend, combined with recession in the Canadian economy and growing disenchantment with off-reservation Indian boarding schools as an effective tool of assimilation, had led to a variety of cost-cutting measures in Indian education programs and greater emphasis on more economical on-reservation boarding and day schools. These policies took shape in particular under Duncan Campbell Scott, who moved to the position of superintendent of education within the Indian Department in 1909 and then to the post of deputy superintendent general in 1913.[8]

It is difficult to compare the relative costs of the different types of teachers, nevertheless, it seems unlikely that there would have been significant savings in replacing the native and lay teachers with an order of teaching nuns. While the salaries the Indian Department paid to the nuns were less than those paid to the native teachers, as a rule the Department paid its native teachers less than its non-native lay teachers. Further, assigning control of Kahnawà:ke's schools to the Sisters of St. Anne involved the additional costs of purchasing and maintaining or renting housing on the reserve for the nuns and providing for their transportation and other needs. In sum, it is unlikely that financial considerations alone explain such a dramatic change in Kahnawà:ke's schools.

A more likely explanation is that the replacement of the native and lay teachers in Kahnawà:ke with an order of teaching nuns was a direct attempt by the Indian Department, now under the direction of a new and aggressive deputy superintendent, to exert control over a community that had shown persistent and widespread opposition to the Indian Act system.[9] The development of traditionalist and nationalist impulses within the community during the 1890s was clearly at odds with the government's policy of assimilation and challenged the Department's authority and control. With regard to local schooling in particular, the community's endeavor to assert its will in the appointment of teachers and the practice of instruction in the native language by some of those teachers was undoubtedly troubling. The replacement of these native teachers with an order of teaching nuns experienced in Indian education not only would have served the Indian Department's goal of assimilation, it would also have made evident in a dramatic way the Department's power and its commitment to carrying out its policies in Kahnawà:ke. Moreover, Duncan Campbell Scott was well acquainted with Kahnawà:ke's resistance to the Indian Act system and its efforts to return to the traditional council of clan chiefs. Soon after his appointment as deputy superintendent general in 1913, Scott initiated negotiations with the archbishop of Montreal for an order of teaching nuns to assume control of the Catholic schools in Kahnawà:ke, and the archbishop selected the Sisters of St. Anne.[10] In short, the government's decision to replace Peter Delisle and the other teachers in Kahnawà:ke's Catholic schools with nuns may be best understood in the context of Kahnawà:ke's recent history of resistance to the Indian Act system and its growing traditionalism and nationalism. The Indian Department's decision may well have been an effort to contain these developments, demonstrate its power, and implement its assimilationist policies.

Opposition and division developed quickly within the community in response to the Department's plan. In June 1914 the Kahnawà:ke band council considered the issues, and three councillors, including the chief councillor or "mayor," Frank McDonald Jacobs, favored the Department's plan, while two were opposed and one abstained from voting.[11] A month later Peter Delisle traveled to Ottawa to meet with Indian Department officials on behalf of Kahnawakehró:non who opposed the replacement of the teachers. The *Ottawa Free Press* reported on Delisle's visit and noted that he brought with him a petition to the minister of the interior that objected to the plan to replace the current teachers with nuns.[12] The petition was written in the native language, carried seventy-one signatures, and emphasized Kahnawakehró:non sovereignty and autonomy in this matter. An Indian Department translation of the petition reads, in part, as follows:

> We the undersigned members of the Iroquois band of Caughnawaga, Quebec, beg to file our strenuous objection to the contemplated admission and residence of a certain or any other congregation of Sisters upon our Reserve.
>
> We have been apprised that the schools in the village are to be placed into the hands of nuns; with all respect due to them as a religious community, we vigorously protest to their admission or permission to reside upon the Reserve conceded for our own special use. Our forefathers have always rigorously barred their entry and now we must persist to refuse to allow their coming on the reserve for manifest and obvious reasons.

... Under a recent enactment we were compelled to submit to the compulsory attendance at schools by our children, now, we are to be impugned in our rights of selection as to who should teach our children; must we resign ourselves to such injustice, or can it be said that we have no legal or moral interest in the matter?[13]

A few months later, in October 1914, 168 Kahnawakehró:non again petitioned the minister, reiterating the concerns and objections expressed in the July petition. In addition, the petitioners suggested that if the minister would not veto the Indian Department's plan, then he should allow the matter to be submitted to a vote by the entire band.[14]

During this time the Indian Department tried on several occasions to purchase land near the St. Francis Xavier mission as a site for the nuns' residence but did not succeed. In a report on the failed efforts over the course of nearly a year, one Schools Branch employee reported that property owners refused to sell land to the government "under any consideration." With time running out before the nuns were to take over the schools, the only alternative was to rent a house in the village for the nuns, which the Indian Department did with the assistance of the chief councillor, Frank McDonald Jacobs. Late in 1914 the nuns moved into the rented residence, and on 1 January 1915 the Sisters of St. Anne officially took charge of the Catholic boys' and girls' schools in Kahnawà:ke.[15]

When the Indian Department resumed efforts to purchase land on the reserve for the nuns' residence in 1916 it was met with written protests that suggest the opposition to the Department's plan was widespread. Letters to Deputy Superintendent General Scott from one of the local Jesuit missionaries, the local Indian agent, and the sister superior in charge of the Catholic schools in Kahnawà:ke confirm this. The leader of the opposition to the nuns and the plan to provide them with a permanent residence on the reserve was Peter Delisle. In 1916, soon after Scott informed the missionary and the nuns that a permanent residence would be built within the year, Delisle wrote to inform him that the band was opposed to having the nuns and whites in general take up permanent residence on the reserve. Scott responded that the Indian Department would make an effort to determine the band's views on the matter before taking action. Subsequently, and without notifying Delisle, the Indian Department, with the assistance of the Justice Department, explored the legality of expropriating reserve land and building a residence for the nuns without the band's consent.[16]

Throughout 1916 and into the following year Delisle kept up the pressure on the nuns, and he became the focus of a stream of concerned letters to the deputy superintendent general. In his letters the missionary, Fr. Joseph Gras, referred to Delisle as "impudent" and "dishonest" and reported that he was "urging the Indians to rebel against constituted authority."[17] In one of her letters the sister superior, Sr. Mary Joseph Edward, suggested that this man "at the bottom of the trouble" be "put in his place," and that if this were done "all the others would cool down, for after all, they are only cowards and make more smoke than fire."[18] Alexander Brosseau, the Indian agent, wrote to complain that the "demagogue" Delisle harassed the nuns and urged his "admirers" to rebellious actions.[19] In a letter to Scott in May 1917, the sister superior wrote:

> I beg to inform you that a certain Peter Delisle is influencing the Indians against our Sisters and their schools. He has been antagonistic to them from the very beginning and has taken every opportunity to undermine their authority. Last Sunday week he harangued the people after church services: among other things he said the Sisters were incompetent and criticized their methods of teaching. He even went so far as to say he would not allow the government to erect the

sisters' dwelling house because he did not want any white people in the village. . . . If you desire that the sisters remain in Caughnawaga I know you will find means to silence this Iroquois because it is a constant strain for them to cope with these inconstant and ignorant people.[20]

The growing controversy over the establishment of the Sisters of St. Anne in Kahnawà:ke and in charge of its schools received widespread public attention. The *Toronto Sentinel*, for example, reported on the developments in May 1917 in an article titled "Nuns Forced upon the Indians." I quote the *Sentinel* article here at some length because it highlights the concerns shared by many Kahnawakehró:non and the division these issues had created within the Kahnawà:ke community.

> The introduction of nuns as teachers on the Reserve at Caughnawaga is causing trouble. It is said that this has been done at the instigation of Indian Affairs. The Sisters supplanted lay teachers, of whom one, P. J. Delisle, . . . heads the campaign against the Sisters and against Rev. Father Gras, S.J., the resident missionary, who has championed the cause of the newly installed teachers. The tribe has split into two factions in the dispute, by far the larger, some claim, being on the side of Delisle. The stronger faction took time by the forelock last Saturday and tore up some 500 feet of fencing around land whereupon it is planned to erect a residence, or school, for the Sisters—and which land the antis claim was illegally transferred to the Jesuits and Sisters for the purpose mentioned.
>
> Since 1915 correspondence has been exchanged between the Department of Indian Affairs at Ottawa and the two antagonistic factions in Caughnawaga concerning the right of the Government to establish a residence for eight nuns, without first obtaining a surrender of land upon which to build the residence, such surrender to be obtained by a majority vote of the Indians. The faction opposing the pro-

posed action of the government is led by P. J. Delisle, the Grand Councilor of the Council of Tribes.

The other faction is under F. McDonald Jacobs, an ex-chief of the Iroquois. The question in dispute, it is said, embodies no religious separate school, or three language controversy, but arises out of the progressive program claimed by both factions for the establishing of a modern, efficient, compulsory system of education. They differ seriously as to the method of attaining this end.

The ambition of the Delisle faction is to avoid having a convent, to oust the teaching Nuns and other white people from the reservation and, instead of the present school curriculum, to have University trained men teachers who can instruct in all the modern sciences as well as a wide range of present-day public school topics. "The modern Indian," says Mr. Delisle, "has taken the war feather from the top of his head and carries it over his ear, signalizing his transition from pursuit of scalping to that of scholarship. We have applied to the Archbishop for other tutors, but he denies our request on the ground that the Jesuits possess seigneurial rights granted them by Louis XIV."[21]

The *Sentinel* article is important in several respects. It emphasizes that the opposition to the Sisters of St. Anne and the plans of the Indian Department was based on several issues and that autonomy was the principle underlying them. These issues included the taking of reserve land without the band's consent, the presence of whites (including the nuns) on the reserve, and the nature of and control over the educational curriculum provided to the schoolchildren of Kahnawà:ke. Led by Peter Delisle, who is also identified as the "Grand Councilor" of an organization known as the "Council of the Tribes," the "Antis" who took this position opposed the use of reserve land for housing the nuns and certainly opposed doing so without the approval of the band; they objected to the presence of whites on the reserve and wanted them removed; and they favored a modern and progressive educational curriculum but did not think the nuns were trained to provide it. The principle underlying the Anti position was the right of Kahnawakehró:non to control their land base, the cultural character of their community, and the education of their children. The *Sentinel* article also indicates that the opposition to the Sisters and the Indian Department was an active resistance that involved some degree of civil disobedience. Antis were willing to try to force an acceptance of their positions and recognition of their autonomy in these matters. It is also important to point out that Anti opposition was political, not religious, in nature. There is no evidence that Anti opposition was based on a rejection of Roman Catholic or Christian values and beliefs. Rather, the Antis were opposed to the interference of the church in the secular life of the community. Finally, the *Sentinel* article indicates that while the Anti position was widely held within the community, the Sisters and the Department also had their supporters. These "Progressives," as they were sometimes called by government officials and others, were led by Frank McDonald Jacobs, who had served as chief councillor of the Kahnawà:ke band council in 1914.

The division within the community between the Antis and Progressives is well illustrated by the band council elections of 1915, held just two weeks after the Sisters of St. Anne had taken over the village schools.[22] In the elections Delisle was selected as one of the six councillors, and Jacobs was turned out of office. In fact, Delisle received the most votes of the thirteen candidates. Moreover, the composition of the entire council was changed in direct response to the issues of the nuns and the plans of the Indian Department. In addition to Jacobs, two other councillors who had supported him and the Department's plans were replaced by new councillors who supported the Anti position led by Delisle. As an Indian Department employee reported following the elections, "The defeat of Ex-Mayor F. McD. Jacobs and his followers was due . . . to his action condoning the residence of the Sisters in the village and their taking charge of the schools."[23]

In response to the pressure of Delisle and the Anti faction, in June 1917 Deputy Superintendent General Scott allowed a community referendum on the question of a permanent residence on the reserve for the Sisters of St. Anne. The result was decisively against the Sisters and the Department's plans. About two-thirds of the community's eligible male voters participated in the referendum, and of these 95 percent (311) were opposed; only 4 percent (14) voted in favor of a permanent residence for the nuns. For the next three years the Indian Department continued to rent housing on the reserve for the nuns. Finally, in 1920 the Department succeeded in securing a permanent residence for them by purchasing land and an existing house within the village, about half a mile from the village schools and the St. Francis Xavier mission.[24]

The Thunderwater Movement

The political situation in Kahnawà:ke surrounding the controversy over the Sisters of St. Anne was associated with another important development that has come to be known as the Thunderwater Movement. Described by one author as a "revitalization movement" and as "nativist" in character and by another as a process of "reconstruction" or "re-invention," the Thunderwater Movement centered on the Council of the Tribes, a pan-Indian organization that sought to address the economic, political, and cultural concerns of native peoples in Canada and the United States. The Thunderwater Movement swept through Kahnawà:ke at precisely the time when the events related to the Catholic schools and the Sisters of St. Anne were unfolding. Though short-lived, it has been viewed as radicalizing some Kahnawakehró:non and intensifying factionalism within the community. Nevertheless, the political and cultural significance of the movement in the community, and in other Rotinonhsiónni communities as well, has not been explored or well understood.

The Council of the Tribes was established in Cleveland, Ohio, about 1913 by a man known as Chief Thunderwater.[25] The purpose of the Council was to address the concerns of Indian people as they related to federal Indian policies and to do so through coordinated political action. The Council sought to provide legal assistance to Indian people with grievances against the government, and it advocated educational advancement, temperance, modern farming practices, and resistance to the sale of reserve lands. The Council of the Tribes consisted of a central governing council, known as the Inner Circle, which was linked to local "Circles" on Indian reserves. The Inner Circle consisted of a number of officers, the most important of which was the "Oghema Niagara," Chief Thunderwater himself. Circles consisted of local Council members, sometimes referred to as "warriors," and a leadership consisting of several officers, including a "Grand Councillor."[26]

The Council of the Tribes promoted its organizational structure as generally "Indian" in nature, and one author has noted at least a superficial resemblance to the structure of the Rotinonhsiónni Confederacy.[27] The Council also adopted various symbols and practices and even a system of reckoning time that were vaguely "Indian" in character. For example, the principal symbol of the organization has the triangular shape of a teepee (see fig. 4). At its center are the images of the sun, a feathered arrow, and a calumet, or long-stemmed pipe. At the base of the triangle are six circles aligned horizontally, an image that some have suggested is a reference to the Six Nations Confederacy. This emblem appeared on the Council's membership certificates and constitution and, reportedly, on the gravestones of Council members. Members used passwords and secret gestures, and some Council proceedings, such as those related to sanctioning and expelling members, were heavily ritualized. In the Council's calendrical system a year was referred to as a "great sun," a month as a "moon," and a day as a "sun," and all time dated from the beginning of native contact with whites, which was established as the year 1492. Along with dedication to the Council's aims and participation in its activities, qualifications for membership included native ancestry and knowledge of one's tribal and clan affiliations. Within just a few years the Council of the Tribes attracted a wide following on reserves in the United States and Canada. By one estimate, at its height about 1917 or 1918 it had 26,000 members. The rapid growth of the Council of the Tribes has been referred to as the "Thunderwater Movement."[28]

Kahnawà:ke was among the reserves where the Council of the Tribes attracted a following. In 1916 a substantial part of the community became involved with the Council, and a variety of fund-raising activities were held to help support Council initiatives. At the time, it was reported that some two hundred Kahnawakehró:non had purchased memberships at a total cost of more than $400. In September of that year Thunderwater visited the community and held a two-day rally with his supporters. By this time a local Circle had been organized, and Peter Delisle, the leader of the opposition to the Sisters of St. Anne, had been appointed as its Grand Councillor. Kahnawà:ke was quickly becoming a principal base of operations for Thunderwater in Canada.[29]

In 1915 the band council elections in Kahnawà:ke became a site of protest and of resistance to the Sisters of St. Anne and the Indian Department's plan to establish them in the community and in charge of Kahnawà:ke's Catholic schools. Peter Delisle and other opponents of the teaching nuns and the Department's plan were voted into office, while the supporters of the nuns and the Indian Department, most notably Frank McDonald Jacobs, were voted out. The following year there was considerably less interest in the band council elections. Neither Delisle nor any other leading Anti candidates sought band council positions, and

4. Council of the Tribes membership certificate. Photograph courtesy of Kanien'kehaka Onkwawen:na Raotitiohkwa.

the numbers of votes polled for the winning candidates were less than half those of the previous year. In assessing the 1916 elections, one Indian Department official noted the lack of interest and said that the resulting quality of the candidates was "the poorest that the band has had in recent years."[30] It was at this time that many Kahnawakehró:non became involved with the Council of the Tribes and Thunderwater himself visited the community. In addition, it was during this year that the Council Circle in Kahnawà:ke was organized and Delisle, who the previous year had won a council seat by a wide margin and had been elected its chief councillor, was appointed its leader. In other words, it appears that in 1916 the political energy that had radically altered the band council in 1915 was diverted to the Council of the Tribes and Chief Thunderwater. But this was only temporary.

In 1917, perhaps energized by the intensity and success of Thunderwater activities during the previous year, there was renewed interest in the band council elections, and Thunderwater supporters won all six council positions. From among them John T. Daillebout was selected as the chief councillor, or "mayor." During the Thunderwater activity of the previous year, Daillebout and four of the other five councillors elected in 1917 had been appointed along with Peter Delisle to form the leadership of the Council of the Tribes Circle in Kahnawà:ke. The only candidate for election in 1917 who was not a Thunderwater supporter was Frank McDonald Jacobs, the councillor voted out in 1915 because of his support for the Sisters of St. Anne. Jacobs received only 38 votes, far less than any of the elected candidates, each of whom received between 181 and 175 votes. The "Thunderwater" band council of 1917 was reelected in 1918, and Thunderwater supporters continued to dominate the council in 1919.[31]

The members of the Thunderwater band councils were involved in two particularly important initiatives during their tenure. One was related directly to the plan of the Indian Department to establish a permanent residence for the Sisters of St. Anne in Kahnawà:ke. In 1917 it was Peter Delisle and the Thunderwater band council who pressured the Indian Department into the referendum on a permanent residence for the teaching nuns on the reserve. The referendum was held in July of that year, and the result was decidedly against the nuns and the plan of the Indian Department. After the referendum, Fr. Gras wrote to Deputy Superintendent General Scott to state that behind the vote against a permanent residence for them was concern over the loss of land and opposition to the government's interference in local affairs.[32] Subsequently the Indian Department temporarily abandoned its effort to buy land and build a permanent residence for the nuns. Instead, they secured a three-year lease on a house in the central part of the village.[33]

The second important initiative the Thunderwater band council was involved in was an attempted incorporation of the Council of the Tribes in Canada in 1918. Its significance is evident only within the context of the spread and popularity of the Thunderwater movement and the Indian Department's response to it. Chief Thunderwater's initial activity in Canada appears to have been at Ahkwesáhsne in late 1914, when his meetings there drew large numbers from both the Canadian and United States portions of the reserve. In 1915 he appears to have been adopted into the St. Regis band, and in that same year he was working with elected band councillors not only at St. Regis but also at Kanehsatà:ke and Tyendinaga. A few months later, in September 1915, a major convention of the Council of the Tribes was held at Deseronto, and in 1916 not only was there a burst of Thunderwater activity in Kahnawà:ke but a Thunderwater rally was held at Six Nations in October, and Thunderwater supporters captured many of the seats on Tyendinaga's band council, just as they would at Kahnawà:ke a year later.[34]

Not surprisingly, Chief Thunderwater and the Council of the Tribes drew the attention of Indian Department officials, and sometimes their concern was heightened by some unusual sources. In April 1915, after Thunderwater had begun to attract attention at Ahkwesáhsne, Deputy Superintendent General Scott learned from Arthur C. Parker of the Society of American Indians in the United States that Thunderwater might be an impostor. Parker was a Seneca from New York, a well-known ethnologist and archaeologist and a cofounder with Charles Eastman of the Society of American Indians.[35] Parker and the Society sought to educate the public about Indian people and were strong advocates of integrating Indians into Euro-American society. Parker said that his organization was disturbed about the "extremely uncomplimentary" reports that it had received about Thunderwater and his activities on the American side of the St. Regis reserve and that he was preparing to take the matter up with the Department of Indian Affairs in Washington DC.[36]

Before Thunderwater's visit to Kahnawà:ke in early September 1916, the Indian agent, Alexander Brosseau, wrote to Department officials to express his worries and warn about Thunderwater activity on the reserve. Brosseau noted in his report that several months earlier the Department had informed him that Chief Thunderwater was already causing a great deal of trouble among native people in Canada. He also noted that he had tried to warn the people of Kahnawà:ke about Thunderwater but that, instead, the councillors had carried on "propaganda" in favor of Thunderwater and that many Kahnawakehró:non were joining his organization. By late August 1916 about two hundred memberships had been purchased. Brosseau reported that Thunderwater himself was planning to hold meetings in the community in early September and suggested that "it would be a good policy to take energetic measures against this individual."[37]

About the time the Kahnawà:ke Indian agent had written to the Indian Department, the Indian agent for St. Regis also wrote to warn about the planned rally at Kahnawà:ke. Further, he suggested that Thunderwater represented a threat to more than just Kahnawà:ke and made it clear that the Department's concern over Thunderwater had been growing:

> Judging from the reports received from time to time as to his activities while in Deseronto . . . and the influence he has had over the Oka [Kanehsatà:ke] Indians, I consider it to the best interests of the Indians throughout Canada that this man should not be tolerated at all. . . . I am aware that you have already stated that it is impossible to keep this man from coming among the Indians, but I believe you should also desire to rid the Indians of this party; you can do so quite easily, as you have plenty of evidence against him, simply by requesting that the Immigration Department notify the Montreal office to deport him should he get to Caughnawaga as he is most certainly an undesirable and an expert agitator.[38]

Throughout the fall of 1916 the Indian Department's anxiety about Thunderwater and the Council of the Tribes continued to grow and took some bizarre turns. In mid-September of that year a court clerk in Belleville, Ontario, wrote to the commissioner of the Dominion police that at the Deseronto "powwow" a "Chief Underwater" addressed the Indians in their own language (unlikely, since he was not Rotinonhsiónni) and that he represented a real threat to the nation as the country found itself in the midst of a world war:

> [Thunderwater's] advice and council was of a nature not in harmony with Loyalty to the Crown, and in fact, it would appear from the information I have received that he is endeavoring to get the Indians throughout Canada to cooperate in causing detrimental action to the Government of Canada. . . . It has been intimated that the funds he uses

so lavishly are furnished from a German Source, and if you have any means of having some one who understands the Indian language, to watch this man at his Caughnawaga Convention, you will be able to satisfy yourself whether he is a safe man to be at large, or not.[39]

After the Council of the Tribes rally in Kahnawà:ke in September 1916, one of the local Jesuit missionaries and Frank McDonald Jacobs, the former band councillor and leader of the Progressive faction, contacted the Department of Immigration to report on Thunderwater's organizing activities and complain that he was an agitator and troublemaker. Subsequently the superintendent of immigration informed Deputy Superintendent General Scott about the complaints. He also told Scott that even before the events in Kahnawà:ke, his department had received troublesome reports about Thunderwater and even that it had attempted, but failed, to block his entry into the country.[40]

According to one Indian Department report, Thunderwater visited Ohsweken in October 1916 as a result of "repeated appeals from many of the Six Nations Indians and lastly on the invitation of the Indian Council." Scott was apprehensive enough about Thunderwater's visit there to direct one Indian Department official to attend his rally and report on his speech. According to the official's report, Thunderwater stated that it was "a deplorable condition of affairs that Indians as intellectual as the Six Nations should have to be treated as children." He went on:

> He assured them that alone they could do nothing to remedy this, but with his help . . . they would be able to get complete control of their own affairs. He warned the Indians against the white men and told of different ways they had of fleecing the Indians. He said that [the Indians] should keep their own council, transact their own business. He asked the Indians not to trust the white men, they have been trying for 300 years to push the Indians back into slavery

and they had partly succeeded. . . . The "Indian Act" is full
of clauses that show the truth of this.

Reportedly, Thunderwater went on to aver that he was a "pagan,"
not a Christian, and that the Christians' God was money.[41]

In concluding his report, the official expressed several concerns with regard to Thunderwater's activity at Tyendinaga. He
said that the children of parents who belonged to the Council of the Tribes were not attending school and that those who
composed the Council Circle at Deseronto were "on the whole
uneducated and unprogressive." He also noted that there was
a bitter division between Thunderwater supporters and opponents at Tyendinaga and that he had it "on good authority" that
a German flag was displayed at Council of the Tribes meetings.
He concluded by expressing his hope that some means would be
found to prevent Thunderwater from returning to the Six Nations reserve, because it would be certain to have a "depressing
effect" on the work of the Indian Department.[42]

In October 1917 Thunderwater and a number of Council supporters traveled to Ottawa to meet with Deputy Superintendent
General Scott. The *Ottawa Citizen* reported that the delegation
had been sent from Deseronto at the request of some eight hundred supporters to explain the purpose of the Council of the
Tribes, to ask for official recognition of the organization, and
to protest various injustices. Scott rejected any such recognition
and even refused to meet with the delegation. Interviewed by
the *Citizen*, Thunderwater claimed that Scott's refusal to meet
with the delegation reflected the Department's view that Indians
had no right to organize to protect their interests. In response,
he said, the Indians of Canada now wanted incorporation of the
Council by a special act of Parliament so that they could fight
in the courts against the abuse of their rights.[43] Less than a year
later, the Council of the Tribes did in fact attempt incorporation. The bill to incorporate the Council of the Tribes derived

from a petition signed by 175 Indians and had its first reading before the House of Commons in early April 1918. According to the petitioners, they sought to incorporate in order to more effectively unite and expand the membership of the Council, improve its ability to advocate for Indian people, promote the social and cultural development of Indian people, and strengthen the Council's influence on the federal government.

It is important to recognize that the attempt to incorporate the Council of the Tribes was largely a Rotinonhsiónni effort. To begin with, Thunderwater's activities and the establishment of Council Circles in Canada between 1914 and 1918 had been centered on Rotinonhsiónni reserves. Further, most of the 175 petitioners whose plea was the basis for the bill introduced to the House of Commons were from Rotinonhsiónni communities. They included Kanien'kehá:ka from Tyendinaga, Ahkwesáhsne, Kahnawà:ke, and Kanehsatà:ke and Onondagas, Cayugas, and Kanien'kehá:ka from Six Nations. In all, they constituted 81 percent (142) of the petitioners. Fourteen were from Kahnawà:ke, and they included Peter Delisle, band council mayor John T. Daillebout, and the other five Thunderwater councillors. The remaining petitioners, representing only 18 percent (33) of the total, were Algonquians from New Credit. Moreover, once the Council was incorporated, the petitioners intended that the central offices of the Council of Indian Tribes of Canada would be at Deseronto on the Tyendinaga reserve.[44]

Once the bill to incorporate the Council of the Tribes had been introduced, Deputy Superintendent General Scott worked quickly behind the scenes to have the introduction revoked. At his request, a report on the activities of Thunderwater and the Council of the Tribes since 1914 was prepared for the interior minister. In the report Scott characterized those who had joined the organization as "unprogressive, shiftless and complaining" and said that the "better class of Indians" were opposed to them and the Council of the Tribes. In addition, he stated that its supporters were "hostile" to departmental control and that they wished to take their affairs into their own hands. As Scott stated in the conclusion of his report,

> The real object or result of the organization among its members is to have them revert to former conditions as much as possible; to look forward to the recovery of their alleged lost privileges and rights rather than to take their places in civilized communities; to conduct their own affairs in their own aboriginal way, absolutely independent of and in defiance of the Government. In view of the above facts the Department would greatly regret the passing of this Bill [to incorporate the Council of the Tribes].[45]

Supporters of the Council of the Tribes learned of the Indian Department's interference in their effort to incorporate when the Department began asking its Indian agents to draw up petitions to be signed by Indians opposed to the incorporation bill. The letter sent to the agent at Kahnawà:ke directed him to give the petition his immediate attention and "see that every available name is procured and the petition forwarded to the Department without delay." In response, Thunderwater supporters in Kahnawà:ke drew up their own petition to protest the Department's interference and urge passage of the incorporation bill. They underscored their identity as Rotinonhsiónni and Kanien'keká:ka and emphasized that their purpose in organizing the Council in this way was to improve the condition and prospects of Indian people. In part, their petition read as follows:

> We the undersigned members of the Iroquois Nation of the Mohawk Tribe of Indians, located on the Caughnawaga Reservation, do hereby respectively and vigorously protest against any action of the Indian Department at Ottawa in endeavoring to obstruct the passage of the bill to incorpo-

rate Council of Tribes of Canada, of which we are members, believing in and recognizing the necessity and advantage of a union of Indians for the protection of the general interests aiming for the advancement of Indian civilization, for the betterment of the social and educational condition and to have a united effort for the prosecution of injustice perpetrated against Indians, as well as to indicate a better understanding with the whiteman and to strive for the improvement of the moral and physical welfare of the Redman, and to give relief to indigent fellow-Indians.[46]

Nevertheless, Scott succeeded in persuading the interior minister, and the prime minister as well, that Chief Thunderwater and the Council of the Tribes were a serious threat, and the bill for incorporation was withdrawn from consideration by Parliament.[47]

Though the attempt to incorporate the Council of the Tribes failed, the efforts of its Rotinonhsiónni supporters to organize around their shared political interests continued. Only a few months after the defeat of the incorporation attempt, Rotinonhsiónni from all the Confederacy nations in Canada and the United States met at Ahkwesáhsne. The immediate purpose of their gathering was the installation of twenty-four chiefs who were to compose a restored council of life chiefs. The council of life chiefs at St. Regis had been abolished and replaced by an elected band council in 1899. The Indian Act system had been established in the face of considerable resistance and, as in Kahnawà:ke, there followed years of persistent opposition and efforts to restore the traditional council. In September 1918 these efforts succeeded, though of course not with the recognition or approval of the Indian Department.[48] As described by the *Montreal Gazette*, the organization and proceedings of the meetings at which the twenty-four chiefs were installed emphasized the vitality of the Confederacy's traditions:

Chiefs of the Mohawks, Senecas, Oneidas, Cayugas, Tuscaroras and Onandagos were on hand to take part in the ancient ceremonies. . . . The Indians sat in different linguistic groups, each nation debating any question brought up and then, when arrived at a decision, allowing their official speaker to announce their decision. As many as six different Indian languages were spoken in the Council. The official speaker of each nation carried the wampum as he recounted the deeds of the ancestors of the tribe, telling off the beads as he did so, describing the formation of the great Peace League by Hiawatha and coming down to the present and present problems.

According to Peter Delisle, who is described as a "chief" and who attended the meeting as a representative of Kahnawà:ke, "The convention was a stirring sight to see to those privileged to witness it."[49]

The Ahkwesáhsne meeting was also an opportunity for those participating to discuss the broader political concerns and interests of the Confederacy. The *Gazette* article reported that at the meeting it was decided to hold another "international council" for the purpose of "organizing to look after the interests and welfare of the Indian." According to the *Gazette*, "The Indians want this organization in order that they can take united action on the question of registration and military service. Considering themselves as still nations who have never given up their Sovereignty, and which are under treaty with the United States and Canadian governments, they also have a project for choosing an ambassador to represent them at Ottawa, and to deal as one sovereign power with another."[50]

Delisle, too, persisted in his advocacy of Kahnawakehró:non autonomy. In March 1919 he was charged with sedition and endured a six-month trial before he was found not guilty. The charge grew out of Delisle's actions at a community meeting at which he encouraged his supporters to obstruct, by force if necessary, any attempts to repair the local church unless Kahnawakehró:non were given control over the secular affairs of the church.[51]

To emphasize a key point, the Thunderwater Movement was largely a Rotinonhsiónni movement that had at its core the goals of addressing shared political and cultural grievances, unifying and revitalizing the Confederacy, and gaining recognition of Six Nations sovereignty. These goals and the evolution of this movement grew out of what many Rotinonhsiónni, including many Kahnawakehró:non, viewed as oppressive policies and conditions in their home communities and throughout Iroquoia.

In its efforts to investigate and discredit the Council of the Tribes, the Indian Department eventually determined that Chief Thunderwater was not an Indian but was a black man named Palmer who was a traveling salesman from the "Negro" neighborhood of Cleveland, Ohio. In 1920 the Department communicated this information to Thunderwater opponents in Kahnawà:ke, who then exposed him as a fraud at a Council rally. According to one source, there was a "dramatic confrontation" between Thunderwater and his accuser, police were called in to break up the meeting, and Thunderwater disappeared from the reserve. Eventually he fled the country, supposedly absconding with some $20,000 in Council funds. In the months that followed, the division between Thunderwater supporters and opponents was played out in the campaign for band council seats. Thunderwater's accuser, who vied for one of the seats, was soundly defeated, while Thunderwater supporters including Peter Delisle, John T. Daillebout, Frank T. Johns, and James Phillips were elected, just as they had been the previous year, and as most would be again in 1921.[52] These events suggest that in the view of many Kahnawakehró:non, the exposure of Thunderwater as an imposter did not undermine the legitimacy of Council leaders and supporters like Peter Delisle or the goals and aspirations they represented. Ultimately the Council of the Tribes failed, but the traditionalist and nationalist impulses behind it did not. In Kahnawà:ke these were significant factors during the 1920s in even more radical developments, including efforts to reestablish the Longhouse within the community.

6. "We Have Our Own Rights and Religion"

The Reestablishment of the Longhouse in Kahnawà:ke

The Organization of a Longhouse Following in the Early 1920s

During the 1920s Rotinonhsiónni people persisted in their efforts to regain and protect their cultural and political sovereignty, which continued to be undermined and threatened by Indian policies in Canada and the United States. In 1920 the Indian Act was amended to empower the Canadian government to order the enfranchisement of any Indians it considered qualified for citizenship, without their request or consent. The new policy of forced enfranchisement was aimed at native people east of Lake Superior who, like the Rotinonhsiónni, were considered more assimilated. The outrage and protests of Rotinonhsiónni and other native people contributed to a repeal of the amendment in 1922, but it was reinstituted in 1933 in order to speed the pace of enfranchisement and assimilation.[1] In the United States many Rotinonhsiónni opposed the passage of the Citizenship Act of 1924, which made all American Indians citizens of the United States.[2] At the Six Nations reserve in Ontario the traditional council of hereditary chiefs was replaced by the elected band council system in 1924, a change imposed without even a referendum on the elective system. Nevertheless, the Confederacy council there continued to meet and remained politically active, particularly in efforts in and outside Rotinonhsiónni communities to gain support for Confederacy sovereignty and the primacy of Confederacy authority.[3] Also, during this period the employment of Kahnawakehró:non and other Kanien'kehá:ka in high steel expanded, with many more men traveling to the United States to work in the building and bridge construction trades.[4] The movement of native ironworkers from Canadian reserves and communities across the international border concerned American immigration authorities, who in 1926 arrested Paul Kanento Diabo, an ironworker from Kahnawà:ke, as a test of their authority and of recently enacted immigration laws. The case was also a political test for many Rotinonhsiónni, who argued that they were part of sovereign nations with the right to pass freely across the Canada–United States border.

In Kahnawà:ke Peter J. Delisle and others who formed the Anti faction during the Thunderwater period and had been engaged with the Council of the Tribes remained politically active in support of sovereignty, both within the community and in concert with other Rotinonhsiónni communities. They continued to pursue their objective of political autonomy through changes in the Indian Act, but they did so largely within the established political channels of the band council system. Following the Reformers of the 1890s and the Progressive faction of the previous decade, others within the community supported the Indian Act, and they too worked within the established system. As a result, within the community there continued to be two opposing factions, each pursuing its agenda within the Indian Act system. Meanwhile a third faction, also opposed to the Indian Act, was developing outside the government's system. This third faction represented a new political direction and laid the foundation for the reestablishment of the Longhouse in Kahnawà:ke.

In the discussion that follows, "Longhouse" refers to a political and religious group that is based on the Rotinonhsiónni clan system, is engaged in traditional Rotinonhsiónni spiritual beliefs and practices, and maintains ties with "Longhouse" groups in other Rotinonhsiónni communities. This broad definition of "Longhouse" includes, but is not limited to, Longhouses organized in the Handsome Lake tradition. Defined in this way, the development of the Longhouse in Kahnawà:ke in the 1920s represents a reestablishment of the Longhouse in the community. At the time of its establishment in the seventeenth century, Kahnawà:ke was settled by both recent converts to Catholicism and others who had not been converted but migrated to Kahnawà:ke for economic and other reasons. It is almost certain that traditional Rotinonhsiónni belief, organization, and practice were part of the social, political, and spiritual life of early Kahnawà:ke. Over time, of course, the traditional forms, beliefs, and practices waned, weakened, or were modified owing to the strong Catholic character of the community and the political and cultural dynamic of its unique history. In other Rotinonhsiónni communities during the nineteenth century, Longhouse political-religious organization and practice was reformulated in the socially progressive but spiritually conservative Handsome Lake movement and church. With the organization of a Longhouse in the Handsome Lake tradition in Kahnawà:ke in the early 1920s, important elements of traditional Rotinonhsiónni political and spiritual belief and practice returned in a formal way to Kahnawà:ke after an absence of more than two centuries.

To understand the process by which the Longhouse was reestablished, it is important to recognize that its system of clan chiefs was still functioning at some level in the early 1920s. This is suggested by two newspaper articles about Kahnawà:ke that appeared in the *Montreal Daily Star* in 1922 and 1923. The first reported on a meeting of native leaders in Canada in February 1922 to protest the Indian Act.[5] I will say more about this meeting later, but here it is important to note that according to the article, "Caughnawaga" was to be represented at the meeting by three chiefs, who included "Grand Chief" Sose Kentaratiron, "Chief" Wise Ariwakenra, and "Chief" American Horse. Sose Kentaratiron, also known as Joseph Beauvais, was an eighty-three-year-old farmer, and Wise Ariwakenra, described in the

5. Joseph Beauvais (Sose Kentaratiron), Mitchell Beauvais
(Wise Ariwakenra), and Angus Montour (American Horse),
Longhouse activists in the early 1920s. Photograph
courtesy of Kanien'kehaka Onkwawen:na Raotitiohkwa.

newspaper article as the son of Kentaratiron, was Mitchell Beauvais.[6] "American Horse" was the professional name of Angus
Montour, who was a well-known and well-traveled performer in
Wild West shows; in 1922 he was about seventy-three years of
age (fig. 5).

The second article in the *Montreal Daily Star*, from March
1923, identified Kentaratiron as a "veteran chief and wise man
of the tribe" who had until recently held the position of Turtle
clan chief.[7] According to that article, two other men were now
rivals for the position of "Tekarihoken," or chief of the Turtle
clan, "Chief Karaienton" and his nephew, "Chief Tamenk," also
known as Dominic Two-Axe. The article notes that Karaienton

was "unanimously" selected over Two-Axe, although it is unclear if this decision was made by the Turtle clan only or by a council of all of the Kahnawà:ke clans. Two-Axe, however, had the support of Kentaratiron and refused to accept the decision of the clan or the council and thereby prompted a meeting of all the Kahnawà:ke clans. In addition to the Turtle clan, these are identified as the "Wolf, Black Bear, White Bear, Rock, Plover [Snipe], and Deer clans." Taken together, the two newspaper articles suggest that in the early 1920s Kahnawà:ke's structure of seven clans constituted a functioning system of some kind that included the selection of clan chiefs. That this system appears to be well established rather than recently reorganized suggests further that the clan system had been in use for some time, perhaps since the abolishment of the traditional council of chiefs in 1889.

From numerous oral histories and a variety of archival sources, it is clear that many of the individuals identified in the 1922 and 1923 newspaper articles played key roles in the reestablishment of the Longhouse in Kahnawà:ke. They included Joseph Beauvais (Sose Kentaratiron), Angus Montour (American Horse), Dominic Two-Axe, and Mitchell Beauvais (Wise Ariwakenra). According to Mary Two-Axe, as a young man her father Dominic had been an ironworker and traveled extensively to jobs in Canada and the United States. About 1920 he was injured at work and returned to live on the reserve. Following his father, Martin Two-Axe, Dominic began to practice as a medicine man. While learning this practice, which included visits to other Rotinonhsiónni communities to study and collect traditional medicines, Two-Axe developed an interest in the Longhouse and the traditional ceremonies (fig. 6).[8]

It is possible that by interacting with ironworkers from other Rotinonhsiónni communities Dominic Two-Axe had already begun to gain an understanding of the Longhouse. His political views may have been influenced by these interactions as well. In

6. Dominic Two-Axe (right), a pivotal figure in the organization of the Longhouse following in the early 1920s. Photograph courtesy of Kanien'kehaka Onkwawen:na Raotitiohkwa.

addition, he may have been influenced politically by the traditionalist and nationalist impulses within his own community during the Thunderwater period, by his contacts as a medicine man with Longhouse groups and other Rotinonhsiónni communities, and by the ongoing, organized effort of many Rotinonhsiónni in Canada to oppose federal Indian policy and advocate their cultural and political sovereignty.

When Two-Axe challenged his uncle, Karaienton, for the position of chief of the Turtle clan in 1923, it was reported that Karaienton's supporters opposed him because he had "brought the Indians in Canada into great disfavor with the Canadian Government over his repeated charges of ill-treatment."[9] In other words, Two-Axe was a troublemaker who had spoken out publicly against government actions with regard to Indian people.

Karaienton's supporters believed that "the Mohawk tribe is being treated with every consideration by the paleface." In this rivalry Two-Axe appears to have had the support of the veteran chief of the clan, Joseph Beauvais (Sose Kentaratiron).

Beauvais himself appears to have been politically active in protesting Indian policy and working with Indian Act opponents in other Rotinonhsiónni communities. For example, many Rotinonhsiónni protested the 1920 amendment to the Indian Act that allowed forced enfranchisement.[10] In April 1922 Rotinonhsiónni from a number of communities gathered at Oshwekon on the Six Nations reserve to express their concern and opposition.[11] As reported by the *Montreal Daily Star* in advance of the meeting, "thousands" were expected to attend the "gigantic pow-wow."[12] According to the *Star*, "Grand Chief" Sose Kentaratiron of Kahnawà:ke was instrumental in initiating and organizing the meeting and was expected to attend along with Chiefs Wise Ariwakenra (Mitchell Beauvais) and Angus Montour. Like Two-Axe, Angus Montour was becoming a Longhouse activist and traveled frequently to other Rotinonhsiónni communities in Canada and the United States to learn more about Longhouse organization and activity and traditional ceremonies.[13]

Developments such as the policy of forced enfranchisement and organized political efforts by Rotinonhsiónni from several communities may have contributed to the political and religious radicalization of Kentaratiron, Mitchell Beauvais, Angus Montour, Dominic Two-Axe, and other Kahnawakehró:non and thereby helped build momentum toward organizing a Longhouse group in their own community. A somewhat similar process did, in fact, take place in the community in the mid-1940s, well after the Longhouse had been reestablished. In 1946 Longhouse membership increased sharply on reports that the federal government was planning to enfranchise the entire Kahnawà:ke community except those who were members of the Longhouse. The reports proved to be untrue, but those who had joined the

Longhouse remained members, and even after the reports were proved false Kahnawakehró:non continued to leave the Catholic and Protestant churches to join the Longhouse.[14]

In early September 1923 Angus Montour, Joseph Beauvais, Dominic Two-Axe, Mitchell Beauvais, and probably others appear to have taken an important step toward organizing a Longhouse group in Kahnawà:ke. At this time several representatives from one or more Rotinonhsiónni communities visited Kahnawà:ke to help organize such a group. According to oral history accounts, the visiting representatives came at the invitation of local Longhouse activists. One of these representatives appears to have been George Thomas, whom one writer described as a "Longhouse preacher" who came to tell the people of Kahnawà:ke about the "native Iroquoian religion as practiced by others."[15] In fact, Thomas was the Thadadaho, one of the fourteen Confederacy chiefs at Onondaga, the central fire of the Confederacy in New York State. The Confederacy chiefs at Onondaga composed the governing council on the reservation and had long been adherents of the Longhouse.[16]

In preparation for the visit of Thomas and the other representatives, Montour, Joseph Beauvais, and a third man named Angus Deer either borrowed or stole—the exact circumstances vary with the source—a very old and valuable wampum belt from the St. Francis Xavier mission. The belt was given to the Rotinonhsiónni at Kahnawà:ke by the Hurons of Lorette in 1676 as a sign of support and goodwill.[17] It was about five feet long and six inches wide and bore a design in white beads on a purple background. The design consisted of six linked rectangles, three on each side of the image of a crucifix at the center of the belt. The belt was considered the property of the Kahnawà:ke band and for most of its history had been held at the St. Francis Xavier mission under the care of the local priests. The Longhouse activists had planned for a "reading" of the belt by the visiting representatives as part of their effort to organize a local Longhouse group.

According to the file the Indian Department maintained on the case, Montour, Beauvais, and Deer stole the belt, and the charge of theft was based on a complaint made by one of the local Jesuit missionaries.[18] The Royal Canadian Mounted Police soon arrested Montour and Beauvais, but Deer disappeared from the reserve. Montour and Beauvais were jailed in Montreal and went on trial for the theft of the wampum belt in late September 1923. During the course of the trial two Kahnawakehró:non, one the "mayor" of the band council and the other a former band councillor, testified against Montour and Beauvais, claiming that the two men had no authority to take the belt and did not have the support of the band council or the majority of the people in the community. During the trial the value of the belt was set at $25,000. A lawyer represented Montour and Beauvais, but they offered no defense and were found guilty. They appealed the verdict and were released on bail, but in late February 1924 their appeal was denied and sentencing was set for early March. In the interim, under the threat of a long prison term, Montour and Beauvais returned the belt to the St. Francis Xavier mission through their lawyer. In the end the men were sentenced to two months in jail. After Montour and Beauvais had served their sentences, the missionary who had laid the charge of theft interceded with the Indian Department on behalf of the third man accused, Angus Deer. Deer's family was in difficult economic circumstances because of his absence, so the missionary requested, and the Department agreed, that Deer be allowed to return to the reserve and not be prosecuted.

Oral history accounts offer a somewhat different version of these events. According to two of Angus Montour's grandsons, the wampum belt was borrowed, not stolen.[19] In their accounts the grandsons recalled that Montour, Beauvais, and Deer asked and received the priest's permission to borrow the belt. When some of the more vocal opponents of Longhouse activism in the community learned of the loan of the belt and its intended use, they forced the priest to report the loan as a theft. One of these men, identified as either a band councillor or a former band councillor, is said to have used his cane to smash the glass case in which the wampum belt had been displayed in order to make the priest's accusation more convincing. In the end, when the belt was presented to Thomas and the other visiting representatives it was determined to be only a "friendship" belt and thus of no real significance, at least with regard to the activists' intentions. At this point the oral history accounts converge with the case as it is presented in the Indian Department file: Montour and Beauvais were arrested, jailed, and found guilty; the belt was returned to the mission; and the two men served short prison terms.

It is possible that the truth about the wampum belt lay somewhere between the accounts offered by oral histories and the Indian Department file. According to one newspaper account, Montour and Beauvais borrowed the wampum belt "to have its mysterious signs and intricate network of figures read by visiting redmen."[20] When they refused to return the belt, a complaint was lodged and the men were charged with theft. As reported in the newspaper, Montour and Beauvais claimed that the belt belonged to the community, not the mission, and that as "chiefs" they had a right to use it at any time. Once they were arrested, the two decided not to return the belt in order to test their claim to it, stating that they would return it if they lost their case but keep it if they won. After their arrest, the judge devised an unusual bail arrangement based on his determination that Montour and Beauvais were not "ordinary thieves" and that they might try flee to another reserve if released on a small bail. The judge required that eight Kahnawakehró:non pledge themselves to go to jail or supply $800 between them if the two men disappeared. The arrangement was apparently completed, and in reaction the lawyer for Montour and Beauvais stated that he would "produce half Caughnawaga to stand behind his clients if necessary."

About a month after the arrest of Montour and Beauvais, in October 1923, the band council of Kahnawà:ke passed a resolution protesting the attempt by "certain individual Indians"— Montour and Beauvais—to deprive the mission and its priest of custody of the wampum belt.[21] The resolution stated that Montour and Beauvais represented "nobody but themselves" and that the council was acting "in conformity with the wishes of the masses of people of this Village and Reserve." The resolution was introduced by the band councillor who is said to have compelled the mission priest to lodge the complaint of theft, and it passed unanimously. In addition to the band council resolution, as the newspaper report quoted below indicates, Montour and Beauvais appear to have undergone some sort of hearing or trial in Kahnawà:ke before their trial in Montreal. Such a hearing or trial probably would have been presided over by Frank McDonald Jacobs, the justice of the peace on the reserve. Reporting on the events that had taken place once the two men were convicted in March 1924, the *Montreal Daily Star* provided this brief account:

> Understanding little English and no French, the old chief [Sose Kentaratiron] had bravely stood throughout his trial in the courthouse of his native village and later in the Court of King's Bench in Montreal. To him the trial and conviction had been something of a novel and exciting experience. His little garden in the woods behind Caughnawaga could not be tended during the winter months and the monotony of things across the river had been broken only by an infrequent pow-wows and evening meetings at the home of Dominique Two Axe, the . . . Tekarihoken of the tribe, while he was out on bail.[22]

After the conviction of Montour and Beauvais, the prosecutor in charge of the case asked the missionary in Kahnawà:ke to be present in court when the expected return of the belt took place. Evidently the prosecutor feared that a replica might have been manufactured and that the original would not be returned. The priest's presence was intended to ensure an accurate identification.[23] The original belt was returned, however, and Montour and Beauvais were sentenced to two months in the Bordeaux jail.

In contrast to the band council resolution of the previous October, which suggested that opposition to the actions of Montour and Beauvais was widespread, almost immediately after their conviction and imprisonment a large number of Kahnawakehró:non—identified as "two hundred warriors and braves"—met in council and decided to send a representative to the Indian Department in Ottawa to plead for pardons. According to Mitchell Beauvais, who was the son of Joseph Beauvais and a member of this group, the supporters of Montour and Beauvais believed that the "theft" of the wampum belt was a tribal matter and that Canadian law should never have been invoked.[24]

The impact of the wampum "theft" case on the development of the Longhouse in Kahnawà:ke is difficult to assess. It seems clear that the case resulted from serious efforts by local activists to organize a Longhouse group, and it is evident that opposition to and support for these efforts split the community.[25] What happened in the years immediately after the trial is less clear. According to oral history accounts provided by a grandson of Angus Montour and a daughter of Dominic Two-Axe, a small Longhouse group had been meeting or began to meet regularly for ceremonies and other activities at the home of one of the families concerned in the main village on the reserve. This group included Angus Montour, Dominic Two-Axe, and some members of the Beauvais and Diabo families, among others.[26]

By 1927 the organization, composition, and activities of this small Longhouse group can be seen in somewhat greater detail through a series of letters Dominic Two-Axe wrote to government officials on a variety of issues. Written in April, July, and August 1927, these were for the most part letters of protest about issues such as the quality of education provided by the Sisters of St. Anne, the disruptive effect of the nuns on the relationship between children and their parents, the withholding of band funds from aged members of the community by Indian Department officials, and the contamination of local streams and the poisoning of livestock by runoff from a local golf course. Two-Axe was particularly concerned with efforts by the Indian Department to purchase land on the reserve for a new school. He objected on the grounds that the land belonged to the band and that the deputy superintendent general of Indian affairs, Duncan Campbell Scott, had "no right to buy one dirt in a private Reservation." He complained that Scott favored the Jesuit priests in this issue even though the band and not the religious order was the recognized owner of the land within the reserve. As support for his claim, Two-Axe provided evidence of the Gage decision of 1763. He went so far as to suggest that Scott be prosecuted and sent "back to Scotland" so that he could "rule his own people over there all he likes."[27]

Using the hereditary title of the Turtle clan, Two-Axe signed his letters as "Grand Chief Dominic Te Ka ri ho Ken." Several of these letters also name two other chiefs who were part of the Longhouse group, identified by the hereditary titles of the Bear and Wolf clans, "Head Chief Sose Te ha na Ka ri ne" and "Head Chief Tier Sa ren ho wa ne."[28] While the identity of "Sose Te ha na Ka ri ne" could not be determined, based on other, slightly later sources, the chief of the Wolf clan appears to have been Peter Canoe.[29] In the last of his series of letters Two-Axe asserts that he and they, "the Original Chiefs," are the chiefs on the reservation, not the "Councillors and Mayor," and that they do not want to be controlled by "any religion or outlaw." This last letter also names the clan mothers, or "mother chiefs," of the three clans. These are "Teres Kwa ra sen ni" of the Turtle clan, "Anies Ka en ti ios ta" of the Black Bear clan, and "Kon wa keri Ken tio kok ta" of the Wolf clan. Oral history accounts identify "Kon wa keri Ken tio kok ta" as the wife of Dominic Two-Axe and "Anies Ka en ti ios ta" as Agnes Blue and the sister of Angus Montour. Teres Kwarasenni's married name was Diabo, and she was the mother of Paul K. Diabo, who would become the subject of an important immigration case and test of Rotinonhsiónni sovereignty in 1925. Her home in the village was the meeting place of the Longhouse group at this time and had been for several years.[30]

Thus, by mid-1927 the Kahnawà:ke Longhouse was organized around three clans, the Turtle, Bear, and Wolf, each with its own chief and clan mother. Each chief was associated with one of the hereditary titles of his clan, but there is no evidence that any were, in fact, chiefs who had been condoled, or officially installed and recognized by the Confederacy. Rather, it appears that the Longhouse group initiated the use of these titles on their own as part of organizing itself, legitimating its activities, and establishing its connection to Longhouses in other Rotinonhsiónni communities. The connection between the seven-clan system that functioned in the early 1920s and the development of a Longhouse based on three clans is not clear. One possibility is that the organization of the Longhouse involved a break with the traditional clan system and a reorganization based on Confederacy law, with which Longhouse activists were becoming more familiar as a result of their interactions with Longhouse groups and Confederacy communities in Canada and the United States. This break may have followed the Dominic Two-Axe's apparently unsuccessful challenge to his uncle for the title of Tekarihoken within the seven-clan system in 1922. Angus Montour and Joseph Beauvais were also chiefs within the seven-clan system, and their involvement with Two-Axe in the organization the Longhouse may have been a part of the break.

Though the effort to reestablish the Longhouse in Kahnawà:ke may have been stimulated and perhaps even promoted by the political activism and developments of which the Thunderwater Movement was a part, a direct connection between the Council of the Tribes and Longhouse activism in Kahnawà:ke is lacking. It is possible, even likely, that some individuals were involved in both Thunderwater and Longhouse activities. For example, Angus Deer, who along with Angus Montour and Joseph Beauvais was accused of the theft of the wampum belt from the St. Francis Xavier mission in 1923, appears to have been a member of the Kahnawà:ke Circle of the Council of the Tribes in 1916.[31] On the other hand, none of the leaders of the Council of the Tribes in Kahnawà:ke are associated with the effort to reestablish the Longhouse in Kahnawà:ke. In particular, Peter Delisle, who remained active in local and pan-Indian politics after the demise of the Thunderwater Movement, does not appear to have been involved in any way with the effort to organize a Longhouse group in Kahnawà:ke in the 1920s. Despite his opposition to the Sisters of St. Anne after they assumed control over Kahnawà:ke's schools in 1915 and his resistance to the interference of local religious officials in the secular life of the Kahnawà:ke community, Delisle appears to have been ardently Catholic throughout his life, and it is unlikely that he would have been associated with the antipathy toward the Catholic Church and the break from it that would soon become associated with the Longhouse. None of the other individuals identified with the leadership of the Kahnawà:ke Circle of the Council of the Tribes or the effort to incorporate the Council in 1918 appear to have been involved in the effort to reestablish the Longhouse in Kahnawà:ke. Further, there is no evidence that key Longhouse activists in Kahnawà:ke in the 1920s, such as Dominic Two-Axe, Angus Montour, or Joseph Beauvais, were members of the Council of the Tribes or part of the Thunderwater Movement.

In addition, the effort to reestablish the Longhouse in Kahnawà:ke in the 1920s involved a small group of activists who faced considerable opposition within the community. While some may have been supportive but not involved, the majority of the community was strongly and actively Catholic, and thus it is unlikely that many approved of the Longhouse activities or participated in them. Some in the community, such as those associated with the band council, appear to have been actively opposed to the Longhouse activists and their efforts. In addition, it is certain that the Indian Department and local church officials also opposed the development of the Longhouse. Thus the Kahnawà:ke Longhouse was, at least indirectly, born out of local political and cultural conflicts and came to represent a third faction within the community, one that not only sought greater sovereignty and opposed the government and its policies but tried to do so outside the established Indian Act system and within the context of the Confederacy.

The Paul K. Diabo Immigration Case and the Development of the Kahnawà:ke Longhouse

Paul Kanento Diabo, who was the son of Teres Kwarasenni, the "mother chief" of the Turtle clan in the early 1920s, was born in Kahnawà:ke in 1891, married there in 1912, and in that year began working high steel in New York City. Between that time and the mid-1920s he traveled back and forth between Kahnawà:ke and various points in the United States where he was employed. In 1925, while living in Philadelphia and working on the construction of the Delaware River Bridge, Diabo was arrested as an illegal alien for having failed to apply for and receive a permit to work in the United States.[32] After a hearing before immigration authorities in May 1926, Diabo was ordered deported to Canada. Subsequently he and his lawyers filed a petition of habeas corpus, which was heard before the U.S. district court in Philadelphia in March 1927. Diabo argued that the Jay Treaty of 1784 recognized the right of the Rotinonhsiónni to pass freely across the border between Canada and the United States and thus that the Immigration Act of 1924 under which he was charged could not be applied to him. Immigration authorities argued that the War of 1812 abrogated the 1794 treaty and that under U.S. immigration laws he was considered a member of an alien nation and subject to the regulations and controls of those laws. The court held for Diabo, and the charges against him were dropped, but immigration authorities immediately filed an appeal. A year later, in March 1928, the appeal was heard before the Third Circuit Court in Philadelphia, which upheld the lower court ruling that freed Diabo and recognized the Rotinonhsiónni right of free passage across the international border.[33]

Seeing Diabo's case as an opportunity to test Rotinonhsiónni sovereignty and treaty rights, the Grand Councils at Onondaga and Six Nations quickly mobilized in support of Diabo after his arrest by helping to organize his legal team and prepare his defense. Diabo also received support from Rotinonhsiónni communities in Canada and the United States, which organized bake sales, raffles, and theatrical productions to raise money to help with his legal costs.[34] In late June 1927, after the victory before the district court in which Rotinonhsiónni border-crossing rights were upheld, the Grand Councils convened in Kahnawà:ke to further demonstrate their support for Diabo, plan for the impending appeal, and discuss the broader issues of Rotinonhsiónni sovereignty. Dominic Two-Axe, Peter Canoe, and Angus Montour, the three chiefs of the Kahnawà:ke Longhouse, played an important role in organizing this meeting. Once it was planned, the local organizers sought to use the church hall as a meeting place, but were denied by the Jesuit pastor. As a result, a separate longhouse-style structure was constructed to house the Grand Council.[35] The building of this structure and the last-minute preparations for the meeting were recorded in the *Montreal Daily Gazette*. Among other things, the report emphasizes the significance of the meeting for the Confederacy as a whole and the role of the Kahnawà:ke chiefs.

Hence the stir and bustle yesterday in the vicinity of a newly erected frame building standing back from the road at Caughnawaga.

This is the Long House. Considerable money and untold manual labor on the part of the Caughnawaga chiefs and braves alike have gone into the building which will house the pow wow. All day yesterday, and far into the night, gangs were hard at work with hammer and saw, with paint pot and paint brush, putting the finishing touches to the structure which today will see the opening of the most important conference the Iroquois have known in decades. . . .

In the houses nearby, the women were busy in their kitchens. Special food must be proferred to the dignitaries of the tribes, which were speeding from New York State, Ontario and other parts of Quebec. . . .

Directing all this was Dominic Teka[r]ihoken, known in these parts as Dominic Two Axes, grand chief of all the Iroquois. Aiding him were chief American Horse [Angus Montour], Chief Peter Canoe, both of Caughnawaga, and willing hands were extended by the first of the fifty-odd visitors from other parts expected. They were four important delegates from the Mohawks of the St. Regis Reserve in New York State. . . . En route by train and automobile from Syracuse, Tonawanda, and Onondaga were parties of chiefs from American reserves. They are expected at noon today.[36]

The *Gazette* article went on to emphasize the larger significance of the meeting of the Grand Councils with respect to unity and goals of the Confederacy.

When the ceremony of centuries ago is over, and the wise men of the tribes have spoken, it is hoped that the Six Nations will have been reborn. Tribal heads would be done with the brave deteriorated into something neither red man nor white man. And they are meeting to bring forth the day

on which the sun shall rise over an Indian people, constituted as they were in the days of old, ruled by their chiefs
under a code of laws which, in their belief, was laid down
in 1372 by De ka na wi dah, the Creator, who warned red
men that the whites were coming.[37]

The Grand Councils met on 29 June, and the proceedings
were again reported in the *Gazette*:

> Women and children were motioned to one corner of the
> House, but a place of honor in that section was given to two
> white-haired tribal mothers of Caughnawaga, whose coun-
> cil is weighty and heard with respect, even by the Grand
> Chief himself.
>
> Motionless, the chiefs sat and waited. The Grand Chief
> rose, took the center of the floor, and his welcome in the
> native tongues opened proceedings of hours in which not
> a single word of English was uttered. Head Chief Gibson
> responded to the welcome in the crisp, expressionless lan-
> guage of his race. The business of the day was broached.
> Caughnawaga had its speakers; Chief Lyons did much of
> the talking for the visitors.
>
> The meeting was impressive. There was none of the
> gesticulation and extravagant language of the Anglo-Saxon
> or Latin conference. And every Indian thought before he
> spoke, he conferred with his brothers, and the meeting sat
> silent until the orator was ready to rise to his feet. One after
> another the chiefs designated as the speakers had their say.
> There was occasional nodding of approval from those who
> listened, once or twice a smile. For the most part, however,
> expression was lacking.
>
> The council continued. Chief Lyons proved himself a
> real linguist when he rose later and addressed his brothers
> and sisters and children in the English language. And he
> gave them some idea of the state of affairs on his own re-
> serve. There, it would seem, an Indian is an Indian. The

chiefs rule. Their word is law, and their word follows the supreme laws laid down in 1372 by De ka na wi dah, the laws which endure for ever through the medium of the wampum of the entire Iroquois family. The Indians have their own church, the Independent Indian Church. They are governed by their tribal rulers, whose power is such that no officer of the white man's government and no white children may set foot on the reservation if the chief objects.[38]

On the following day a council of the Kanien'kehá:ka nation was held with representatives from Kahnawà:ke, Kanehsatà:ke, and Ahkwesáhsne. At this meeting, with Peter J. Delisle translating, a lawyer from Philadelphia spoke about the Diabo case and its importance to the Rotinonhsiónni.[39]

A few months later, in November 1927 the members of the Kahnawà:ke Longhouse, led by Dominic Two-Axe and Angus Montour, held an extraordinary three-day meeting in which they publicly announced their break from the Catholic Church and their commitment to the "religion of their forefathers." Reporting on the meeting under the title "Changing Religion," the *Montreal Daily Star* stated the following:

> Today marked the close of the pow-wow, and a sensational close it was. The ultimate result was the abandonment of the Christian religion by Indians of the Six Nations, and the return to the old Indian deities made famous in Longfellow's "Hiawatha." Members of the Six Nations have turned their backs to Christianity and its churches, and adopted the gods they worshipped prior to the white man's coming to America's shores. With their return to the worship of Gitchie Manitou and other Indian deities, the old pagan ceremonies and rituals will prevail. They will be adopted after having been abandoned for over three hundred years.
>
> According to the reformation leaders Chief Dominic Two Axe and Chief American Horse and other Six Nations members, 1928 will mark the year the Redmen officially

abandoned the cross and returned to the religion of their forefathers. But to date the white man's religion has only been unofficially abandoned by them, and the old Indian rites, unofficially adopted. . . .

With the coming of the white man to America, evil befell the Indians, claimed the chiefs during the three-day pow-wow. Deprived [of] all privileges, rights, and liberties, the Six Nations declare through their alleged leaders that the only thing the Indians have left is their old religion. That cannot be taken away from them they say.

In the cabin in which the pow-wow was held since Sunday, the atmosphere considerably enhances the "religious services" conducted inside. Dark and devoid of any furnishings used by white men, the cabin is about a mile from the village of Caughnawaga, in a little wood, and is entirely surrounded by a barbed wire fence. The darkness within the cabin lends it an air of mystery.

The pow-wow was held both morning and afternoon. In reality it was not a pow-wow, but inaugural religious services, in which those present were taught the "constitution" or basis of their forefather's religion. Following each service, a dance was held, typically Indian. Wild cries, leaping in the air, and the beat of the tom-tom, with the dancers pirouetting around the room in a frenzy, featured the dance. . . .

With the pow-wow over today, the "reformation" will by no means die out. Chief Two Axe and Chief American Horse will conduct daily the old religious services in the "long-house," the council-meeting place of the members of the Six Nations in the Caughnawaga reservation.[40]

Its ethnocentrism aside, the newspaper account of the "religious meeting" is significant in a number of ways. To begin with, Two-Axe and Montour are identified as important leaders of the Longhouse group and this event. The article also refers to two other leaders of the "religious meeting" by the terms "Farahowanna" and "Tannacarina," which are undoubtedly references to two of hereditary titles of chiefs in the Bear and Wolf clans of the Kanien'kehá:ka, Sharenhowaneh, and Dehennakarineh.[41] Further, the report in the *Daily Star* suggests that the Longhouse activists understood themselves to be involved in a radical movement. They had "abandoned the Cross" and were returning to the "old religion," and thus, of course, this movement had an important spiritual dimension. But it was a radical political movement as well. The "white man" is seen as having deprived Indian people of their "privileges, rights, and liberties," which the leaders of the movement have taken a position to oppose and resist. In addition, the activists have identified themselves as "Six Nations" people, clearly allying themselves with the Confederacy.

The description of the "religious services" at the November meeting is also important. Taking place over three days and involving a daily routine in which the "basis of their forefather's religion" was taught, followed by "typically Indian" dances, the "religious services" are a rough approximation of the general pattern of the traditional thanksgiving ceremonies. Interesting, too, is the reference to the meeting place for future "old religious services" as the "long-house." Finally, and not surprisingly, it is important to note that the November Longhouse meeting did not go without local concern and opposition. According to the *Daily Star* report, one local resident interviewed considered the meeting "illegal" and the leaders "self-appointed and self-styled chiefs" who had no authority, a view also held by the local Indian agent.

In that same month of November 1927, there was a second meeting of the Grand Council in Kahnawà:ke. This meeting was held to discuss border issues, but also issues related to education and the Indian Act. It was prompted by recent developments at Ahkwesáhsne in which one of the traditional chiefs was arrested and jailed for refusing to send his children to school, as the Indian

Act dictated. The chief argued that the Indian Act violated Rotinonhsiónni sovereignty and that education in non-Indian schools undermined the Confederacy, a position that was supported by some in Kahnawà:ke and other Rotinonhsiónni communities.[42] The Indian Department and some members of the Kahnawà:ke community sought to block the meeting but failed. As reported by an area newspaper, one of the clan mothers from Kahnawà:ke stated that the purpose of the meeting was to condemn the nonnative laws directed at native people and their culture and to reaffirm the priority of the Great Law of Peace.[43] In short, the Paul K. Diabo immigration case and the developments surrounding it, and the meetings of the Grand Councils in Kahnawà:ke in particular, energized the small Longhouse group in Kahnawà:ke. Though still faced with opposition within the community, it had gained a level of external support and legitimacy that encouraged local interest and participation and emboldened its members to a more aggressive declaration of its goals and a more open practice of its activities.

The Evolution of the Kahnawà:ke Longhouse in the 1930s

After a few years the number of people involved in the Longhouse meetings and ceremonies at Kwarasenni's house grew too large and so the people began to look for a new location. They asked the band councillors for land and were given a small plot "up the hill" near the Old Malone Highway to build a longhouse. The Longhouse people raised money and collected donations and eventually built a longhouse on the site given to them. This Longhouse group continued to grow.[44]

When I was born [1931] I was baptized in the Catholic Church. Right after, soon after, I don't know when, but soon after that [my father] moved to the Longhouse when he changed, he came out. Well, everybody was Catholic here anyway, so they all moved to come out to the Longhouse. My father, the way he used to tell us . . . he joined about 1932 or 1933, 1932, I guess, right after I was born. . . . The [Longhouse] that I know, that was there [on a small hill a short distance the intersection of the Old Malone Highway and the St. Isadore Road]; it was John Beauvais and Agnes Beauvais. They got six kids, three boys and three girls. There was Wilfred Beauvais, Tommy Beauvais, Roger Beauvais; and sisters, there was Lillian Beauvais, who was married to John, and Edith Beauvais, who was married to Norman McGregor, and Lorna Beauvais, who was not married. That's where we used to go to the Longhouse. So all these people were there. . . . Mr. McGregor, he used to go to the Longhouse, his neighbor, Mike McGregor, they're gone now . . . and Louie, John's brother, Louie Beauvais . . . and Sa-ha-na-je, Frank Beauvais.[45]

These two accounts, the first provided by Mike Woodrow, a grandson of Angus Montour, and the second by Frank "Casey" Nolan, whose family joined the Longhouse when he was a young boy, suggest several important developments in the Longhouse during the late 1920s and early 1930s. After its initial organization, the Longhouse following in Kahnawà:ke began to grow and to include more than the few families who were central to its initial reestablishment. The Beauvais family, it appears, was becoming particularly prominent within the group. With this growth, the need for a formal meeting place became more pressing. Eventually a longhouse was built some distance from the center of the village near today's intersection of the Old Malone Highway and the St. Isadore Road (Highway 227). Other oral history accounts confirm this version of Longhouse development and the location of the new building.[46] It is not clear when this longhouse was built or if it was the same "long-house" that activists used in November 1928 to publicly announce their break from Catholicism and commitment to the way of the Longhouse.

Woodrow's and Nolan's accounts also suggest that the larger community and the band council in particular were not entirely opposed to the Longhouse at this time. It appears that the Longhouse group was given common land to build a permanent meeting place, an action that would almost certainly have involved approval by the band council. Further, it appears that at least some in the community must have directly or indirectly supported the fund-raising the Longhouse group undertook to raise money for the construction of a longhouse.

Nevertheless, opposition to the Longhouse continued to exist within the community, as is suggested by Stewart Beauvais's account of hearing his grandfather, Joseph Beauvais (Sose Kentaratiron), cautioning his father and his uncle, Mitchell Beauvais, about Mitchell's Longhouse activities: "My uncle started that. . . . His name was Mitchell, Mitchell Beauvais. My grandfather told my father, and I was there, he said, 'Look, your brother's starting this . . . don't make any enemies, don't talk about it when you're together, talk about other things. . . . [Mitchell] was on the farm . . . all my uncles were on the farm. . . . As far as I know, him and a few others got [the Longhouse] going."[47] In their accounts of growing up as part of the Longhouse, Frank "Casey" Nolan and Mary Two-Axe both recalled being shunned by others in the community and having hostility directed toward them because their families belonged to the Longhouse.[48] They were not permitted to attend the Catholic schools on the reserve, so they had had to attend the Protestant school. "[It] was only the Catholics," Nolan recalled. "They call us down, we call them down, so we had to fight all the time. But not all of them, just a few of them." On the whole, though, according to Nolan, Longhouse people, Catholics, and Protestants associated rather easily, often helping one another out in hard times or when someone's crops needed harvesting. With time, perhaps, their relations eased. As Stewart Beauvais recalled, "A lot of people were against it, but then, gradually, once they understood what was going on, they sort of mellowed down and just let it go."[49]

As the Longhouse following grew, internal divisions emerged. According to most accounts, these divisions were a result of rivalries for leadership within the Longhouse group and led to fissioning and the establishment of new Longhouse groups. Frank "Casey" Nolan remembered:

> Well, we had this Joe Martin. . . . Next thing I know, they came out, some people followed Joe Martin, he built a new longhouse. He went down to his father's, they used to have meetings there, but they still belonged to [the first] Longhouse and go back and forth, you know, they separate here and there. . . . They would go from one house to house. . . . Next thing I know it's, "We're going over there now . . . that one is no good because its not right." That's all I heard. . . . [My family went] with Joe Martin . . . they used [his father's] house, a small group, eh? They came out from Joe Martin's . . . then they went to Frank Diabo's house.[50]

Joe McGregor, whose aunt, uncle, and cousins joined Nolan's family in the Longhouse, had a similar account of this phase of the Longhouse. According to McGregor, the members of this Longhouse included several members of the Beauvais family, including John and Joseph Beauvais. Joe K. Martin, who was a blacksmith and a barber, was also a member of this Longhouse group. Competing for leadership, Martin left the group, taking several members with him, and established a second Longhouse group. Later they built a meeting place a short distance down the hill from the Beauvais longhouse. This split took place sometime in the 1930s, and sometime after it formed this second Longhouse group itself divided, with several members following Frank Beauvais in establishing a third Longhouse group on his family's farm outside the village in the eastern part of the reserve along the St. Lawrence River.[51] In his account of the early development of the Longhouse, Stewart Beauvais noted that the third Longhouse established on the Beauvais farm outside the village was organized by his uncle, John Beauvais. John Beauvais was the brother of Mitchell and the father of the Frank Beauvais identified by McGregor. According to Stewart Beauvais, Frank Beauvais became prominent in this third Longhouse after the death of his father.

Mike Woodrow also provided an account:

> In the 1930s, because of conflicts and arguments, this group split, with a second Longhouse group forming around Joe Martin. This second Longhouse group built a meeting place down the hill from the first Longhouse. Eventually a third Longhouse group was formed that located itself on the Beauvais farmland out along the [St. Lawrence] river. This took place before the St. Lawrence Seaway was constructed, because it was later forced to relocate because of the Seaway construction.[52]

Archival sources also provide some insight into the course of the Kahnawà:ke Longhouse in the 1930s, much of it from a file the Indian Department maintained on the effort some Longhouse members made to obtain land for their own cemetery. The file, labeled "Petition of Indians Who Call Themselves 'Life-Chiefs and Clan-Mothers of the Longhouse of the Caughnawaga Reservation' for a Site for a 'Pagan' or 'Longhouse' Cemetery," contains a variety of letters, petitions, and other documents dating between 1935 and 1942.[53] According to documents in the file, in March 1935 "a certain group of Indians belonging to a religious sect, called the Longhouse, of the Pagan sect" requested that the band council of Kahnawà:ke provide common land for use as their burial ground. The band council deferred ruling on the request, seeking first to determine the Indian Department's judgment on the status of the group, which was also described as the "sect of aboriginal beliefs." In this connection, F. Brisebois, the Indian agent for Kahnawà:ke, wrote to the secretary of the DIA to forward the band council's request. In his letter Brisebois stated that "this Sect is not recognized by the Laws of the Province or any other province." He also noted that the "presumed Chief" of the Longhouse was "arrested and convicted of performing illegal marriages in the reserve." In response to Brisebois's letter, the secretary wrote that "the pagan element on the Caughnawaga Reserve have no status as such" but also said the Department had no objection if the band council wanted to allot land for a Longhouse burial ground. He even said that, with the permission of the Department, the council could use band funds to purchase land that might then be allotted for use as a Longhouse cemetery. Subsequently the band council rejected the request of the "Pagan element" by a vote of seven to three, and the Department approved its action.[54]

After the band council's decision, in April 1936 a "Mrs. J. K. Beauvais" wrote to the king of England to protest and seek his intercession in the matter. "Mrs. J. K. Beauvais" is almost certainly Agnes Beauvais, the wife of John Kanatasa Beauvais, who is identified in oral history accounts as an important figure in the Longhouse in the 1930s and in later documents in Indian Department files as a Longhouse chief. Mrs. Beauvais wrote as follows:

> We are not subject to the Indian Act laws. We have our own Indian rights and religions which was made by our dearest God, our Father in Heaven, who taught the Red Indians are His people and will have his own laws and religion. They do not want to servey the cemetery, we have none. So here we are Our Wampum Keeper that is our priest, and his wife are very sick, the wife is dying. Where shall we bury her when her death comes and what Church shall we

bring [her] to, we want to have the service in our own long house, and everything else. That is my wishes for you to grant us please. Please give notice to the Governor General of Ottawa of our wish. I am very sorry that I did not have a chance to send a word at the time of your father's funeral.[55]

Evidently there was no resolution of the matter, because in 1939 Longhouse members were still seeking land for a burial ground. In January of that year "Chief" Joe K. Martin wrote to the secretary of the Indian Department to demand a burial ground. The Longhouse members had a right to their own cemetery, he stated, because they were "people in the Six nation confederacy league." "We have our own religion aboriginal belief," he wrote. "There is all kinds of religion, and every religion has a grave yard ground. So we want to have one." In addition, his letter states that there were sixty-one Longhouse members at Kahnawà:ke.[56] An exchange of communications between Indian Department officials on Martin's demand concluded with this memorandum from the Kahnawà:ke Indian agent to the Department secretary:

> In this connection I wish to say that Martin apparently is a member of a certain sect of Indians who are calling themselves "Pagans" or members of the Long House Church. They have a place of meeting on the Reserve and they are reported to worship the Sun, the Moon and Stars. The members of this sect also state that they are the only Indians belonging to the Six Nations. Relative to their request for a grave yard I may say that they should make their request to the Council for a piece of land on the Commons.[57]

In March 1939 Martin wrote the provincial authorities a letter that not only takes up the cemetery issue but also includes a long discourse tying the Kahnawà:ke Longhouse to the Confederacy and the Kahnawà:ke, Kanehsatà:ke, and Ahkwesáhsne communities to the Kanien'kehá:ka Nation, argues the primacy of Confederacy and Kanien'kehá:ka sovereignty relative to the Canadian and American governments, and rejects the authority of the band council, the church, government officials, and enfranchised Indians within the reserve. I quote the letter at length to emphasize these points and present them in Martin's own words:

> We the Mohawks members of the long house one part of the six nations Confederate League [write] to you in [behalf] of the conditions on the said Caughnawaga Reservation the Confederate League and its democracy is the oldest democracy in the world which is known by the Indian nation and other nations [existing] outside the red race. Whereby under the laws customs and regulations of the Confederate League has a Sepreme Power just like any other nations and its courts.
>
> Therefore the white mans laws and rules and regulations has no power whatever inside of said Indian Territory and the enfranchised Indians cannot inforce such laws on said Reservation. The Confederate League has a treaty with the Federal Government which is known to be original treaty of 1784 which was ratified by the Confederate League the United States and the Eleven kings of the foreign. So therefore we wish to inform you we members of the Longhouse will not be ruled by the elected chiefs and priest local agents doctor or nurse for we are going under sovereignty and independency of Iroquois nation those that are your laws are the ones who protest against the people of the Longhouse for them to have a cemetery on the Reservation and it is your place to stop such people who have enfranchised themselves to the white mans laws and regulations they are outcast from the confederate League and have given under the Indian rights and the Indian Act does not concern the members of the Longhouse and said six nations Indians. So therefore we are going to have and own the cemetery whereby that we

shall act to purchase land which will be owned by members of the Longhouse and if the elected chiefs and members of the Indian Act hinder us from getting land we demand our rights and for you to stop such people and you have a right to do so for they are your people and have enfranchised according to themselves laws and regulations if not, we will [illegible] Uncle Sam and his troops. For we are wards of the Federal Government and the original treaty was made by the Confederate League and the United States which is known to be the only treaty and existants in the world. All other treatys that have been made before and after the treaty of 1784 are not inforest because they have not been ratified by any power of any foreign nation. So therefore this petition will give you reports of members of the Longhouse and what this petition wants and the three Reservations had declared to stand as a nation the Caughnawaga, St. Regis, Oka have made up their minds to join hands again for we have nothing to do whatever with the International line which divides Canada the United States. And there is no white living soul under the sun and heaven that has the power to divide the mohawks nation into two or three bodies that means those who are under the old democracy and treaty rights of 1784.

So when you see this petition we demand that shall acted upon if not we will take it to headquarters and you will have to do what we have wish so bare in mind it is up to you to do so. Govern General sent me a telegram on March the 13 1939 and he told me that I should communicated authorities of province of Quebec in regards the [illegible] cemetery. We have two cemeteries here one is a Catholic cemetery and one is at the United Church of Canada cemetery. So we want to have our own cemetery. The Six Nation Confederacy League. So don't throw this question to one another. From Indian Department to Province of Quebec. Please answer as soon as possible.[58]

A month later Martin, clearly frustrated by the inaction of the Indian Department, wrote again to provincial authorities. The letter concluded with this statement:

> I thought I would send in a report of all the names that believe aboriginal beliefs, Long-house is our meeting house. This petition passed through the meeting. Kindly send the report into the religion Office. And we have nothing to do with Dr. Harold W. McGill [the director of Indian affairs]. I think he takes charge of the elected Chiefs, you have right to see this matter. And you have to fixed it and have to answer. So kindly answer as soon as possible.[59]

Martin's list of the "members of the Long-house" included a total of twenty-five individuals. Among them are four chiefs. Besides Martin himself, who was thirty-nine years old, there was "Chief" Frank Diabo, age fifty-nine, "Chief" Joseph Jacobs, age seventy-two, and "Chief" Frank Beauvais, age twenty-seven. Among the other members identified are Joe Martin's father, the family of Frank "Casey" Nolan, and relatives of Joe McGregor. The group included sixteen males and nine females ranging from six months to seventy-nine years; eight members were twenty or younger, twelve were between twenty-one and fifty-nine, and five were sixty or older.

Less than one month after Martin's letter to provincial authorities, John K. Beauvais wrote to the governor general of Canada on behalf of the "Chiefs of the Long-House" requesting recognition of "an independent Indian religion." Beauvais identified himself as the "Head Chief" and, employing the hereditary titles of the clans, named the "Chiefs of the Longhouse" as Grand Chief Sawatis Tekarihoken (Turtle Clan), Head Chief Sawatis Sarenhowane (Wolf Clan), and Head Chief Sose Tehanakarine (Bear Clan). "Head Chief Sawatis Sarenhowane" probably refers to Beauvais himself. While the identity of the two other chiefs is not known, the names do not appear to refer to Joe K. Martin or the other "Head Chiefs" that Martin identified in his members list of 1939. Beauvais followed with a similar letter to the governor general in June 1939. Subsequently the secretary of the Indian Department directed the Indian agent in Kahnawà:ke to inform Beauvais that "it is not possible to meet [his] requests."[60]

A third letter from Beauvais, dated to April 1941, indicates that the burial ground issue persisted. In this letter Beauvais identified himself as a "Chief" and "The Wampum Keeper" and wrote as follows:

> We the Life-Chiefs and Clan-Mothers of the Long-house of Caughnawaga Indian Reservation known as the Mohawk branch of Six Nations Iroquois
> Do hereby wish to warn you. Now we choose the cemetery for the Long-house fifty feet wide one hundred feet long on the Common grounds on the eastern side of the Protestant cemetery.
> Furthermore we do wish you notify the Indian agent to measure the Land of exact size.

Importantly, Beauvais claimed that in this matter his group had the support of the mayor of the band council, Andrew Delisle, but the Indian Department appears to have taken no action in response to Beauvais's letter.[61] In response, in early January 1942 Chief Frank Bova, acting as secretary to the "Life-Chiefs," wrote to the Indian Department requesting an answer to the April 1941 letter and asked that their response be sent to "Head Chief" John K. Beauvais. The Department's only response was to direct the local Indian agent to inform Beauvais that any communications with the DIA should be made through the elected band council.[62]

The evolution of the burial ground issue during the late 1930s and early 1940s suggests several points about the growth of the Longhouse during this period. First, though participation in the Longhouse was increasing, its membership was still limited and probably included no more than a hundred or so people. This estimate is in line with Voget's estimate of about three hundred Longhouse members in 1950, after a period of increased defections from the Catholic Church in the mid-1940s.[63] Second, it appears that the divisions in the Longhouse recorded in oral history accounts took place during the late 1930s, and by about 1941 the split into three separate Longhouse groups had taken place. Third, though the burial ground issue was never resolved to the satisfaction of the Longhouse members, the issue demonstrates a split within the band council in which some members accepted and perhaps even tacitly supported the Longhouse and others remained opposed. Finally, the burial issue also demonstrates the continuing opposition of the Longhouse people to the Indian Act system and their desire to take control of their own affairs. Significantly, this claim of autonomy is framed within the context of an identification with the Confederacy and the legal basis of its sovereignty.

Conclusion

The Economy and Politics of Community Division
in Kahnawà:ke in the Late Nineteenth Century

B y the 1870s, decades of white encroachment had resulted
in a significant loss of land to the Kahnawà:ke reserve
and caused a severe scarcity of land and resources, exacerbated by considerable inequality in landownership among the
residents. These conditions led four of the Kahnawà:ke chiefs to
try to sell the reserve in 1875. Their plan had wide support in
the community, but it also met with some opposition and may
have contributed to local dissatisfaction with the chiefs and the
traditional council system. In general, the problems of land and
resource scarcity and inequalities of landownership were divisive, intensifying antagonism and violence toward whites and
métis who lived on the reserve and even encouraging some Kah-
nawakehró:non to try to separate from the band. The antagonism
toward whites and métis was widespread in the native community and strongest among those who owned little or no land. On
the other hand, the white and métis families did have supporters, or at least sympathizers, who tended to be more assimilated
large landowners and entrepreneurs. It is possible that that these
landowners and business owners benefited from the presence of
the whites and métis on the reserve and may even have shared
some economic interests with them.

The problems of land and resource scarcity and inequality and
the divisions within the Kahnawà:ke community to which they
contributed were evident in the Walbank survey and subdivision
of the reserve, which the Department of Indian Affairs initiated
in 1884 in an effort to expand private landownership and further
its goal of assimilation. In their role in the land claims process

that was part of the Walbank subdivision, the Kahnawà:ke chiefs had some success in limiting the number of people who could legitimately claim band membership and a right to land allotment. In general, however, the Indian Department's effort failed, and the problems of land and resource scarcity, unequal landownership, antagonism toward whites and métis, and division within the native community persisted. Further, these problems constituted an important dimension of a split that developed within the community during the 1870s and 1880s over its council of clan chiefs and the Indian Act system.

Some scholars have suggested that Kahnawà:ke's council was a "traditional" Kanien'kehá:ka council composed of nine chiefs, three each from the Turtle, Bear, and Wolf clans.[1] But this was clearly not the case. Kahnawà:ke's council consisted of seven chiefs, each representing one of seven clans within the community: the Ratiniáhton (Turtle), Rotiskeré:wakekó:wa (Great Bear), Rotiskeré:wakaká:ion (Old Bear), Rotikwáho (Wolf), Rotinehsí:io (Snipe), Rotihsennakéhte (Deer), and Rotineniothró:non (Rock) clans. The council of seven chiefs was based on traditional principles of equal participation and voice, but it reflected the unique composition and history of the Kahnawà:ke community. Each chief was selected by his clan and held his position for life; lacking a suitable candidate, a clan could select its chief from one of the other clans in the community. This council structure was probably instituted during the 1840s as a result of government action, was a modification of a preexisting system that was also based on the seven clans, and remained in place until the establishment of the band council system in 1889.

Blanchard has suggested that there was near total opposition to the Indian Act within Kahnawà:ke and that the band council system was established only through a forged petition and the deceit of a local missionary.[2] The evidence, however, shows that during the 1870s and 1880s the Kahnawà:ke community was divided in its backing for the traditional council of chiefs and that there was significant and persistent support for the Indian Act system. During this period a Reform faction emerged that opposed the clan chiefs and the council of chiefs system and repeatedly sought to apply the Indian Act to the reserve and establish an elective band council system. Under the elective system periodic elections would be held, a councillor's term of office would be limited to three years, and clans and clan chiefs would no longer have an official role in local government. Dissatisfaction with the character and leadership of the chiefs, frustration with the rigidity of the traditional system, and political ambition all played a role in the development of the Reform faction. Large landowners and business owners were an important part of the Reform faction, whose core was the "young warriors," more progressive and assimilated young men who sought to open up opportunities for political leadership within the community. Most prominent among them was Thomas Jocks (Atonwa Karatoton).

In response to the Reform effort to establish the elective system, a Conservative countermovement developed that opposed the Indian Act system and supported the sitting chiefs and Kahnawà:ke's "old rules"—the traditional system of seven clan chiefs serving for life. The Conservative countermovement drew much of its support from those with little or no land, who suffered most from land and resource scarcity and were most strongly opposed to the presence of whites and métis on the reserve. By the late 1870s some leaders of the Reform faction had gained positions on the traditional council, and thus the political divide within the community was reflected in the council itself. The Conservative position had wide support within the community, and Conservatives successfully countered several efforts by the Reform faction to abolish the community's old rules, but in time the young warriors and the Reform faction prevailed. In 1889 the Indian Advancement Act was applied to the reserve, Kahnawà:ke's old rules were abolished, and the elective band council system was established. While there was considerable support within Kahnawà:ke for the Indian Act system, the government's policy of assimilation and its decision to allow the council of chiefs to lapse into ineffectiveness were significant factors in these changes.

Kahnawà:ke's experience with the establishment of the Indian Act system represents a course different from that of other Rotinonhsiónni communities in Canada. One scenario was that at Ahkwesáhsne on the St. Regis reserve, where the band council system was instituted in 1888. According to Frisch, Indian Department officials used accusations of corruption and irresponsibility against the life chiefs at St. Regis as a pretext for abolishing the traditional council and instituted the band council system without much opposition. Very soon, however, dissatisfaction with the new system emerged and became a source of considerable conflict and even violence between traditionalists and government authorities.[3]

The experience at Grand River was quite different from that at Ahkwesáhsne and had some parallels to the situation in Kahnawà:ke. At Six Nations a traditional council of hereditary chiefs persisted through the 1870s and 1880s, but it was a fully functioning body and even expanded its responsibilities into areas typically associated with band councils under the Indian Act system. In the late 1880s a reform movement emerged and, as in Kahnawà:ke, young, more assimilated men were at its center. These "progressive warriors," as they became known, were welleducated men who owned large farms or were engaged in specialized trades, spoke English, gained seats on the traditional council, and occupied other positions of leadership and service within the reserve community. Like the young warriors at Kahnawà:ke, the progressive warriors at Six Nations were opposed to the conservative bent of the council, which they viewed as the result of the closed basis for council positions. They supported the application of the Indian Act and the establishment of a band council system. In 1890 they drafted a petition to this effect that was signed by about 20 percent of the adult males on the reserve, but the government took no action. In 1906 they formed the Indian Rights Association and continued their campaign to unseat the traditional chiefs, earning them the label "dehorners." Petitions for application of the Indian Act were made in 1907 and 1910, but again the government took no action. According to Weaver, government authorities, fearing local unrest if steps were taken toward a change, followed a policy of noninterference until after World War I. By 1920 many of the reformers had died or retired from the council, and the council itself had been taken over by more militant chiefs who sought to save the traditional system and, in addition, were actively claiming sovereignty. The leader of the council during this period was Levi General, also known as Deskahe. The federal government was concerned with the militancy of Deskahe and others on the council, and in September 1924 it imposed a band council system on the reserve. A month later the first band council elections were conducted under the supervision of the Royal Canadian Mounted Police.[4]

In Kahnawà:ke, as in Ahkwesáhsne, the elective system met with almost immediate resistance. The opposition came from Conservatives who sought to elect new chiefs to the traditional council in order to keep it functioning and prevent the application of the Indian Advancement Act. Their leader was Louis Jackson (Rowi Tawehiakenra), and their main objective was to increase the autonomy of Kahnawà:ke's band council, a goal they sought to achieve by working within the Indian Act system. Jackson and two supporters gained election to the first band council, as did Thomas Jocks and two other members of the Reform faction. As a result, in a pattern that would persist for several years, Kahnawà:ke's band council was split into two factions that mirrored the Conservative/Reform divide within the larger community. During Kahnawà:ke's first years under the Advancement Act, Jackson and his supporters frequently disrupted the operation of the band council and proved so difficult to deal with that the Indian Department sought ways to remove them. It failed owing in large measure to the high level of support for them within the community. In 1890 they sought greater autonomy for the band council through an amendment to the Advancement Act that would free Kahnawà:ke's council from the authority of the superintendent general of Indian affairs. The proposed amendment had support among Liberals in the government but was opposed by the Reform faction in Kahnawà:ke, the Indian Department, and the Conservative Party that controlled Parliament at the time, so it was never enacted. For the most part, those in Kahnawà:ke who opposed the amendment were large landowners, the base of the Reform faction, who feared the prospect of an unchecked council dominated by the likes of Jackson and others who owned little or no land, the base of the Conservative faction.

The Development of Traditionalist and Nationalist Impulses in Kahnawà:ke in the 1890s and the Early Twentieth Century

Alfred has argued that Kahnawà:ke accepted the elective band council system and eagerly supported it. As evidence for this assertion, he notes that over three hundred votes were cast in the first band council election.[5] Clearly, however, Kahnawà:ke's response to the band council system was more complicated. To begin with, it was the Indian Advancement Act, not the Indian Act, that was applied to Kahnawà:ke, and the distinction is important.[6] Compared with the Indian Act of 1876, the Advancement Act was a more aggressive attempt to assimilate native political institutions that aimed to replace traditional forms of government with a system modeled on the municipal governments of Euro-Canadian townships. In particular, it entailed establishing a council of representatives elected annually, with one of the representatives holding a position equivalent to "mayor." In addition, there were strict guidelines for ensuring proportional representation of the band members on a reserve. While the

Indian Act also aimed at political assimilation, it allowed bands greater flexibility in the type of elective system that would be established and the conditions under which elections would be conducted. For example, under the Indian Act chiefs would be elected every three years instead of annually, and the limitations on the number of chiefs and on representation were less rigid. In other words, compared with the Indian Act, the Advancement Act represented a much more dramatic and disruptive change for Kahnawà:ke's political institutions.

Government officials themselves recognized the Advancement Act as a more aggressive policy and intended it for those bands they considered more assimilated. This was reflected in the full title of the policy when it was enacted by Parliament in 1884 as the "Act for conferring certain privileges on the more advanced Bands of the Indians of Canada, with the view of training them for the exercise of municipal power." Not only did many bands reject the Advancement Act, but many were deemed by Indian Department officials to be unprepared for so dramatic a change in local government. In fact, most bands had the elective system applied to them under the Indian Act of 1876, and Kahnawà:ke was one of only a few to which the Advancement Act was applied. Another important aspect of the Advancement Act was an 1886 amendment that permitted a band to return to its former government if the municipal system was not successful. In the eyes of many Kahnawakehró:non in the 1890s, the new band council system clearly was not successful, but when they sought a return to the council of clan chiefs and reminded Indian Department officials of the conditions under which the Advancement Act was applied, their petitions were rejected and the band council system remained.[7]

While it is evident that some Kahnawakehró:non supported the Indian Act system and application of the Advancement Act, many others did not. This split within the community was evident through the 1870s and 1880s and persisted after 1889, and almost as soon as the band council system was established there were calls to revoke the Advancement Act and return to the traditional council of clan chiefs. Participation in the first band council election was not an indication of acceptance and support for the new system but reflected a decision by some of its Conservative opponents to resist and obstruct the system from within and use it to gain greater autonomy for the Kahnawà:ke council. For a time this strategy appears to have had considerable support within the community, but the "ill feeling" generated under the new system, particularly between the Conservative and Reform factions, eventually led many to abandon this position and support a more traditionalist goal that sought greater political autonomy *and* a return to the traditional council of clan chiefs.

The Traditionalist movement within Kahnawà:ke in the 1890s was accompanied by a strong identification with the Confederacy, with other Rotinonhsiónni communities in Canada that faced similar problems, and with the larger issue of Rotinonhsiónni sovereignty that began to emerge from their common concerns and actions. By the late 1890s this Traditionalist position had widespread support within the Kahnawà:ke community, and Louis Jackson and other former Conservatives who sought to work for greater autonomy within the Indian Act system were a small minority and politically isolated. Traditionalists persisted in their effort to restore the council of clan chiefs through the 1890s and into the early twentieth century, but they did not succeed.

During the second decade of the twentieth century many Kahnawakehró:non continued to struggle against the Indian Act system and the control the Indian Department exercised over their community. However, they also continued to struggle among themselves over these issues, as some in the community supported the government's policies and cooperated with the Indian Department in its efforts to institute and administer those policies. Continuing a pattern set in the 1890s in response to the application of the Indian Advancement Act, these struggles brought some Kahnawakehró:non, most notably Peter Delisle, into closer political interaction and alliance with Rotinonhsiónni in other communities in Canada and the United States who faced similar struggles and issues. Out of this closer political relationship emerged a stronger connection to the Confederacy and intimate engagement with the issues of political and cultural sovereignty with which it was becoming involved. Two pivotal events for Kahnawà:ke in this regard were the decision by the Department of Indian Affairs to establish an order of teaching nuns on the reserve in 1914–15 and, after that, the spread of a pan-Indian revitalization movement known as the Thunderwater Movement.

In important ways the political developments within Kahnawà:ke involving the Sisters of St. Anne and the Thunderwater Movement represented continuity with the pattern of political divisions within the community two decades earlier. At this time the community split into two factions—the "Antis," who opposed the Sisters of St. Anne and formed the basis of the Thunderwater Movement in the community, and the "Progressives," who supported the Department's plan to bring the nuns onto the reserve and opposed the Thunderwater Movement. As supporters of the Indian Act system, the Progressive faction represented continuity with the Reform faction of the 1890s. Led by Frank McDonald Jacobs, they worked with the Indian Department to implement its policies and undermine support for Chief Thunderwater and local participation in the Council of the Tribes. Theirs was a minority position among Kahnawakehró:non, but it prevailed because of the support of the Indian Department.

In its opposition to the nuns and the Department's plan for the schools in Kahnawà:ke, the Anti faction expressed a number of concerns; but echoing the Conservative and Traditionalist factions of the 1890s, at the core of its position was an emphasis on local political autonomy. Like the earlier Conservative faction but unlike the Traditionalist faction that grew out of it during the 1890s, Anti strategies included working within the Indian Act system to pursue the group's objectives. Perhaps because of the Traditionalists' earlier failure to realize one of their central objectives—the reestablishment of the traditional system of clan chiefs—Antis were discouraged from working entirely outside the band council system. Rather, they saw it as one viable means of attaining their objectives. As had been the case in the 1890s, the pursuit of local autonomy brought Antis into close association with similar factions in other Rotinonhsiónni communities, and their objective became tied to the larger issue of Rotinonhsiónni sovereignty. These concerns and efforts found expression in the Council of the Tribes, which provided a basis for organizing the interests and actions of Anti-like factions in several Rotinonhsiónni communities in Canada. Common local interests merged in the Council of the Tribes, and through the Thunderwater Movement Kahnawà:ke's identification with other Rotinonhsiónni communities was strengthened.

In "Hoax Nativism at Caughnawaga," Susan Koessler Postal argued that the Council of the Tribes attracted followers in Kahnawà:ke because the community had been experiencing a slow but steady disintegration of its native character and cultural elements, which she referred to as "cultural drift."[8] She claimed that the community was unable to reverse or redirect this process and thus was receptive to any organized effort that offered revitalization. Further, she argued that Kahnawakehró:non "awakened" by Chief Thunderwater initiated "nativist" impulses within Kahnawà:ke. This interpretation, however, does not consider other political and cultural developments taking place in the community before and during this time, nor does it take into account the essentially Rotinonhsiónni basis of the Thunderwater Movement.

The Thunderwater Movement was largely a Rotinonhsiónni social and political interest group that sought to address their shared political and cultural grievances, unify and revitalize the Confederacy, and gain recognition of Six Nations sovereignty. These goals and the evolution of this movement grew out of what many Rotinonhsiónni, including many Kahnawakehró:non, viewed as oppressive policies and conditions in their home communities and throughout Iroquoia. The Council of the Tribes served as a means for the expression and organization of political and cultural concerns, resistance to government policies, and nationalist aspirations that had been developing in Rotinonhsiónni communities for some time. In Kahnawà:ke these traditionalist and nationalist impulses had been growing for more than two decades as the community struggled to respond to the Indian Act system. Considering all of this, Postal's assertion that Chief Thunderwater and the Council of the Tribes "awakened" nativist impulses in Kahnawà:ke is not reasonable.

Also not reasonable is Postal's assertion that the "nativist" impulses expressed in the Thunderwater Movement were less than genuine because Thunderwater himself proved to be an imposter. While Thunderwater's exposure as a fraud must certainly have been disturbing to his followers in Kahnawà:ke, it is clear that it did not undermine the legitimacy of local Council leaders and supporters or the goals and aspirations they represented and worked for. Describing the Thunderwater Movement in Kahnawà:ke as "hoax" nativism denies the traditionalist and nationalist developments that had been taking place within the community for nearly two decades, developments that led to and were reinforced by stronger ties to the Confederacy and other Rotinonhsiónni communities.

Finally, Postal argued that the exposure of Chief Thunderwater as a fraud and the supposed rapid disintegration of his movement left the desire for cultural revitalization unfulfilled and thereby predisposed many Kahnawakehró:non to accept a more genuine revitalization in the form of the Longhouse in the 1920s. It is clear, however, that while the Council of the Tribes was short-lived, the cultural and political impulses in Kahnawà:ke and other Rotinonhsiónni communities that generated interest in it were already growing at the time of the Council and continued to be important after its demise. Given this more complete understanding of Kahnawà:ke's political and cultural course in the late nineteenth and early twentieth centuries, it is more reasonable to view Longhouse development in Kahnawà:ke in the 1920s as the outcome of traditionalist and nationalist impulses within the community and ties to Confederacy communities that had been emerging over nearly three decades.

The Reestablishment of the Longhouse in Kahnawà:ke
The 1920s saw numerous challenges to Rotinonhsiónni sovereignty, but it was also a dynamic period in the history of the Confederacy as Six Nations people rose to meet them. For Kahnawà:ke, these were years when its ties to the Confederacy were solidified and the Longhouse was reestablished. As a product of the internal and wider political developments that engaged the community during the second decade of the twentieth century, there was growing interest in the Longhouse within Kahnawà:ke. For the most part, this interest arose outside the existing Anti and Progressive factions, among people who had not been prominent in the Thunderwater Movement or the opposition to it. Those few who became caught up in reestablishing the Longhouse in the community included men and women and the young and the old. They included some, such as farmers, who spent most of their lives on the reserve and others, such as ironworkers and entertainers, who had traveled widely outside Kahnawà:ke and whose wider experience probably brought them into contact with Rotinonhsiónni familiar with the Longhouse traditions and contributed to their own activism. Most prominent among them were Dominic Two-Axe, Angus Montour (American Horse), and

Joseph Beauvais (Sose Kentaratiron). These Longhouse activists held meetings and ceremonies in their own homes and sought assistance from Longhouse groups in other Rotinonhsiónni communities. At this very early stage in its reestablishment, the Kahnawà:ke Longhouse was organized around three clans—the Turtle, Bear, and Wolf—not the seven clans that had been the basis of its traditional council of clan chiefs. Each clan had a clan mother and a chief, and though the chiefs used the hereditary titles of their clans, they were not condoled.

The arrest and trial of Kahnawà:ke ironworker Paul K. Diabo as an illegal alien in 1926 challenged Rotinonhsiónni claims to sovereignty, but their response strengthened the unity, identity, and influence of the Confederacy. In particular, the meetings of the Grand Councils in Kahnawà:ke in the summer of 1927 marked an important moment in the twentieth-century renaissance of the Confederacy and the efforts to promote Rotinonhsiónni cultural and political sovereignty, efforts that had been building for more than a decade. The impact of the Diabo case on the future of the Longhouse in Kahnawà:ke was also very important, but not in the seminal way some have claimed. Alfred, for example, claims that the Diabo case and the meeting of the Grand Councils in Kahnawà:ke in the summer of 1927 impressed upon Kahnawakehró:non a sense of the unity and power of the Confederacy and the value of membership in their own efforts to resist assimilation and government interference.[9] This view is shared by Jocks.[10] Both conclude that the energizing effect of these events stimulated interest in the Longhouse and then the organization of a following in the community. However, as this book has demonstrated, interest in the Longhouse had been growing in Kahnawà:ke since at least the early 1920s, and an organized Longhouse following was already established by the time of the Grand Council meetings in 1927. The effect of the Grand Councils was to reinforce and promote the growth of the Kahnawà:ke Longhouse by expanding local participation and building ties to other Rotinonhsiónni communities at a time when it faced considerable local opposition and, of course, the disapproval of government and religious authorities.

Alfred also argues that the meeting of the Grand Councils in Kahnawà:ke marked the end of the community's political isolation from the Confederacy.[11] He emphasizes the energizing and integrating developments of this period in the community's history by referring to it as Kahnawà:ke's "first traditional revival."[12] But if indeed there ever was such a complete break in Kahnawà:ke's ties to the Confederacy, these were being reforged at least a decade earlier with the Council of the Tribes and the Thunderwater Movement around the very issues of sovereignty, national identity, and cultural revival that were growing concerns of Rotinonhsiónni people in the 1920s and 1930s. In fact, it can be argued that these ties were being reestablished as far back as the 1890s, when Conservatives and Traditionalists who sought greater political autonomy and a return to traditional government found themselves engaged with Rotinonhsiónni from other communities who had similar political and cultural objectives. Kahnawakehró:non were central actors in those developments. In the early 1920s activists in Kahnawà:ke established ties with Longhouse groups in other Rotinonhsiónni communities in support of their efforts to organize a Longhouse in their own community. This successful early phase of Longhouse activism in Kahnawà:ke was undoubtedly influenced and facilitated by the political ties to and interactions with Confederacy communities that formed before and during the Thunderwater period. In short, traditionalist and nationalist impulses, which included the reestablishment of the Longhouse and ties to the Confederacy, had been developing in Kahnawà:ke for more than three decades before the events of the Diabo immigration case. One could even argue that these trends within Kahnawà:ke generated conditions that contributed to the very occurrence of the Diabo case. In its impact on Kahnawà:ke the importance of the Diabo immigration case is not as a beginning point for traditionalist and nationalist revival in the community but as a transition point that affirmed the changes of the previous decades and encouraged more open and radical political and cultural activism.

Participation in the Kahnawà:ke Longhouse expanded in the 1930s, reaching about one hundred members by the end of the decade.[13] With this growth, however, came strain. The Longhouse was fractured by leadership rivalries, resulting in its reorganization into two, then three Longhouse groups by the late 1930s or early 1940s. Despite these divisions, the Longhouses were united by the common goals of reviving traditional spirituality and government, promoting political sovereignty, resisting assimilation and the Indian Act system, and working with and through the Confederacy. At the local level, the common goals of Longhouse members encouraged them to work together to obtain land for a Longhouse burial ground. While there continued to be opposition to the Longhouse within the community, especially from Progressives who supported the Indian Act system, there was growing tolerance for the Longhouse and its members, particularly among those who were opposed the Indian Act system but had continued to work within it to advance Kahnawakehró:non and Rotinonhsiónni sovereignty.

Longhouse membership continued to expand during the 1940s. In large measure, this growth was a response to two events. According to Kennedy, Longhouse membership jumped dramatically in the spring of 1946 on rumors that the federal government planned to enfranchise all Kahnawakehró:non who were not members of the Longhouse.[14] Though the rumors proved to be false, the effect was to double the number of people participating in the Longhouse. The second significant event was the federal government's initiative to revise the Indian Act, discussions of which began in Kahnawà:ke in the summer of 1947. Some Kahnawakehró:non favored a more assimilationist revision of the Indian Act that would encourage deeper integration into Euro-Canadian society, while others favored a revision that provided for greater political and cultural autonomy. The intensity of the feeling this issue provoked and the split it created within the community expanded interest and participation in the Longhouse.[15] According to Voget, by 1950 Longhouse membership had reached three hundred.[16]

The pattern of division within the Kahnawà:ke Longhouse that developed during the 1930s persisted through the 1940s. According to Voget's observations of the Longhouse in 1950, three Longhouse groups existed at that time, the smallest composed of some of the original members of the 1920s Longhouse. This original Longhouse group had been declining in membership for some time, and the growth in Longhouse participation had been related mainly to the other two groups that had broken away during the 1930s. Of these two other Longhouse groups, the larger was affiliated with the Confederacy Council at Grand River and the other was affiliated with the Grand Council at Onondaga in New York. All three Longhouses operated within the "Handsome Lake" tradition. Continuing a pattern that started with Conservatives and Traditionalists in the 1890s and continued with Antis during the Thunderwater period, these three Longhouse groups sought greater political sovereignty, revocation of the Indian Act, and reestablishment of native political institutions. They opposed the band council system and did not participate in it. In addition, they asserted the importance of native descent, emphasized clan membership and exogamy, and opposed intermarriage with whites and white settlement on their reserve.[17]

The Political Landscape of Kahnawà:ke in the 1940s
Alfred has argued that a traditionalist revival in the 1920s generated the conditions out of which in the 1940s there emerged two political factions with opposing goals with respect to integration

into Euro-Canadian society. These included "modernists" who favored deeper integration and "traditionalists" who favored less integration and greater political and cultural autonomy. In his view, the "traditionalist" faction was composed of Longhouse members and some elected band councillors. The evidence presented in this book suggests some alternative views. First, the sort of division and factionalism Alfred sees developing in the 1940s was not new but was decades old. It began with the divide between Conservatives and Reformers in the 1870s and 1880s, persisted with the Conservative and Reform factions and the rise of a Traditionalist faction after the establishment of the band council system in the 1890s, and continued with Antis and Progressives during the Thunderwater period of 1915 to 1920.

Second, a more appropriate reading of Kahnawà:ke politics in the 1930s and 1940s would emphasize the existence of three factions rather than just two. One faction would be the "modernists" who supported the Indian Act system and favored further assimilation and integration into Euro-Canadian society. Described by Alfred as Kahnawakehró:non who were "entrepreneurs" and more educated and who sometimes lived off the reserve, they represented continuity with the Progressive faction of the Thunderwater period and the Reform faction of the 1890s. During the late 1940s they identified themselves as the "Intelligent Party" and supported a more assimilationist and integrationist revision of the Indian Act.[18] The Longhouse constituted a second faction. Its members rejected the Indian Act, assimilation, and Christianity, favored greater political and cultural autonomy, and sought to realize their goals through the support and influence of the Confederacy. The Longhouse represented a relatively new political element within the community, but one that grew out of the conditions of earlier factionalism and traditionalist and nationalist impulses that began in the 1890s. A third faction consisted of those within the band council and the community at large who shared many of the political and cultural concerns and objectives of the Longhouse but did not reject Christianity and sought to change the Indian Act system by working within it. They represent continuity with Peter J. Delisle and the Anti faction of the Thunderwater period. Voget used the term "marginal Christian" to describe this group, a label that does not adequately reflect its political objectives and strategy.[19] As band councillors, members of this faction supported the Longhouse (for example, in its effort to obtain land on the reserve for its own cemetery), and during the late 1940s the two factions joined to oppose a more assimilationist revision of the Indian Act and support a revision that would give Kahnawakehró:non, Rotinonhsiónni, and native people in general greater political and cultural autonomy.[20]

Alfred has conceptualized Kahnawà:ke's political and cultural revival in the twentieth century in terms of a model of "ethnonationalism" that emphasizes a shift in its pattern of community-state interaction, politics and governance, and collective identity. From the perspective of this model, in the nineteenth and early twentieth centuries Kahnawà:ke's interaction with the state was "cooptive," a relationship in which the community came to accept the colonial framework that had been imposed on it by the British and Canadian governments. Within this colonial framework, Kahnawà:ke is seen to occupy a politically subordinate status that undermined its autonomy and its political and cultural institutions and practices. In the 1920s dissatisfaction with these political and cultural consequences led Kahnawakehró:non to challenge the colonial framework, provoking government efforts to "moderate" Kahnawà:ke opposition and resistance and thereby a displacement of the "cooptive" relationship by a "confrontational" pattern of interaction between the native society and the state. Out of these conditions a consensus emerged among Kahnawakehró:non for a revival of native political and cultural principles, institutions, and practices and the establishment of new institutional framework that recognized and respected native cultural and political autonomy.[21]

The difficulty with this conceptualization is that it paints a picture of Kahnawà:ke with strokes too broad to reveal the fine grain of the community's internal political and cultural dynamics, its interaction with other communities, or its interaction with the state. More specifically, this conceptualization imagines the community as uniform in its perceptions, actions, and goals as these relate to community-state interaction, local political institutions, and identity. The model does not take account of the probability of internal political divisions and factionalism and that themselves may drive the growth of "ethno-nationalism."

As this book suggests, political consensus rarely if ever existed in Kahnawà:ke between 1870 and 1940. During the stage of its political development that Alfred describes as "cooptive" (roughly the nineteenth century to the mid-1920s), there was intense and persistent internal division and conflict over the desired community-state relationship and the goals to be pursued within it. During the 1870s, through their efforts to abandon Kahnawà:ke's "old rules" and apply the Indian Act system, some Kahnawakehró:non supported a "cooptive" interaction and a "colonial" political framework. However, by supporting the established system of clan chiefs and opposing application of the Indian Act, others resisted and pursued a more "confrontational" course, even as the state succeeded in applying its colonial framework to the reserve, as it did with the Indian Advancement Act and the band council system in 1889. "Cooptive" and "confrontational" patterns of interaction, institutions, and identity developed side by side in response to one another and thereby divided the community. In these circumstances, the establishment of the colonial apparatus on the Kahnawà:ke reserve in the form of the Indian Act system, and the band council system in particular, did not generate consensus around a "cooptive" relationship. Instead, it intensified the political division within the community and generated the first traditionalist and nationalist impulses in Kahnawà:ke in the modern era.

The political divisions, incipient nationalism, and efforts to revive traditional political institutions persisted within the Kahnawà:ke community and then intensified from 1915 to 1920. One product of this was Longhouse activism. Another result was wider opposition to the Indian Act system and greater support for political autonomy. Political sentiment within the community gradually shifted toward "confrontation," but the shift was never complete, consensus was never reached, and factionalism remained a central feature of Kahnawà:ke's political landscape. In Alfred's terms, the "cooptive" pattern persisted even in the 1930s and 1940s as the community entered the "confrontational" stage of its political development. In short, Alfred's model does not allow for Kahnawà:ke's internal complexities or for how these complexities drove political development within the community, particularly the growth of traditionalism and nationalism.

In the second half of the twentieth century the Kanien'kehá:ka community of Kahnawà:ke more fully reestablished its ties with the Rotinonhsiónni Confederacy and emerged as a central source of energy, activism, and controversy in the growth of Rotinonhsiónni traditionalism and nationalism. This pattern should be viewed as the continuation of a complex, century-long process in which the people of Kahnawà:ke, sometimes together and sometimes in opposition, have sought to respond to and shape the problems and circumstances they have been confronted with in their individual and collective lives. It is out of this process that their identity as Kahnawakehró:non, as Kanien'kehá:ka, and as Rotinonhsiónni has evolved, strengthened, and been made more secure.

Notes

Introduction

1. Until recently the community was more commonly referred to as "Caughnawaga," an anglicized version of its name in Kanien'kéha, the Mohawk language. In 1982 the community switched to the Kanien'kéha spelling and pronunciation, a practice that has gradually gained currency among scholars and the public at large. "Kahnawakehró:non" refers to the Kanien'kehá:ka, or Mohawks, of Kahnawà:ke. "Kanien'kehá:ka" is used here in preference to the more commonly employed "Mohawk." "Mohawk" derives from an anglicized version of an Algonquian term applied to the people that translates as "man-eaters" or "cannibal monsters." Kanien'kehá:ka ("people of the flint") is the name by which the people traditionally referred to themselves. For more information on the synonymy of "Mohawk" and "Kanien'kehá:ka," see Fenton and Tooker, "Mohawk," 478.

2. Reid, *Mohawk Territory*.

3. National Archives of Canada (hereafter NAC), *Records relating to Indian Affairs*, Record Group 10, vol. 2320, file 63812-2, Saro Tekaniatarekwen et al. to governor general, 4 December 1890.

4. NAC, vol. 6076, file 305-1G, pt. 1, Dr. A. O. Patton et al. to minister of the interior, 9 July 1914.

5. NAC, vol. 3178, file 449628-1, Sr. M. Joseph Edward to Duncan Scott, 21 May 1917.

6. Alfred, *Heeding the Voices of Our Ancestors*. I use the term "Longhouse" to refer to a group of Iroquois people who are organized formally on the basis of the Iroquois clan system, engage in traditional Iroquois spiritual beliefs and practices, and are recognized by and maintain ties with similar Longhouse groups. For further discussion of the use of the term with respect to the Kahnawà:ke community, see chapter 6.

7. Throughout this study I use the term "Rotinonhsiónni" to refer to the people commonly known as the Iroquois. In their lan-

guages, the Iroquois referred to themselves as the "people of the extended house," or "Rotinonhsiónni" in Kanien'kéha. The term "Haudenosaunee," derived from the Seneca, has gained common usage and has a similar reference.

8. Salisbury and Silverman, "Introduction: Factions and the Dialectic," 1–7, and Nicholas, "Factions: A Comparative Analysis," 23–29.

9. Fenton, "Factionalism in American Indian Society."

10. Berkhofer, "Faith and Factionalism among the Senecas"; Nicholas, "Factions: A Comparative Analysis," 21–61; and Frisch, "Factionalism, Pan-Indianism, Tribalism, and the Contemporary Political Behavior of the St. Regis Mohawks."

11. Salisbury and Silverman, "Introduction," 1–20.

12. Salisbury and Silverman, "Introduction," 6–7.

13. Campisi, "Fur Trade and Factionalism of the 18th Century Oneida Indians" and "Oneida Treaty Period, 1783–1838." See also Horsman, "Wisconsin Oneidas in the Preallotment Years."

14. Richter, "Iroquois versus Iroquois."

15. Shimony, "Conflict and Continuity."

1. "At the Rapids"

1. Brandão, *Your Fyre Shall Burn No More*, 19–30; Richter, *Ordeal of the Longhouse*, 30–49.

2. Dennis, *Cultivating a Landscape of Peace*, 76–115.

3. Brandão, *Your Fyre Shall Burn No More*, 43–44.

4. Richter, *Ordeal of the Longhouse*, 31 and 300n2; Fenton, *Great Law and the Longhouse*, 67–73; Tooker, "League of the Iroquois," 418–22; and Snow, *Iroquois*, 60.

5. Snow, *Iroquois*, 88. For an extended discussion of Rotinonhsiónni population estimates at this time and the problems in making such estimates, see Brandão, *Your Fyre Shall Burn No More*, 153–68.

6. Snow, *Iroquois*, 88–89. Brandão, *Your Fyre Shall Burn No More*, 161, suggests a lower estimate for this period of between 5,400 and 7,200.

7. Alfred, *Heeding the Voices of Our Ancestors*, 26–29; Fenton and Tooker, "Mohawk," 466–67.

8. Fenton, *Great Law and the Longhouse*, 244–45; Trelease, *Indian Affairs in Colonial New York*, 41, 46–51.

9. Alfred, *Heeding the Voices of Our Ancestors*, 29–31; Brandão, *Your Fyre Shall Burn No More*, 146; Snow, *Iroquois*, 89–90 and 94–100.

10. Brandão, *Your Fyre Shall Burn No More*, 5–18.

11. Others have advanced this thesis, but it has been most recently and fully developed by Brandão. For example, see Richter, *Ordeal of the Longhouse*, 65–71, and Snow, *Iroquois*, 110–11, 114–15, 127.

12. Richter, *Ordeal of the Longhouse*, 70–74.

13. Richter, *Ordeal of the Longhouse*, 102–3; Havard, *Great Peace of Montreal of 1701*, 38.

14. Brandão, *Your Fyre Shall Burn No More*, 113–16.

15. Brandão, *Your Fyre Shall Burn No More*, 113–15; Fenton, *Great Law and the Longhouse*, 251–53; Havard, *Great Peace of Montreal of 1701*, 50; Richter, *Ordeal of the Longhouse*, 102–4.

16. Snow, *Iroquois*, 117–19.

17. Fenton and Tooker, "Mohawk," 469–70; Havard, *Great Peace of Montreal of 1701*, 35–37; Richter, *Ordeal of the Longhouse*, 119–20; Green, "New People in an Age of War," 25–28.

18. Alfred, *Heeding the Voices of Our Ancestors*, 36–43; Fenton and Tooker, "Mohawk," 469–70; Green, "New People in an Age of War," 25–29 and 35–40; Richter, *Ordeal of the Longhouse*, 119–20, 124–28.

19. Alfred, *Heeding the Voices of Our Ancestors*, 39–40; Green, "New People in an Age of War," 30–31; Richter, *Ordeal of the Longhouse*, 119–20.

20. Fenton, *Great Law and the Longhouse*, 47, 50; Snow, *Iroquois*, 7, 24, 37, 70, 89, 124, 134, 162; Tooker, *Iroquois Ceremonial of Midwinter*, 7–37; Wallace, *Death and Rebirth of the Seneca*, 50–59.

21. Fenton, *Great Law and the Longhouse*, 41, 50; Richter, *Ordeal of the Longhouse*, 25–28; Snow, *Iroquois*, 7; Wallace, *Death and Rebirth of the Seneca*, 59–75.

22. Blanchard, " . . . To the Other Side of the Sky."

23. Axtell, "Were Indian Conversions *Bona Fide*?"

24. Green, "New People in an Age of War," 33–35.

25. Richter, *Ordeal of the Longhouse*, 125–28.

26. Jocks, "Relationship Structures in Longhouse Tradition at Kahnawà:ke," 193–94.

27. Alfred, *Heeding the Voices of Our Ancestors*, 37–38.

28. Green, "New People in an Age of War," 55–56.

29. Alfred, *Heeding the Voices of Our Ancestors*, 47–48; Brandão, *Your Fyre Shall Burn No More*, 117–22; Fenton and Tooker, "Mohawk," 470–71; Green, "New People in an Age of War," 62–72 and 94–103; Richter, *Ordeal of the Longhouse*, 133–61.

30. Havard, *Great Peace of Montreal of 1701*, 55–57; Richter, *Ordeal of the Longhouse*, 156–59, 167–69, 196–97.

31. Alfred, *Heeding the Voices of Our Ancestors*, 40–41; Fenton and Tooker, *Iroquois Ceremonial of Midwinter*, 470–71; Blanchard, *Kahnawake*.

32. Fenton, *Great Law and the Longhouse*, 316; Fenton and Tooker, "Mohawk," 470–71; Green, "New People in an Age of War," 68–168; Richter, *Ordeal of the Longhouse*, 184–86; Snow, *Iroquois*, 126–27.

33. Fenton and Tooker, "Mohawk," 471; Havard, *Great Peace of Montreal of 1701*, 91–141; Richter, *Ordeal of the Longhouse*, 214–80; Snow, *Iroquois*, 131–40; Calloway, *New Worlds for All*, 119–20.

34. Fenton and Tooker, "Mohawk," 473; Snow, *Iroquois*, 140.

35. Snow, *Iroquois*, 140 and 152.

36. Alfred, *Heeding the Voices of Our Ancestors*, 47; Blanchard, "Patterns of Tradition and Change," 181–92.

37. Snow, *Iroquois*, 141–45.

38. Alfred, *Heeding the Voices of Our Ancestors*, 151–52 and 195; Fenton and Tooker, "Mohawk," 471.

39. Green, "New People in an Age of War," 282–84.

40. Green, "New People in an Age of War," 283–98.

41. Alfred, *Heeding the Voices of Our Ancestors*, 43–47.

42. Alfred, *Heeding the Voices of Our Ancestors*, 49–50.

43. Calloway, 149; Fenton and Tooker, "Mohawk," 475–76; Tooker, "Iroquois since 1820," 452–53; Wallace, "Origins of the Longhouse Religion," 443–44.

44. Fenton and Tooker, "Mohawk," 478, Tooker, "Iroquois since 1820," 452–53; Wallace, "Origins of the Longhouse Religion," 445–48.

45. Devine, *Historic Caughnawaga*, 379–80. See also Blanchard, *Seven Generations*, 328–30.

46. Easterbrook and Aitken, *Canadian Economic History*, 293–319, 381–444; Marr and Paterson, *Canada: An Economic History*, 1–10; Norrie and Owram, *History of the Canadian Economy*, 169–200, 217–25.

47. Alfred, *Heeding the Voices of Our Ancestors*, 52–53; Devine, *Historic Caughnawaga*, 390–93.

48. Blanchard, *Seven Generations*, 277–80 and "Patterns of Tradition and Change," 277–78.

49. Blanchard, *Seven Generations*, 350; Devine, *Historic Caughnawaga*, 404–5.

2. "Serious Troubles"

1. Alfred, *Heeding the Voices of Our Ancestors*, 151–53.

2. Canada, House of Commons, *Official Report of the Debates of the House of Commons of the Dominion of Canada*, fourth session, sixth Parliament, 1709–10.

3. National Archives of Canada (hereafter NAC), *Records relating to Indian Affairs*, Record Group 10, vol. 1963, file 5209, "Caughnawaga Reserve—Petition from four chiefs requesting to sell the whole of the reserve at $25 per acre, 1875." See also NAC, vol. 1969, file 5348, "Caughnawaga Agency—J. E. Pinsonneault stating that the chiefs wish to sell all of their land at $25 per acre, 1875."

4. NAC, vol. 1880, file 1081, "Caughnawaga Reserve—Illegal sale of liquor, sale of wood by the Indians to white people, request to remove Narcisse Desparois from the reserve, 1873."

5. According to Alfred, the proposal to sell the reserve had the support of some 800 of the reserve's population of 1,557. See Alfred, *Heeding the Voices of Our Ancestors*, 53.

6. The referendum on the council of chiefs system is discussed in chapter 3.

7. NAC, vol. 2018, file 8268, Cherrier to minister of the interior, 5 February 1878.

8. NAC, vol. 2070, file 10556, "Caughnawaga Agency—Agent Georges Cherrier reports that Martin Sakoriatakwa illegally occupies land along the Primeau Road, 1878."

9. NAC, vols. 8969–72, "Walbank Reference Books—Caughnawaga. According to the survey, 26 percent (3,227 acres) was in cultivated land, 14 percent (1,679 acres) was in pasture, 43 percent (5,304 acres) was in bush, and 11 percent (1,380 acres) was in sugarbush. The remaining 6 percent (738 acres) consisted of land in the village and in roads and railways.

10. NAC, vol. 2920, file 188062, Indian Department memorandum to deputy minister, 24 April 1896.

11. Landownership in this instance refers to cultivated or hay land and land that was in pasture, bush, or sugarbush. It does not include the small privately owned house lots in the village.

12. The clan system and the council of chiefs in Kahnawà:ke are discussed in detail in chapter 3.

13. NAC, vols. 8968 and 8969, "Walbank Reference Books—Caughnawaga."

14. NAC, vol. 8972, schedules 525 and 505; NAC, vol. 8971, schedule 395; and NAC, vol. 1880, file 1081.

15. NAC, vol. 8971, schedules 283–87.

16. NAC, vol. 8969 and vol. 8971, schedules 287 and 302–4.

17. NAC, vol. 8970, schedule 116; NAC, vol. 8971, schedule 288; and NAC, vol. 8972, schedules 501 and 605.

18. NAC, vol. 8970, schedule 98; NAC, vol. 8971, schedule 404; NAC, vol. 8972, schedules 517 and 518; and NAC, vol. 1880, file 1081.

19. NAC, vol. 8971, schedules 471–76 and NAC, vol. 1880, file 1081.

20. NAC, vol. 1933, file 3408, Vankoughnet memorandum, 1 June 1874.

21. NAC, vol. 1880, file 1081, Chiefs of the Iroquois Indians of Sault St. Louis to Howe, n.d., and NAC, vol. 1933, file 3407, Vankoughnet memorandum, 1 June 1874.

22. NAC, vol. 1880, file 1081, DeBouchonvilles to Howe, 9 February 1873.

23. NAC, vol. 1933, file 3408, Pinsonneault to Laird, 30 June 1874.

24. NAC, vol. 2057, file 9702, Cherrier to minister of the interior, 28 April 1878.

25. NAC, vol. 2057, file 9702, Cherrier to minister of the interior, 1 May 1878.

26. NAC, vol. 2057, file 9702, Cherrier to minister of the interior, 1 May 1878.

27. NAC, vol. 2057, file 9702, Cherrier to minister of the interior, 13 May 1878.

28. NAC, vol. 2057, file 9702, Cherrier to Vankoughnet, 16 May 1878.

29. NAC, vol. 2057, file 9702, Giasson to Girouard, 28 April 1879.

30. NAC, vol. 2057, file 9702, Cherrier to minister of the interior, 14 May 1879.
31. NAC, vol. 2057, file 9702, 19 June 1879.
32. NAC, vol. 2057, file 9702, Giasson to MacDonald, 16 June 1879.
33. NAC, vol. 2057, file 9702, Bergeron to MacDonald, 18 September 1879.
34. NAC, vol. 2057, file 9702, Cherrier to minister of the interior, 18 September 1879.
35. NAC, vol. 2057, file 9702, Cherrier to minister of the interior, 2 April 1880.
36. NAC, vol. 2057, file 9702, Cherrier to minister of the interior, 15 May 1880.
37. NAC, vol. 2057, file 9702, Vankoughnet to minister of the interior, 22 June 1880, and Cherrier to superintendent general of Indian affairs, 20 July 1880.
38. NAC, vol. 2057, file 9702, Cherrier to minister of the interior, 14 May 1879.
39. NAC, vol. 2057, file 9702, Cherrier to minister of the interior, 19 June 1879.
40. NAC, vol. 2057, file 9702, Bergeron to McDonald, 25 June 1879.
41. The political developments in Kahnawà:ke relating to the council of chiefs and the Indian Act system are discussed in detail in chapter 3.
42. NAC, vol. 2069, file 10376, "Cherrier reporting on the opening of a school by a Miss Desparois, 1878."
43. At the time the Indian Department initiated its plan to survey, subdivide, and allot the land of the reserve, it did not specify the actual extent of the land contained within the reserve. It appears that what the Indian Department had in mind was the survey, subdivision, and allotment of the land that was owned by the band and those individuals who claimed to have membership in the band. The survey, which was completed in 1884, determined that this included 12,328 acres. Apparently not included in the survey was some 28,000 acres of land in the original seigneury that had passed to non-native hands through illegal land sales, rents, and occupations.
44. NAC, vol. 2113, file 21156, Dawes to Vankoughnet, 3 June 1880.

45. NAC, vol. 2113, file 21156, Vankoughnet to Dawes, 18 June 1880.

46. The survey of the reserve and of individual and tribal landhold-ings produced several reports detailing the specifics of land and landownership on the reserve. See NAC, vol. 8968, "Whole Book, Walbank's Reference—Caughnawaga, Index of Indian Holdings," and NAC, vol. 8969, "List of Lots Held by Indians."

47. NAC, vol. 2693, file 139964, pt. 1, Vankoughnet to Brosseau, 24 September 1884.

48. NAC, vol. 2693, file 139964, pt. 1, Walbank to Vankoughnet, 30 September 1884.

49. NAC, vol. 2693, file 139964, pt. 1, Walbank to Vankoughnet, 25 October and 5 November 1884, and NAC, Vankoughnet to Walbank, 31 October and 12 November 1884.

50. NAC, vol. 2693, file 139964, pt. 1, "Public Notice," 15 January 1885.

51. NAC, vol. 2693, file 139964, pt.1, "Subdivision of the Caughnawaga Reserve: Preliminary Report on Contested Claims," by W. McLea Walbank, July 1885.

52. The claims process conducted as part of the Walbank survey and subdivision of the Kahnawà:ke reserve is documented in several types of records contained in DIA files. These records include the completed interview schedules used in the claims process, a prelimi-nary report written by Walbank on the contested claims, a report by the deputy superintendent general concerning the DIA's final deter-mination on the contested claims, and a report of a meeting of the council of chiefs held to consider the Department's response. See NAC, vols. 8970–72, "Walbank's Reference Books—Caughnawaga," and NAC, vol. 2693, file 139964, pt. 1, "Subdivision of the Caugh-nawaga Reserve: Preliminary Report on Contested Claims," by W. McLea Walbank, July 1885; Vankoughnet to Brosseau, 26 January 1886; and Report on meeting of the council of chiefs, 9 February 1886.

  As part of the claims process, it was the practice to note the chiefs' objections to a particular claimant on that individual's completed in-terview schedule. Presumably Walbank, the Indian agent, or some other person working under their supervision made these notations. Agreement among the chiefs in their objection to an individual's claim to band membership is usually indicated by the statement "Objected to unanimously by the chiefs" or some similar phrasing, which is then usually followed by a brief statement concerning the reason or reasons for contesting the claim. Disagreement among the chiefs is usually indicated by stating which chiefs objected to the individual's claim and why, and which chiefs recognize the individual's membership in the band. A typical example is the following: "Chiefs Asennase & S[h]atekaienton do not recognize him as an Indian of this band, as his father belonged to another Band. Chiefs Jocks [Karatoton] and Sakoentineta recognize him as an Indian of this Band" (NAC, vol. 8970, schedule 7). Based on the notations made on the schedule for each of the claims contested by the chiefs, it is possible to examine chiefs' judgments on the claims and determine the criteria by which they recognized membership within the band.

53. To this group can be added the cases of a white man and a black woman whose claims were based on their adoption in infancy into native families in Kahnawà:ke. The chiefs did not dispute the fact of their adoptions, but neither did they recognize any rules by which adoptees could become recognized band members. Thus the claims of these two individuals also were unanimously contested because they were considered "non-Indian" and not members of the band.

54. This does not include five white men whose claims were denied but whose wives' claims were recognized.

55. In a study with some parallels to the discussion here, Hayden has examined the determination of band membership by the council of chiefs at Six Nations during the late nineteenth and early twentieth centuries. As in Kahnawà:ke, he found that the chiefs did not automatically apply government rules as they related to band membership and that their decisions reflected political interests and issues. Specifically, according to Hayden, the chiefs used their authority in determining band membership questions and the availability of two sets of rules for descent—the provisions of the Indian Act, with its emphasis on patrilineal descent, and the traditional rules of descent, which emphasized matrilineality—as a means to exercise social control on the reservation. See Hayden, "Patrilineal Determination of Band Membership at the Six Nations Reserve."

56. The aftermath of the claims process and the failure of the Walbank survey and subdivision are detailed in NAC, vol. 2693, file 139964, Department correspondence 4 March 1886 to 12 January 1894.

57. NAC, vol. 2920, file 188062, Memorandum to deputy minister, 24 April 1896.

3. "For Three Years" or "For Life"

1. Blanchard and Alfred both suggest that before the establishment of the band council system Kahnawà:ke's council was composed of nine chiefs, three each from the three Kanien'kehá:ka clans, the Turtle, Bear, and Wolf. As the following discussion argues, the archival record does not support this view. See Blanchard, "Patterns of Tradition and Change," 84–93 and 290, and Alfred, *Heeding the Voices of Our Ancestors*, 56–57.

2. National Archives of Canada (hereafter NAC), *Records relating to Indian Affairs*, Record Group 10, vol. 1953, file 4452, Caughnawaga Reserve—Request from the band to elect their chiefs every three years and to reduce the number of chiefs from 7 to 3, 1875; NAC, vol. 2018, file 8268, Caughnawaga Agency—Election of chiefs, 1877–78; and NAC, vol. 7921, file 32-5, pt. 1, Caughnawaga Agency—Elections of chiefs and councillors and a petition stating that the Indians of Caughnawaga would like their community made into a municipality, 1887–97.

3. "Election" is the term most frequently used in Indian Department and DIA documents to refer to the selection of chiefs for the council. I place the term in quotation marks to indicate this, but also to show that the term may not accurately reflect the process by which council chiefs were selected in Kahnawà:ke. This point is discussed in more detail below.

4. NAC, vol. 1953, file 4452, Pinsonneault to Laird, 17 February 1875, and de Lorimier to Vankoughnet, 10 March 1875.

5. NAC, vol. 2018, file 8268, Cherrier to minister of the interior, 8 June 1877 and 19 March 1878.

6. NAC, vol. 2018, file 8268, Cherrier to minister of the interior, 8 June 1877 and 19 March 1878. A variant of the Confederacy council name for the Onondaga meaning "name bearers" or "they carry the name," "Rotisennaketekowa" refers to the Deer clan of the

Onondaga. As used in this context the term "band" refers to what are commonly known as clans or lineages within clans. The identity and names of the Kahnawà:ke clans and the significance of the term "band" as used in the DIA files consulted in this research are discussed in more detail below.

7. NAC, vol. 2018, file 8268, minister of the interior to Cherrier, 18 June 1877.

8. Daugherty and Madill, *Indian Government under Indian Act Legislation*, 2–4.

9. NAC, vol. 2018, file 8268, Cherrier to minister of the interior, 4 February 1878.

10. NAC, vol. 2018, file 8268, Department to Cherrier, 18 February 1878.

11. NAC, vol. 2018, file 8268, Cherrier to minister of the interior, 26 February 1878.

12. NAC, vol. 2018, file 8268, minister of the interior to Cherrier, 26 February 1878.

13. Cherrier's letter to the minister of the interior concerning the "election" of the three new chiefs referred to the Rotiskerewakekowa as the "Tiskariwaki." See NAC, vol. 2018, file 8268, Cherrier to minister of the interior, 19 March 1878.

14. There is also evidence that on the council and within each clan there existed a level of subchiefs below the "grand" or "principal" chiefs. For example, in the mid-nineteenth century Doutre noted that subchiefs were an integral part of Kahnawà:ke's council. See Doutre, *Sauvages du Canada en 1852*, 204–5. I thank Gunther Michelson for alerting me to Doutre's work and for providing me with a translation of that part referred to in the text. In an 1875 affidavit concerning the council of chiefs, an individual identified himself as an "assistant chief," and in 1885, as part of a land claims process associated with the Walbank survey and subdivision of the reserve, another identified himself as a "subchief." See NAC, vol. 1953, file 4452, Affidavit of Louis Osahetakenra, 28 June 1875, and NAC, vol. 8970, Walbank's Reference Books—Caughnawaga, Interview Schedule 89.

15. Doutre, *Sauvages du Canada en 1852*, 204–5.

16. NAC, vol. 7921, file 32-5, pt. 1, Seven petitions to elect chiefs, January 13, 1889; see also Brosseau to superintendent general, January 16, 1889.

17. Fenton, "Northern Iroquoian Culture Patterns," 313. I am indebted to Roy Wright and Joe Deer for their assistance in helping me understand the significance of the "band" names.

18. Fenton, "Northern Iroquoian Culture Patterns," 313; Blau, Campisi, and Tooker, "Onondaga," 499; Campisi, "Oneida," 489–90.

19. NAC, vol. 1953, file 4452, de Lorimier to Vankoughnet, 10 March 1875.

20. NAC, vol. 717, "Minutes of proceedings of an inquiry held at Lachine to investigate complaints of Indians of Caughnawaga expressed in a petition to the governor-general of Canada, 27 February 1840." In Jennings, *Iroquois Indians*, reel 48. It is interesting that the report of the inquiry recommended that each band "select," rather than "elect," its chief. I thank Mattieu Sassoyan for alerting me to this document.

21. I am grateful to Gunther Michelson for providing me with the information about the inscription deposited in the cornerstone of the St. Francis Xavier Mission church. A reference to this inscription can be found in *Eastern Door* 4, no. 44 (1995): 13.

22. Fenton notes that a similar practice was followed among the Rotinonhsiónni in New York during the mid-eighteenth century. Once chiefs were condoled, or installed in office, they were presented to the state governor, who accepted and installed them. See Fenton, *Great Law and the Longhouse*, 408.

23. Fenton and Tooker, "Mohawk," 477.

24. Hamori-Torok, "Acculturation of the Mohawks of the Bay of Quinte," 132, and "Structures and Factions in Tyendinaga Politics," 32–33.

25. Frisch, "Revitalization, Nativism, and Tribalism among the St. Regis Mohawks," 77, 81, and 102–6.

26. Weaver, "Six Nations of the Grand River, Ontario."

27. Information on the land owned by Williams, Jocks, and Murray was obtained from the records of the Walbank survey and subdivision

of the reserve, which took place in 1884 and 1885. Landownership and the Walbank survey are discussed detail in chapter 3.

28. Daugherty and Madill, *Indian Government under Indian Act Legislation*, 2–3; Tobias, "Protection, Civilization, Assimilation," 131.

29. According to an Indian Department file, there were 366 adult males living on the reserve in 1874. Since the adult male population would not be expected to change significantly in just one year, I assume that this number was a good estimate of the adult male population in 1875. The suggestion that approximately 37 percent of the adult male population had signed the 1875 petition is based on this figure. See NAC, vol. 1937, file 3738, School and census returns for the Iroquois of Oka and Caughnawaga, 1874.

30. NAC, vol. 1953, file 4452, Affidavit A (translation), Louis Thotsenhowane, 16 March 1875; Affidavit B (translation), Watio Karhahienton, 16 March 1875; and Affidavit C (translation), David Ohonwanoron, 16 March 1875.

31. NAC, vol. 1953, file 4452, Thomas Karatoton to David Laird, 28 June 1875.

32. NAC, vol. 1953, file 4452, Karatoton to minister of the interior, 28 June 1875.

33. NAC, vol. 1976, file 5752, Caughnawaga Reserve—Petition to have Chief Francis Otonharishon removed from office owing to his poor conduct, 1875.

34. NAC, vol. 1858, file 97, Thomas Karatoton to Joseph Howe, 12 April 1872.

35. NAC, vol. 1953, file 4452, E. N. de Lorimier to Lawrence Vankoughnet, 10 March 1875.

36. The birth date and age could be determined for thirteen of the eighteen voters who favored limiting a chief's term of office to three years and for fifteen of the twenty-four voters who favored chiefs "for life."

37. NAC, vol. 2018, file 8268, Cherrier to minister of the interior, 5 February 1878.

38. In the 1878 referendum twenty-four favored chiefs "for life," and eighteen voted "for three years." Of those who voted in the referendum, twenty-nine could be identified in the records of the Wal-

bank survey; of these, sixteen voted "for life" and thirteen voted "for three years." Among those who voted "for life," 75 percent (twelve) were landowners, with an average landholding of 16.4 acres. All were small to middling landowners, owning between 1 and 50 acres. Among those who voted "for three years," 85 percent (eleven) were landowners, with an average landholding of 73.1 acres. In land owned, they ranged from 15 to 261 acres.

39. NAC, vol. 2018, file 8268, Georges Cherrier to minister of the interior, 19 March 1878.

40. NAC, vol. 2057, file 9706, Geo. E. Cherrier to minister of the interior, 29 April 1878.

41. NAC, vol. 2057, file 9706, Department to G. E. Cherrier, 9 May 1878.

42. NAC, vol. 2018, file 8268, Georges Cherrier to minister of the interior, 19 March 1878. Note that at about this time Chief Martin Sakoriatakwa had resigned his position; thus there would have been only three remaining chiefs on the council at the time of the 1878 elections.

43. This percentage is based on an estimated adult male population of 366, which was the number of adult males resident on the reserve in 1874. See note 29.

44. NAC, vol. 2101, file 18268, Petition that Chiefs Joseph Williams, Thomas Jocks, Peter Murray, and Thomas Rice may be deposed and another election held, January 1880.

45. NAC, vol. 2222, file 43633, Correspondence regarding the right of Thomas Rice to be chief after his two-year absence, 1883.

46. It is unclear why the position became vacant. Murray (Kaheroton) may have died, resigned, or been deposed. NAC, vol. 2298, file 59289, Correspondence regarding an investigation into the alleged conduct of Chief Thomas Rice, 1885.

47. Daugherty and Madill, *Indian Government under Indian Act Legislation*, 1–27; Tobias, "Protection, Civilization, Assimilation," 132–35.

48. Canada, House of Commons, *Official Report of the Debates of the House of Commons of the Dominion of Canada*, second session, sixth Parliament, 1888, 900.

49. Daugherty and Madill, *Indian Government under Indian Act Legislation*, 4.

50. Daugherty and Madill, *Indian Government under Indian Act Legislation*, 10–27.

51. The following discussion is based on documents in NAC, vol. 7921, file 32-5, pt. 1.

52. NAC, vol. 7921, file 32-5, pt. 1, Rowi Tawehiakenra et al. to the honorable superintendent general of Indian affairs, 21 January 1888.

53. Canada, House of Commons, *Official Report of the Debates of the House of Commons of the Dominion of Canada*, second session, sixth Parliament, 1888, 900.

54. NAC, vol. 7921, file 32-5, pt. 1, Department correspondence, 14 February to 28 April 1888.

55. NAC, vol. 7921, file 32-5, pt. 1, Brosseau to Vankoughnet, 9 January 1889.

56. NAC, vol. 7921, file 32-5, pt. 1, Petitions from the Rotinesiioh, Rotisenakete, Ratiniaten, Rotiskerewakekowa, Rotik8ho, Onkwaskerewake, and Rotineniotronon, 13 January 1889, and Brosseau to the superintendent general of Indian affairs, 16 January 1889.

4. *"An Ill-Feeling Which Is Yet Burning"*

1. National Archives of Canada (NAC), *Records relating to Indian Affairs*, Record Group 10, vol. 7921, file 32-5, pt. 1, Brosseau to Vankoughnet 10 April 1888.

2. For a description of the boundaries of the election districts, see NAC, vol. 7921, file 32-5, pt. 1, Walbank to Vankoughnet, 16 March 1888, and Order-in-Council, 5 March 1889.

3. As discussed in chapter 3, the subdivision and allotment process was not completed in the 1880s, and the problems of unequal access to and ownership of land persisted. In 1896 Indian Department officials were still dealing with these problems and again discussing the need for subdivision and allotment.

4. NAC, vol. 7921, file 32-5, pt. 1, Department correspondence, 24 February to 10 April 1888.

5. NAC, vol. 7921, file 32-5, pt. 1, Brosseau Report of Caughnawaga Elections, 26 March 1889. Generally, in this and subsequent chapters individuals are identified by their English names, which is how

they are typically identified in Indian Department records. Whenever possible, I have also included their names in Kanien'kéha.

6. NAC, vol. 7921, file 32-5, pt. 1, Department correspondence 26–28 March 1889.

7. NAC, vol. 7921, file 32-5, pt. 1, Basil Montour et al. to superintendent general, 1 April 1889.

8. Jackson, *Our Caughnawagas in Egypt*. See also Stacey, *Records of the Nile Voyageurs*.

9. NAC, vol. 8969, Reference Sheet 15; vol. 8970, schedule 116; vol. 8972, schedules 503 and 553.

10. NAC, vol. 7921, file 32-5, pt. 1, Brosseau to superintendent general, 8 April 1889, and Petition of Bourdeau et al. to superintendent general, 8 April 1889.

11. NAC, vol. 7921, file 32-5, pt. 1, Brosseau to superintendent general, 27 March 1889, and Department of Justice to Vankoughnet, 9 April 1889. The Indian Department file on the case of Jackson's election indicates that Jackson purchased his home from his brother-in-law shortly before the March elections.

12. NAC, vol. 7921, file 32-5, pt. 1, Bourdeau, Daillebout, and Jackson to superintendent general, 22 April 1889.

13. NAC, vol. 7921, file 32-5, pt. 1, Brosseau to superintendent general, Department correspondence 11 October to 25 November 1889, and Jackson to Vankoughnet, 21 October 1889.

14. Canada, Department of Indian Affairs, *Annual Report of the Department of Indian Affairs for the Year Ended 31st December 1889*, xxi.

15. NAC, vol. 7921, file 32-5, pt. 1, Department correspondence 25 October 1889 to 22 March 1890.

16. Daugherty and Madill, *Indian Government under Indian Act Legislation*, 21–22.

17. NAC, vol. 7921, file 32-5, pt. 1, Brosseau to Vankoughnet and superintendent general, 12, 22, and 29 March 1890.

18. The details of the debate, including those discussed and recorded here, are reported in the *Official Report of the Debates of the House of Commons of the Dominion of Canada*, fourth session, sixth Parliament, 1890, 2718–39.

19. Canada, House of Commons, *Official Report*, 1890, 2718.

20. Canada, House of Commons, *Official Report*, 1890, 2724.

21. Canada, House of Commons, *Official Report*, 1890, 2724,

22. Canada, House of Commons, *Official Report*, 1890, 2733–34.

23. Canada, House of Commons, *Official Report*, 1890, 2730.

24. Canada, House of Commons, *Official Report*, 1890, 2726–27.

25. NAC, vol. 7921, file 32-5, pt. 1, Sawatis Karoniaktatie et al. to superintendent general, 3 April 1890.

26. NAC, vol. 7921, file 32-5, pt. 1, Department correspondence 26 March to 29 April 1891.

27. NAC, vol. 7921, file 32-5, pt. 1, Department correspondence 3 February to 28 April 1892.

28. NAC, vol. 2320, file 63812-2, Petition of 4 December 1890.

29. Of the 121 petitioners who signed the 4 December 1890, petition, at least 41 percent (fifty) had signed the January 1888 petition and at least 47 percent (fifty-seven) had signed one of the January 1889 "clan" petitions.

30. NAC, vol. 2320, file 63812-2, Petition of the Iroquois women residing at Caughnawaga Village or Reserve, 8 December 1890.

31. It is interesting to note the reference in the petition to the "Seven Nations of Caughnawaga Indians." It is possible that this is a reference to the Seven Nations or Seven Fires of Canada, but it is more likely a reference to the seven clans of Kahnawà:ke. The petition is clearly referring to the people of Kahnawà:ke, not the peoples who composed the Seven Nations Confederacy in the eighteenth century, and it explicitly identifies Kahnawà:ke with the Rotinonhsiónni Confederacy, not the Seven Nations Confederacy.

32. NAC, vol. 2320, file 63812-2, Saro Tekaniatarekwen et al. to governor general, 4 December 1890.

33. NAC, vol. 2320, file 63812-2, Wati Kawennerate et al. to governor general, December 1890.

34. Blanchard, *Seven Generations*, 363–66, and Frisch, "Revitalization, Nativism, and Tribalism among the St. Regis Mohawks," 102–3.

35. Frisch, "Nativism, and Tribalism among the St. Regis Mohawks," 102–3.

36. NAC, vol. 2320, file 63812-2, "Convention of Indians," 26 August 1890.

37. Shimony, *Conservatism among the Iroquois at the Six Nations Reserve*, xxxiii–xxxiv, and Weaver, "Six Nations of the Grand River, Ontario," 531.

38. Weaver, "Six Nations of the Grand River, Ontario," 532.

39. Shimony, *Conservatism among the Iroquois at the Six Nations Reserve*, xxxiii–xxxiv; Snow, *Iroquois*, 183–84; and Tooker, "League of the Iroquois," 437.

40. Snow, *Iroquois*, 183.

41. NAC, vol. 2320, file 63812-2, Statement to the Honorable T. M. Daly, 22 September 1894.

42. NAC, vol. 2320, file 63812-2, Statement to superintendent general (translation), 22 September 1894.

43. NAC, vol. 2320, file 63812-2, Petition to the Honorable T. M. Daly, 22 September 1894.

44. NAC, vol. 2320, file 63812-2, Petition to the Honorable T. Mayne Daly, November 1894.

45. NAC, vol. 2320, file 63812-2, Brosseau to deputy superintendent general, 7 December 1894.

46. NAC, vol. 2320, file 63812-2, Stacey to superintendent general, 3 January 1895.

47. The superintendent-general had attended a similar meeting at Ahkwesáhsne a few months before in December 1894. See Frisch, "Revitalization, Nativism, and Tribalism among the St. Regis Mohawks," 104–5.

48. NAC, vol. 2320, file 63812-2, Summary of proceedings at a meeting of Caughnawaga Indians, 13 February 1895.

49. NAC, vol. 2320, file 63812-2, "Caughnawaga Heard From," *Montreal Daily Witness*, 7 March 1895.

50. NAC, vol. 2320, file 63812-2, Daly to governor general, 9 April 1894.

51. NAC, vol. 2320, file 63812-2, Reed to Brosseau, 10 April 1895. The deputy superintendent also directed the Indian agent for St. Regis to inform the Indians there of the Department's decision.

52. Canada, Department of Indian Affairs, *Annual Report of the Department of Indian Affairs for the Year Ended 30th June 1895*, 30.

53. NAC, vol. 2320, file 63812-2, Department correspondence 12 December 1896 to 2 February 1897.

54. NAC, vol. 7921, file 32-5, pt. 2, Department correspondence 6 July 1906 to 25 February 1907. After this, there were a number of other developments in the band council election system at Kahnawà:ke. In 1907 the band council sought to eliminate the residency requirement for voter eligibility, and in 1913 elections were moved to January of each year in an effort to increase voter participation. During this period the Kahnawà:ke council continued to consist of six councillors elected at large. In 1935 the reserve returned to a six-district election system, but with two councillors from each district, thereby increasing the size of the council to twelve. See NAC, vol. 7921, file 32-5, pt. 2, Department correspondence 20 June 1906 to 1 June 1934.

55. NAC, vol. 2320, file 63812-2, Letter to the superintendent general of Indian affairs, 2 November 1896.

56. Canada, Department of Indian Affairs, *Annual Report of the Department of Indian Affairs for the Year Ended 31st December 1897*, xxv.

57. NAC, vol. 2320, file 63812-2, Anen Katenre et al. to Sifton, 5 February 1897.

58. Canada, Department of Indian Affairs, *Annual Report of the Department of Indian Affairs for the Year Ended 30th June 1898*, 495.

59. NAC, vol. 2320, file 63812-2, Petition of six councillors to Sifton, 1 February 1901; Petition of Louis Satekaienton et al., 21 November 1901; and Petition of the chiefs and warriors of the Caughnawaga band to Sifton, 23 January 1905.

60. Devine, *Historic Caughnawaga*, 367–69.

61. Canada, Department of Indian Affairs, *Annual Report of the Department of Indian Affairs for 1880*.

62. The details about the Kahnawà:ke schools summarized here and the following paragraph are reported in a number of sources, including the 1899 annual report for the Department of Indian Affairs and NAC, vol. 6076, file 305-1B, pt. 1.

5. *"Must We Resign Ourselves to Such Injustice?"*

1. Canada, Department of Indian Affairs, *Annual Report of the Department of Indian Affairs for the Year Ended 31st December 1890; Annual Report of the Department of Indian Affairs for the Year Ended June 30,*

1900; and *Annual Report of the Department of Indian Affairs for the Year Ended March 31, 1910*.

2. Canada, *Annual Reports* for 1890, 1900, and 1910, and Johnston, *Indian School Days*.

3. A brief obituary from the *Catholic Record* included in an Indian Department file states that Delisle was sixty-four years old at the time of his death. The obituary is undated but is found in association with other documents in the file that are dated between February 1941 and January 1942. See NAC, vol. 7922, file 32-5, pt. 7, Delisle obituary, 5 April 1941.

4. NAC, vol. 6076, file 305-1B, pt. 1, Delisle to McLean, 10 September 1900.

5. Canada, *Annual Reports* of 1890, 1900, and 1910.

6. NAC, vol. 6076, file 305-1B, pt. 1, Department memoranda and correspondence 15–19 January 1903, Benson to deputy superintendent general, 19 August 1903, and Department correspondence 1 April 1902, 19 March 1908, and 24 October 1912; Canada, *Annual Report* for 1910.

7. Roy, *Sisters of Saint Anne*, 209–10; NAC, vol. 6076, file 305-1G, pt. 1, "Trouble Brewing," 25 August 1902; and Department correspondence December 1913 and February and March 1914.

8. Barman, Hebert, and McCaskill, "Legacy of the Past," 1–22, and Titley, *Narrow Vision*, 38–39 and 75–93.

9. Titley, *Narrow Vision*, 37–38.

10. NAC, vol. 6076, file 305-1G, pt. 1, Department correspondence 2 December 1913 to 10 March 1914, and Roy, *Sisters of Saint Anne*, 210.

11. NAC, vol. 6076, file 305-1G, pt. 1, General meeting of the Caughnawaga Reserve, 6 June 1914.

12. NAC, vol. 6076, file 305-1G, pt. 1, "Indians Protest against Nuns in Their Community," *Ottawa Free Press*, 8 July 1914.

13. NAC, vol. 6076, file 305-1G, pt. 1, Dr. A. O. Patton et al. to minister of the interior, 9 July 1914.

14. NAC, vol. 6076, file 305-1G, pt. 1, Mitchell Delorimier et al. to minister of the interior, 15 October 1914. Shortly after the petition was received in Ottawa, the head of the Schools Branch of the In-

dian Department informed Deputy Superintendent General Scott of the petition and reported to him that this and the earlier petition "appear to be the fine work of Delisle and Dr. Patton." See NAC, vol. 6076, file 305-1G, pt. 1, Benson to Scott, 19 October 1914.

15. NAC, vol. 6076, file 305-1G, pt. 1, Department correspondence 25 March to 7 July 1914; vol. 3178, file 449628-1, Department correspondence 10 September to 14 December 1914; and vol. 6075, file 305-1, pt. 1A, Department correspondence 19 December 1914.

16. NAC, vol. 3178, file 449628-1, Department correspondence 30 August 1916 and 1 and 18 September 1916.

17. NAC, vol. 3178, file 449628-1, Gras to Scott, 30 January 1917.

18. NAC, vol. 3178, file 449628-1, Sr. M. Joseph Edward to Scott, 26 February 1917.

19. NAC, vol. 3179, file 449628-2, Brosseau to Scott, 21 May 1917.

20. NAC, vol. 3179, file 449628-2, Sr. Marie Melanie to Scott, May 1917.

21. NAC, vol. 3179, file 449628-2, "Nuns Forced upon the Indians," Sentinel, 31 May 1917.

22. By 1915 band council elections had been moved from March to January in an effort to increase voter participation.

23. NAC, vol. 7921, file 32-5, pt. 3, Brosseau to McLean and Cooke to McLean, 18 January 1915.

24. Two of the votes cast in the 1917 referendum, representing 1 percent of the total cast, were judged "unacceptable" and not included in the final tally. NAC, vol. 3179, file 449628-2, Department correspondence 18–20 July 1917, and file 449628-2A, Department correspondence 24 March to 21 July 1920.

25. Little was known about the identity of Chief Thunderwater at the time he established the Council of the Tribes and began attracting followers in Canada. In 1919 the Indian Department determined that he was an imposter and sought to discredit the council by exposing him as a fraud. See below.

26. Postal, "Hoax Nativism at Caughnawaga," 268–69; Titley, Narrow Vision, 97.

27. Postal, "Hoax Nativism," 269.

28. Postal, "Hoax Nativism," 267–69; Titley, Narrow Vision, 97–98. Additional sources of information include copies of membership cer-

tificates in my possession and the correspondence of Chief Thunderwater included in the Indian Department's file on Thunderwater and the Council of the Tribes. For the latter, see NAC, vol. 3184, file 458168, pt. 1.

29. NAC, vol. 3184, file 458168, pt. 1, Brosseau to secretary, 21 August 1916; Postal, "Hoax Nativism," 268–71; and Titley, *Narrow Vision*, 100.

30. NAC, vol. 7921, file 32-5, pt. 3, Cook to secretary, 16 and 18 January 1916.

31. NAC, vol. 7921, file 32-5, pt. 3, Department correspondence, January 1917 and file 32-5, pt. 4, Department correspondence January 1919.

32. NAC, vol. 3179, file 449628-2, Gras to Scott, 20 July 1917.

33. For the details of the referendum, see NAC, vol. 3179, file 449628-2, McKenzie to Scott, 18 July 1917. For details on the lease of housing for the Sisters of St. Anne in Kahnawà:ke, see NAC, vol. 3179, files 449628-2A, -2B, and —2D.

34. NAC, vol. 3184, file 458168, pt. 1, Memorandum to Hon. Mr. Meighen, 23 April 1918.

35. During World War I the Society of American Indians became divided over the issue of integration and assimilation, but Parker continued to be a strong advocate for this position. See Hertzberg, "Nationality, Anthropology and Pan-Indianism in the Life of Arthur C. Parker (Seneca)."

36. NAC, vol. 3184, file 458168, pt. 1, Parker to Scott, 21 April 1915.

37. NAC, vol. 3184, file 458168, pt. 1, Brosseau to secretary, 21 August 1916, and Scott to deputy SGIA 21 September 1916.

38. NAC, vol. 3184, file 458168, pt. 1, Taillon to secretary, 1 September 1916.

39. NAC, vol. 3184, file 458168, pt. 1, Clarke to Sherwood, 11 September 1916.

40. NAC, vol. 3184, file 458168, pt. 1, superintendent of immigration to deputy superintendent general of Indian affairs, 21 September 1916.

41. NAC, vol. 3184, file 458168, pt. 1, Abraham to Scott, 2 October 1916.

42. NAC, vol. 3184, file 458168, pt. 1, Abraham to Scott, 2 October 1916.

43. NAC, vol. 3184, file 458168, pt. 1, *Citizen*, 26 October 1917.

44. NAC, vol. 3184, file 458168, pt. 1, An act to incorporate a council for the Indian tribes in Canada, 1918.
45. NAC, vol. 3184, file 458168, pt. 1. Memorandum to Hon. Mr. Meighen, 23 April 1918.
46. Quoted in "Indians Petition the Government," *Montreal Star*, 13 April 1918. See copy in NAC, vol. 3184, file 458168, pt. 1.
47. Titley, *Narrow Vision*, 97–100.
48. Frisch, "Revitalization, Nativism, and Tribalism among the St. Regis Mohawks," 103–8, and Blanchard, *Seven Generations*, 366–74.
49. "Indians Want to Have Ambassador," *Montreal Gazette*, 2 October 1918. Copy in NAC, vol. 3184, file 458168, pt.1.
50. "Indians Want to Have Ambassador."
51. "Indians Present at Trial of Chief," *Montreal Gazette*, 19 December 1919, and "Chief Delisle Was Acquitted," *Montreal Gazette*, 24 December 1919.
52. Postal, "Hoax Nativism," 271; Titley, *Narrow Vision*, 100; and "Elections of Chiefs and Councilors, 1919–1928," NAC, vol. 7921, file 32-5, pt. 4.

6. "We Have Our Own Rights and Religion"
1. Frideres, *Native Peoples in Canada*, 30; Ponting and Gibbins, *Out of Irrelevance*, 13; and Tobias, "Protection, Civilization, Assimilation," 137–38.
2. Snow, *Iroquois*, 194–95.
3. Snow, *Iroquois*, 191; Weaver, "Six Nations of the Grand River, Ontario," 533.
4. Mitchell, "Mohawks in High Steel," 20–21.
5. "Many Redmen Meet to Protest Alleged Wrongs," *Montreal Daily Star*, 25 February 1922.
6. The identities of Sose Kentaratiron and Wise Ariwakenra were established in part based on a series of newspaper articles in 1923 and 1924 that related to the involvement of Kentaratiron and American Horse in the alleged theft of a valuable wampum belt from the St. Francis Xavier Mission. Those events are discussed elsewhere in the chapter. The identities of Kentaratiron and Ariwakenra were also established based on oral histories provided by Stewart Beauvais, a

grandson of Kentaratiron; Mike Woodrow, a grandson of American Horse; and the "Elders" language group of the Kanien'kehaka Onkwawen:na Raotitiohkwa.

7. "Bitter Rivalry in Fight for Job as 'Tekarihoken' at Indian Reservation," *Montreal Daily Star*, 26 March 1923.

8. Mary Two-Axe, interview by Gerald F. Reid, Kahnawà:ke, 3 August 2000.

9. "Bitter Rivalry."

10. Ponting and Gibbins, *Out of Irrelevance*, 13; Frideres, *Native Peoples in Canada*, 30; and Tobias, "Protection, Civilization, Assimilation," 138.

11. As reported in the *Montreal Daily Star* in April 1922, the meeting to protest the government's new forced enfranchisement policy was to be attended by members of the "Seven Nations Indians." "Seven Nations Indians" could be understood as a reference to the Seven Indian Nations of Canada, the eighteenth-century confederation of French-allied Christian Rotinonhsiónni, Huron, and Algonquian communities, of which Kahnawà:ke was a member and the central fire. However, this may not be a correct interpretation. To begin with, the groups meeting are referred to as the "Seven Nations Indians" rather than the "Seven Indian Nations." The difference is subtle, but it may be important. The phrasing as written in the newspaper report recalls "Six Nations," which of course refers to the Rotinonhsiónni, or Six Nations Confederacy. In at least one documented instance, "Seven Nations" has been used to refer to a grouping of the Six Nations and the Hurons rather the eighteenth-century confederation. Further, the groups identified as involved in the meeting did not include any mention of Algonquian nations or communities. Finally, according to the newspaper article, the meeting was to be held at "Oswego," Ontario, which is almost certainly a reference to Oshwekon on the Six Nations reserve. If the meeting was to be one of the Seven Indian Nations of Canada, a more likely location would be Kahnawà:ke or one of the other constituent communities, such as Ahkwesáhsne (St. Regis), Kanehsatà:ke (Oka), St. Francis, or Lorette. Certainly, because the Grand River communities were composed mainly of descendants of Rotinonhsiónni who

had been allied with the English rather than the French, Oshwekon would have been an unlikely meeting place for the members of eighteenth-century confederation. On the other hand, Oshwekon would have been a likely meeting place if the protestors were mainly Rotinonhsiónni peoples. A traditional council of chiefs still functioned on the Six Nations reserve, and it had been active in efforts to maintain Rotinonhsiónni sovereignty. In addition, the reserve had been the site of numerous political rallies and meetings, such as those connected to the Thunderwater Movement, held to promote Rotinonhsiónni political interests and oppose government policies and interference. In short, it seems more likely that the "Seven Nations" meeting at "Oswego" was a meeting primarily of representatives from Rotinonhsiónni communities. See "Many Redmen Meet to Protest Alleged Wrongs."

12. "Many Redmen Meet to Protest Alleged Wrongs."
13. Joe Deer, interview by Gerald F. Reid, Kahnawà:ke, 20 October 1997, and Mike Woodrow, interview by Gerald F. Reid, Kahnawà:ke, 14 June 2001. Deer and Woodrow are both grandsons of Angus Montour. Mr. Woodrow preferred that his interview not be tape-recorded. His account presented here and elsewhere in this chapter is based on notes taken during and immediately after the interview.
14. Kennedy, "Unrest in the Religious Life of the Indians Living on the Caughnawaga Reserve during the Year 1946," 1–2.
15. Postal, "Hoax Nativism," 272.
16. Blau, Campisi, and Tooker, "Onondaga," 497, and Fenton, "Funeral of Tadodáho."
17. McFadden, *Wampum Belts*, 9.
18. NAC, vol. 6817, file 486-8-2, pt. 1, Correspondence regarding theft of wampum belts at the Caughnawaga Agency, 1923–32.
19. Joe Deer interview and Mike Woodrow interview.
20. "Eight Indians to Pledge for Chiefs," *Montreal Daily Star*, 17 September 1923. I am indebted to Fr. Cyr at the St. Francis Xavier mission for alerting me to this article and other related documents discussed below and providing me with copies.

21. Resolution 225, Council of the Indian Reserve of Caughnawaga, 19 October 1923.

22. "Paleface Judge Sends Two Indian Chiefs to Jail for Stealing Belt," *Montreal Daily Star*, 11 March 1924.

23. NAC, vol. 6817, file 486-8-2, pt. 1, W. Patterson to Fr. Lacouture, 7 March 1924.

24. "Indian Delegates Will Plead Case of Two Chiefs in Jail," *Montreal Daily Star*, 21 March 1924.

25. There is an interesting footnote to the wampum belt case of 1923–24. In 1926 one of the Jesuit missionaries in Kahnawà:ke attempted to sell the belt to the McCord Museum in Montreal. As noted, during the trial in 1923 the belt was valued at about $25,000, and the missionary was seeking to raise money for repairs to the mission buildings. He had not received permission from the band council or anyone else in Kahnawà:ke to sell the belt. An assistant curator at the museum informed Indian Affairs about the missionary's plan, and the deputy superintendent general interceded to prevent the sale of the belt. See NAC, vol. 6817, file 486–8-2, pt. 1, Department correspondence 26 December 1925 to 10 January 1927.

26. Mike Woodrow, interview by Gerald F. Reid, Kahnawà:ke, 14 June 2001, and Mary Two-Axe, interview by Gerald F. Reid, Kahnawà:ke, 3 August 2000.

27. NAC, vol. 6083, file 305-9, pt. 1, Grand Chief Dominic Tekarihoken to governor general, 30 April, 27 July, 3 August, and 17 August 1927.

28. Based on the March 1924 *Daily Star* article referred to above on the wampum theft case, Two-Axe may have been named to the position of chief of the Turtle clan at least by early 1924.

29. "Big Chiefs at Caughnawaga Pow-Wow," *Montreal Star*, 27 June 1927.

30. Woodrow interview, Two-Axe interview, and "Elders" Language Group interview by Gerald F. Reid, Kahnawà:ke, 10 January 2002.

31. A membership certificate dated 1916 identifies "Angus Deer" of the "Iroquois Nation, Mohawk Tribe, and Black Bear Clan, residing at Caughnawaga Reservation . . . aged 31 years" as belonging to the "Second Circle" of the Council of the Tribes. A copy of the

membership certificate, made available by Joe Deer of Kahnawà:ke, is in the author's possession.

32. Blanchard, "High Steel!" 45, and Snow, *Iroquois*, 193. For details about Diabo's status at the time of his arrest in Philadelphia, see "Transcript of Record," John B. McCandless v. U.S., ex rel. Paul Diabo, no. 3672, October term, 1927, 3–4.

33. *Federal Reporter* 18F (2d), 282, and *Federal Reporter* 25F (2d), 7. See also "Transcript of Record," John B. McCandless v. U.S., ex rel. Paul Diabo, no. 3672, October term, 1927, 3–4.

34. "Fight Indian's Exclusion," *New York Times*, 29 December 1926, 25; Blanchard, *Seven Generations*, 410–11; Blanchard, "High Steel!" 50; and Alfred, *Heeding the Voices of Our Ancestors*, 59.

35. Blanchard, "Patterns of Tradition and Change," 285–87 and Jocks, "Relationship Structures," 216.

36. *Montreal Gazette*, 28 June 1927; quoted in Blanchard, *Seven Generations*, 412–14.

37. "Iroquois Pow Wow Aims at Rebirth of Six Nations," *Montreal Gazette*, 28 June 1927, quoted in Jocks, "Relationship Structures," 214–15.

38. Blanchard, *Seven Generations*, 414–16.

39. Blanchard, *Seven Generations*, 416; Transcript of Record in the United States Court of Appeals for the Third Circuit, "John B. McCandless, Appellant v. United States of America, ex rel. Paul Diabo, Appellee," no. 3672, October term, 1927.

40. "Changing Religion," *Montreal Daily Star*, 11 November 1927.

41. Tooker, "League of the Iroquois," 424.

42. Dominic Two-Axe appears to have been a strong opponent of mandatory schooling. According to his daughter, Mary Two-Axe, she and her siblings started school later than most other children because her father refused to send them until after he was jailed by the local constable.

43. Blanchard, *Seven Generations*, 418.

44. Mike Woodrow, interview by Gerald F. Reid, Kahnawà:ke, 14 June 2001.

45. Frank "Casey" Nolan, interview by Gerald F. Reid, Kahnawà:ke, 27 October 1997 and 3 August 2000.

46. Mary Two-Axe, interview by Gerald F. Reid, Kahnawà:ke, 3 August 2000, and Joe McGregor, interview by Gerald F. Reid, Kahnawà:ke, 2 August 2000.

47. Stewart Beauvais, interviews by Gerald F. Reid, Kahnawà:ke, 2 August 2000 and 21 October 1997.

48. Nolan interviews and Two-Axe interview.

49. Beauvais interview.

50. Frank "Casey" Nolan, interview by Gerald F. Reid, 3 August 2000.

51. Joe McGregor, interview by Gerald F. Reid, 2 August 2000. Mr. McGregor did not consent to a recording of his interview but did permit me to take notes of our conversation. The account presented here is based on the notes recorded during and after that conversation.

52. Mike Woodrow, interview by Gerald F. Reid, Kahnawà:ke, 14 June 2001. Mr. Woodrow did not consent to a recording of his interview but did permit me to take notes of our conversation. The account presented here is based on the notes recorded during and after that conversation.

53. NAC, RG10, vol. 10261, file 373/36-7, "Petition of Indians Who Call Themselves 'Life-Chiefs and Clan-Mothers of the Longhouse of the Caughnawaga Reservation' for a Site for a 'Pagan' or 'Longhouse' Cemetery, 1935–1958."

54. NAC, vol. 10261, file 373/36-7, correspondence 11 March to 23 April 1936.

55. NAC, vol. 10261, file 373/36-7, Mrs. J. K. Beauvais to His Majesty King Edward VIII, 23 April 1935.

56. NAC, vol. 10261, file 373/36-7, Chief Joe K. Martin to F. T. Hooker, 21 January 1939.

57. NAC, vol. 10261, file 373/36-7, Indian Department correspondence 30 January to 15 February 1939, and Brisebois to MacInnes, 17 February 1939.

58. NAC, vol. 10261, file 373/36-7, Chief Joe K. Martin to F. F. Hecker, 16 March 1939.

59. NAC, vol. 10261, file 373/36-7, Chief Joe K. Martin to undersecretary of Province of Quebec, 24 April 1939.

60. NAC, vol. 10261, file 373/36-7, Chief John K. Beauvais to governor general, 11 May and 25 June 1939, and MacInnes to Brisebois, 5 July 1939.

61. NAC, vol. 10261, file 373/36-7, Chief J. K. Beauvais to H. W. McGill, 7 April 1941.

62. NAC, vol. 10261, file 373/36-7, Chief Frank Bova to H. W. McGill, 23 January 1942, and MacInnes to Brisebois, 28 January 1942.

63. Voget, "Acculturation at Caughnawaga," 223.

Conclusion

1. See Blanchard, "Patterns of Tradition and Change," 138, 179, 206–61, and 273–74, and Alfred, *Heeding the Voices of Our Ancestors*, 55–57.

2. Blanchard argues that the establishment of the band council system in Kahnawà:ke resulted from a fraudulent petition asking the governor general to apply the Indian Act. He suggests that the petition, signed with the names of twenty Kahnawakehró:non, may have been written by a local Jesuit missionary. See Blanchard, *Seven Generations*, 262–63.

3. Frisch, "Revitalization, Nativism, and Tribalism among the St. Regis Mohawks," 91, 102–8.

4. Weaver, "Six Nations of the Grand River, Ontario," 530–33.

5. Alfred, *Heeding the Voices of Our Ancestors*, 55–57.

6. Alfred states incorrectly that the Indian Act system was applied to Kahnawà:ke in 1890; in fact this occurred in 1889.

7. Daugherty and Madill, *Indian Government under Indian Act Legislation*, 1–27.

8. Postal, "Hoax Nativism at Caughnawaga," 266–81.

9. Alfred, *Heeding the Voices of Our Ancestors*, 59–60.

10. Jocks, "Relationship Structures in Longhouse Tradition at Kahnawà:ke," 214–16.

11. Alfred, *Heeding the Voices of Our Ancestors*, 59–60.

12. Alfred, *Heeding the Voices of Our Ancestors*, 58–60.

13. Kennedy suggests that Longhouse members in 1939 numbered about sixty. See Kennedy, "Unrest in the Religious Life of the Indians Living on the Caughnawaga Reserve during the Year 1946," 24.

14. Kennedy, "Unrest in the Religious Life of the Indians Living on the Caughnawaga Reserve during the Year 1946," 1–4.

15. Alfred, *Heeding the Voices of Our Ancestors*, 60–61.

16. Voget, "Acculturation at Caughnawaga," 223.

17. Voget, "Acculturation at Caughnawaga," 222–29.

18. Alfred, *Heeding the Voices of Our Ancestors*, 60–61.

19. Voget, "Acculturation at Caughnawaga," 221–23.

20. Phillips has some further discussion of these factions and their association in resistance to the Indian Act in the late 1940s and to the expropriation of land for the construction of the St. Lawrence Seaway during the 1950s. See Phillips, "Kahnawake Mohawks and the St. Lawrence Seaway."

21. Alfred, *Heeding the Voices of Our Ancestors*, 178–83.

Bibliography

Alfred, Gerald R. *Heeding the Voices of Our Ancestors: Kahnawake Mohawk Politics and the Rise of Native Nationalism.* Toronto: Oxford University Press, 1995.

Axtell, James. "Were Indian Conversions *Bona Fide?*" In *After Columbus: Essays in the Ethnohistory of Colonial North America*, 100–121. New York: Oxford University Press, 1988.

Barman, Jeanne, Yvonne Hebert, and Don McCaskill. "The Legacy of the Past: An Overview." In *Indian Education in Canada*, vol. 2, edited by Jean Barman, Yvonne Hebert, and Don McCaskill. Vancouver: University of British Columbia Press, 1986.

Berkhofer, Robert F. "Faith and Factionalism among the Senecas: Theory and Ethnohistory." *Ethnohistory* 12, no. 2 (1965): 99–112.

"Big Chiefs at Caughnawaga Pow-wow." *Montreal Daily Star*, 27 June 1927.

"Bitter Rivalry in Fight for Job as 'Tekarihoken' at Indian Reservation." *Montreal Daily Star*, 26 March 1923.

Blanchard, David. "High Steel!" Kahnawake Mohawk and the High Construction Trade." *Journal of Ethnic Studies* 11, no. 2 (1983): 41–60.

———. *Kahnawake: A Historical Sketch.* Historic Kahnawake Series no. 1. Kahnawake: Kanien'kehaka Raotitiohkwa Cultural Center, 1980.

———. "Patterns of Tradition and Change: The Re-creation of Iroquois Culture at Kahnawake." Ph.D. diss., University of Chicago, 1982.

———. *Seven Generations.* Kahnawake: Kahnawake Survival School, 1980.

———. " . . . To the Other Side of the Sky: Catholicism at Kahnawake, 1667–1700." *Anthropologica* 24 (1982): 77–102.

Blau, Harold, Jack Campisi, and Elizabeth Tooker. "Onondaga." In *Northeast*, vol. 15 of *Handbook of North American Indians*, edited by

Bruce Trigger, 491–99. Washington DC: Smithsonian Institution, 1978.

Brandão, José António. *Your Fyre Shall Burn No More: Iroquois Policy toward New France and Its Native Allies to 1701*. Lincoln: University of Nebraska Press, 1997.

Calloway, Colin G. *New Worlds for All: Indians, Europeans, and the Remaking of Early America*. Baltimore: Johns Hopkins University Press, 1997.

Campisi, Jack. "Fur Trade and Factionalism of the 18th Century Oneida Indians." In *Studies on Iroquoian Culture*, edited by Nancy Bonvillain, 37–46. Occasional Publications in Northeastern Anthropology, no. 6. Rindge NH: Department of Anthropology, Franklin Pierce College, 1980.

———. "Oneida." In *Northeast*, vol. 15 of *Handbook of North American Indians*, edited by Bruce Trigger, 481–90. Washington DC: Smithsonian Institution, 1978.

———. "The Oneida Treaty Period, 1783–1838." In *The Oneida Indian Experience: Two Perspectives*, edited by Jack Campisi and Laurence M. Hauptman, 48–64. Syracuse NY: Syracuse University Press, 1988.

Canada. Department of Indian Affairs. *Annual Report of the Department of Indian Affairs for the Year Ended 30th June 1879*. Ottawa: McLean, Rogers, 1880.

———. *Annual Report of the Department of Indian Affairs for 1880*. Ottawa: Maclean, Rogers, 1881.

———. *Annual Report of the Department of Indian Affairs for the Year Ended 31st December 1889*. Ottawa: Brown Chamberlain, 1890.

———. *Annual Report of the Department of Indian Affairs for the Year Ended 31st December 1890*. Ottawa: Brown Chamberlain, 1891.

———. *Annual Report of the Department of Indian Affairs for the Year Ended 30th June 1895*. Ottawa: S. F. Dawson, 1896.

———. *Annual Report of the Department of Indian Affairs for the Year Ended 31st December 1897*. Ottawa: S. F. Dawson, 1898.

———. *Annual Report of the Department of Indian Affairs for the Year Ended 30th June 1898*. Ottawa: S. F. Dawson, 1899.

————. *Annual Report of the Department of Indian Affairs for the Year Ended June 30, 1900*. Ottawa: S. F. Dawson, 1901.

————. *Annual Report of the Department of Indian Affairs for the Year Ended March 31, 1910*. Ottawa: C. H. Parmelee, 1910.

Canada. House of Commons. *Official Report of the Debates of the House of Commons of the Dominion of Canada*. Second session, sixth Parliament, 1888. Ottawa: McLean, Roger, 1888.

————. *Official Report of the Debates of the House of Commons of the Dominion of Canada*. Fourth session, sixth Parliament, 1708–10. Ottawa: Brown Chamberlain, 1890.

"Changing Religion." *Montreal Daily Star*, 11 November 1927.

Daugherty, Wayne, and Dennis Madill. *Indian Government under Indian Act Legislation, 1868–1951, Part I*. Ottawa: Department of Indian and Northern Affairs of Canada, 1980.

Dennis, Matthew. *Cultivating a Landscape of Peace: Iroquois-European Encounters in Seventeenth-Century America*. Ithaca NY: Cornell University Press, 1993.

Devine, E. J. *Historic Caughnawaga*. Montreal: Messenger Press, 1922.

Doutre, Joseph. *Les sauvages du Canada en 1852*. Montreal: Institut Canadien, 1855.

Easterbrook, W. T., and Hugh G. J. Aitken. *Canadian Economic History*. Toronto: University of Toronto Press, 1988.

"Eight Indians to Pledge for Chiefs." *Montreal Daily Star*, 17 September 1923.

Fenton, William N. "Factionalism in American Indian Society." *Actes du IV Congrès International des Sciences Anthropologiques et Ethnologiques* 2 (1955): 230–40.

————. "The Funeral of Tadodáho: Onondaga Today." In *An Iroquois Sourcebook*, vol. 1, *Political and Social Organization*, edited by Elisabeth Tooker. New York: Garland, 1985.

————. *The Great Law and the Longhouse: A Political History of the Iroquois Confederacy*. Norman: University of Oklahoma Press, 1998.

————. "Northern Iroquoian Culture Patterns." In *Northeast*, vol. 15 of *Handbook of North American Indians*, edited by Bruce Trigger, 296–321. Washington DC: Smithsonian Institution, 1978.

Fenton, William N., and Elizabeth Tooker. "Mohawk." In *Northeast*, vol. 15 of *Handbook of North American Indians*, edited by Bruce Trigger, 466–80.Washington DC: Smithsonian Institution, 1978.

"Fight Indian's Exclusion." *New York Times*, 29 December 1926.

Frideres, James S. *Native Peoples in Canada: Contemporary Conflicts*. Scarborough, Ont.: Prentice-Hall Canada, 1988.

Frisch, Jack Aaron. "Factionalism, Pan-Indianism, Tribalism, and the Contemporary Political Behavior of the St. Regis Mohawks." *Man in the Northeast* 2 (1971): 75–81.

———. "Revitalization, Nativism, and Tribalism among the St. Regis Mohawks." Ph.D. diss., Indiana University, 1971.

Green, Gretchen. "A New People in an Age of War: The Kahnawake Iroquois, 1667–1760." Ph.D. diss., College of William and Mary, 1991.

Hamori-Torok, Charles. "The Acculturation of the Mohawks of the Bay of Quinte." Ph.D. diss., University of Toronto, 1966.

———. "Structures and Factions in Tyendinaga Politics." *Anthropologica* 14, no. 1 (1972): 31–42.

Havard, Gilles. *The Great Peace of Montreal of 1701: French-Native Diplomacy in the Seventeenth Century*. Translated by Phyllis Aronoff and Howard Scott. Montreal: McGill-Queen's University Press, 2001.

Hayden, Robert. "The Patrilineal Determination of Band Membership at the Six Nations Reserve: A Case Study of Semi-autonomy and Cultural Change." In *Studies on Iroquoian Culture*, edited by Nancy Bonvillain, 27–36. Occasional Publications in Northeastern Anthropology, no. 6. Rindge NH: Department of Anthropology, Franklin Pierce College, 1980.

Hertzberg, Hazel Whitman. "Nationality, Anthropology and Pan-Indianism in the Life of Arthur C. Parker (Seneca)." *Proceedings of the American Philosophical Society* 123, no. 1 (1979): 47–72.

Horsman, Reginald. "The Wisconsin Oneidas in the Preallotment Years." In *The Oneida Indian Experience: Two Perspectives*, edited by Jack Campisi and Laurence M. Hauptman, 65–82. Syracuse NY: Syracuse University Press, 1988.

"Indian Delegates Will Plead Case of Two Chiefs in Jail." *Montreal Daily Star*, 21 March 1924.

"Iroquois Pow Wow Aims at Rebirth of Six Nations." *Montreal Gazette*, 28 June 1927.

Jackson, Louis. *Our Caughnawagas in Egypt*. Montreal: Drysdale, 1885.

Jennings, Francis. *Iroquois Indians: A Documentary History of the Diplomacy of the Six Nations and Their League*. Woodbridge CT: Research Publications, 1984. Microfilm.

Jocks, Christopher. "Relationship Structures in Longhouse Tradition at Kahnawà:ke." Ph.D. diss., University of California at Santa Barbara, 1994.

Johnston, Basil H. *Indian School Days*. Norman: University of Oklahoma Press, 1988.

Kennedy, J. Stanley. "Unrest in the Religious Life of the Indians Living on the Caughnawaga Reserve during the Year 1946." Undergraduate research paper, McGill University, 1947.

"Many Redmen Meet to Protest Alleged Wrongs." *Montreal Daily Star*, 25 February 1922.

Marr, William L., and Donald G. Paterson. *Canada: An Economic History*. Toronto: Gage, 1980.

McFadden, Ray. *Wampum Belts*. Onchiota NY: Six Nations Indian Museum, 1947.

Mitchell, Joseph. "The Mohawks in High Steel." In *Apologies to the Iroquois*, by Edmund Wilson, 1–36. Syracuse: Syracuse University Press 1991.

National Archives of Canada. *Records relating to Indian Affairs*. Record Group 10. Volume 1858, file 97.

———. Volume 1880, file 1081.

———. Volume 1933, file 3407.

———. Volume 1937, file 3738.

———. Volume 1953, file 4452.

———. Volume 1963, file 5209.

———. Volume 1969, file 5348.

———. Volume 1976, file 5752.

———. Volume 2018, file 8268.

———. Volume 2057, files 9702 and 9706.

———. Volume 2069, file 10376.

———. Volume 2070, file 10556.

———. Volume 2101, file 18268.

———. Volume 2113, file 21156.

———. Volume 2222, file 43633.

———. Volume 2298, file 59289.

———. Volume 2320, file 63812-2.

———. Volume 2693, file 139964, pt. 1.

———. Volume 2920, file 188062.

———. Volume 3178, file 449628-1.

———. Volume 3179, files 449628-1, 449628-2A, 449628-2B, 449629-2D.

———. Volume 3184, file 458168, pt. 1.

———. Volume 6075, file 305-1. pt. 1A.

———. Volume 6076, files 305-1B, pt. 1, 305–1G, pt. 1.

———. Volume 6083, file 305-9, pt. 1.

———. Volume 6817, file 486-8-2, pt. 1.

———. Volume 7921, files 32-5, pt. 1, and 32-5, pt. 4

———. Volumes 8968–72.

———. Volume 10261, file 373/36-7.

Nicholas, Ralph W. "Factions: A Comparative Analysis." In *Political Systems and the Distribution of Power*, edited by Michael Banton. ASA Monographs 2. New York: Frederick Praeger, 1965.

Norrie, Kenneth, and Douglas Owram. *A History of the Canadian Economy*. Toronto: Harcourt Brace, 1996.

"Paleface Judge Sends Two Indian Chiefs to Jail for Stealing Belt." *Montreal Daily Star*, 11 March 1924.

Phillips, Stephanie. "The Kahnawake Mohawks and the St. Lawrence Seaway." Master's thesis, McGill University, 2000.

Ponting, J. Rick, and Roger Gibbins. *Out of Irrelevance: A Socio-political Introduction to Indian Affairs in Canada*. Toronto: Butterworths, 1980.

Postal, Susan Koessler. "Hoax Nativism at Caughnawaga: A Control Case for the Theory of Revitalization." *Ethnology* 4, no. 3 (1965): 266–81.

Reid, Gerald F. *Mohawk Territory: A Cultural Geography*. Kahnawà:ke: Kahnawà:ke Survival School, 1981.

Richter, Daniel. "Iroquois versus Iroquois: Jesuit Missions and Christianity in Village Politics, 1642–1686." *Ethnohistory* 32, no. 1 (1985): 1–16.

———. *The Ordeal of the Longhouse: The Peoples of the Iroquois League in the Era of European Colonization*. Chapel Hill: University of North Carolina Press, 1992.

Roy, Louise. *The Sisters of Saint Anne: A Century of History*. Vol. 2. Lachine, Quebec: Éditions Sainte Anne, 1994.

Salisbury, Richard F., and Marilyn Silverman. "An Introduction: Factions and the Dialectic." In *A House Divided? Anthropological Studies of Factionalism*, edited by Richard F. Salisbury and Marilyn Silverman. Institute of Social and Economic Research, Memorial University of Newfoundland Social and Economic Papers no. 9. Toronto: University of Toronto Press, 1977.

Shimony, Annemarie Anrod. "Conflict and Continuity: An Analysis of an Iroquois Uprising." In *Extending the Rafters: Interdisciplinary Approaches to Iroquois Studies*, edited by Michael K. Foster, Jack Campisi, and Marianne Mithun. New York: State University of New York Press, 1984.

———. *Conservatism among the Iroquois at the Six Nations Reserve*. Syracuse NY: Syracuse University Press, 1994.

Snow, Dean R. *The Iroquois*. Cambridge MA: Blackwell, 1994.

Stacey, C. P., ed. *Records of the Nile Voyageurs, 1884–1885: The Canadian Voyageur Contingent in the Gordon Relief Expedition*. Toronto: Champlain Society, 1959.

Titley, E. Brian. *A Narrow Vision: Duncan Campbell Scott and the Administration of Indian Affairs in Canada*. Vancouver: University of British Columbia Press, 1992.

Tobias, John L. "Protection, Civilization, Assimilation: An Outline History of Canada's Indian Policy." In *Sweet Promises: A Reader on Indian-White Relations in Canada*, edited by J. R. Miller. Toronto: University of Toronto Press, 1991.

Tooker, Elizabeth. *The Iroquois Ceremonial of Midwinter*. Syracuse NY: Syracuse University Press, 1970.

―――. "Iroquois since 1820." In *Northeast*, vol. 15 of *Handbook of North American Indians*, edited by Bruce Trigger, 449–64. Washington DC: Smithsonian Institution, 1978.

―――. "The League of the Iroquois: Its History, Politics, and Ritual." In *Northeast*, vol. 15 of *Handbook of North American Indians*, edited by Bruce Trigger, 418–41. Washington DC: Smithsonian Institution, 1978.

Trelease, Allen W. *Indian Affairs in Colonial New York: The Seventeenth Century.* Lincoln: University of Nebraska Press, 1997.

Voget, Fred. "Acculturation at Caughnawaga: A Note on the Native-Modified Group." *American Anthropologist* 53, no. 2 (1951): 220–31.

Wallace, Anthony F. C. *The Death and Rebirth of the Seneca.* New York: Knopf, 1970.

―――. "Origins of the Longhouse Religion." In *Northeast*, vol. 15 of *Handbook of North American Indians*, edited by Bruce Trigger, 442–48. Washington DC: Smithsonian Institution, 1978.

Weaver, Sally M. "Six Nations of the Grand River, Ontario." In *Northeast*, vol. 15 of *Handbook of North American Indians*, edited by Bruce Trigger, 525–43. Washington DC: Smithsonian Institution, 1978.

Index

Abenakis, 12–13

acculturation, xvi, xxii. *See also* assimilation

Adirondack Mountains, 6

adoption, 4, 6, 14, 197n53

agriculture, 14–15, 17–19, 22–23

Ahkwesáhsne reserve: council of chiefs, 57; and Council of the Tribes, 123–24, 128; establishment of, 12; and Indian Act system, 171; traditionalist movement, 93–96. *See also* St. Regis reserve

Albany (formerly Fort Orange), 2, 5

alcohol: factionalism and, 8, 88; Indian Act system and, 85; land cessions and, 17; social problems and, 6

Alfred, Gerald, 181–85

Algonquians, 2, 12, 128, 189n1

Allegheny reserve, 17

allotments. *See* land ownership

American Horse. *See* Montour, Angus

American Revolution, 16, 57

Anenharontonkwas, Sose. *See* Foster, Joseph

Anglican church, 108

Anti faction: autonomy and sovereignty, 135; band council elections, 120–22; Sisters of St. Anne and, 116–17; Thunderwater Movement, 176, 179, 183–85. *See also* factionalism

Antoine, Herbert (Tewen Tawennaronkwas), 26–27

Ariwakenra, Wise. *See* Beauvais, Mitchell

Asennase, Atonwa. *See* Deer, Thomas

assimilation: autonomy and, 82–83; and forced enfranchisement, 134; and Handsome Lake movement, 17; and Indian Act system, 60, 182–83; and Indian Advancement Act, 69–74, 170–71, 174–75; Indian policies, xvi,

xxii, 20; Kahnawà:ke, 4, 14–15, 183–87; and land privatization, 36–38, 168–69; and schools, 110–11; and Society of American Indians, 124, 210n35

Atawenrate, Pierre, 56

Atewenniiostha, Teres, 25

Atonwa Karatoton. *See* Jocks, Thomas

autonomy, local: and assimilation, 82–83; and factionalism, 176–79; of the Longhouse, 167; and politics, 184–87; and schools, 112–17; and traditionalist movement, 90–94. *See also* nationalism and sovereignty

band council system: elections, 75–90, 120–22; factionalism, 50; and the Indian Act system, 82–90; Indian Advancement Act and, 69–74, 170–71; Kahnawà:ke reserve, 173–79, 207n54; Longhouse and, 158; objections to, 90–102, 217n2; Thunderwater Movement and, 122–23. *See also* Indian Advancement Act of 1884; tribal government

Bande du Loup. *See* Wolf clan

Bande la Tortue. *See* Turtle clan

band membership: and adoption, 197n53; allotments, 38–49, 169; defined, 55; and the Indian Act system, 197n55; and land claims, 196n52; and women, 28

bands. *See* clans

Bear clan: clan system and, 55–56, 138; council of chiefs, 169; Kahnawà:ke Longhouse, 146–47, 154–55, 165–66, 180; women and, 90–92

Beauvais, Frank, 157, 165

Beauvais, John K., 161, 165–66

Beauvais, Joseph (Sose Kentaratiron), 136–38, 140–45, 158, 180

cultural values: adoption of, 4–5; Council of the Tribes and, 177–78; Grand Council and, 181–85; Kahnawà:ke, 14–15; Longhouse and, 180; traditionalist movement and, xviii, 90–94. *See also* Longhouse; values, traditional

Daillebout, John T., 122, 128, 132
Daillebout, Michel, 76–81
Daly, T. Mayne, 95, 97–101
Dawes, James, 37
Dayodekane. *See* Newhouse, Seth
Deblois, Edouard, 25, 28–29, 44
Deer, Angus, 141
Deer, Thomas (Atonwa Asennase), 40–41, 46, 60
Deer clan, 52–53, 55–56, 138, 169
Deganawida ("the Peacemaker"), 1
Delisle, Andrew, 166
Delisle, Joseph (Sose Kentarontie), 53, 61
Delisle, Louis (Rowi Ronwarahare), 76–81
Delisle, Peter J.: and band council elections, 120–22; and Council of the Tribes, 128, 131–33; death of, 208n3; Longhouse and, 148; politics and, 176, 185; and Sisters of St. Anne, xvi–xvii, 108–18; teaching of, 105–6
DeLorimier, E. N., 63–64
DeLorimier family, 24, 27–28, 34–35, 44
Denonville expedition, 10–11
Deskahe. *See* General, Levi
Desparois, Narcisse (Narsis Karatoton), 26, 28, 36
Dewdney, Edgar, 77, 79, 83
Diabo, Frank, 159, 165
Diabo, Paul Kanento, 135, 147, 149–56, 180–82
disease epidemics, 2–5
dream interpretation, 7
drunkenness. *See* alcohol
Dutch alliances and trade, 2, 5

Eastman, Charles, 124
economic development, 18–19

education: factionalism and, 115–17; and Handsome Lake movement, 17; rejection of, 127, 155–56, 215n42; and Society of American Indians, 124. *See also* schools; Sisters of St. Anne
Edward, Sr. Mary Joseph, 114
employment, 18–20, 135
encroachment, white, 20–22, 50, 67–68, 168. *See also* land ownership
enfranchisement, 82–84, 163–64, 182, 212n11. *See also* Indian Act system
Enfranchisement Act of 1869, 60, 92

factionalism: Ahkwesáhsne, 12; alcohol and, 8; band council, 77–82, 87–88, 90–102; Christianity and, 5–6; and council of chiefs, 49, 169–70; defined, xix–xxi; and Longhouse, 134–35, 141–49, 158–60; Reform vs. Conservative, 68–69, 73, 89–90, 170–79, 184–87; schools and, 112–18; and Thunderwater Movement, 118–33; and traditionalist movement, 183–84
family longhouses, 14, 17. *See also* Longhouse
famine, European trade and, 5
farming. *See* agriculture
fasting, 7–8
Fort Niagra, 16
Fort Orange. *See* Albany
Foster, Joseph (Sose Anenharontonkwas), 73, 95
France, alliances and trade, 2–5, 10–14
fraud and corruption: in band council system, 169, 217n2; and Chief Thunderwater, 132, 178–79, 209n25, 209n28; Department of Indian Affairs, 171; land cessions and, 16–17
Frontenac expedition, 10
fur trade, 4–6, 15–18

Gage, Thomas, 14, 21, 146
gender roles, 17. *See also* women
General, Levi (Deskahe), 172

Seven Nations Confederacy, 90–102,
205n31
Shatekaienton, Rowi. *See* Beauvais,
Louis
Sifton, Clifford, 103
Sisters of St. Anne, xvi–xvii, 106, 110–
18, 146, 176
Six Nations Confederacy: and Council
of the Tribes, 119–21, 126–28; de-
fined, 212n11; and Grand Council,
93–96, 150–56, 183; Longhouse and,
162–63; and progressive warriors,
171; and sovereignty, 84, 91–92, 178
Six Nations reserve (formerly Grand
River reserve), 16–17, 57, 93–94, 171
Skaniatariio (Handsome Lake), 17. *See
also* Handsome Lake movement
Skatsienhati, Sosi. *See* Williams, Joseph
Sky, John, 98
Small Bears clan, 55
smallpox. *See* disease epidemics
Snipe clan, 55–56, 138, 169
Society of American Indians, 124,
210n35
Society of Jesus. *See* Jesuits
Sotienton, Wishe. *See* Bourdeau, Michel
sovereignty. *See* autonomy, local; nation-
alism and sovereignty
spiritual beliefs, religious conversion
and, 7–9
Stacey, Peter, 97–98
Standup, John, 98
St. Francis Xavier Mission, 56, 113, 118,
141–45, 148
St. Lawrence River, 2, 5–6, 10, 12, 160
St. Peter Claver's Indian Residential
School, 108
St. Regis reserve: establishment of, 12;
and Grand Council, 103, 151; and
Indian Act system, 127, 171; nationalism, 164; and Thunderwater Movement, 123–24. *See also* Ahkwesáhsne
reserve
subsistence economy, 14–15, 22–23
sweat lodges, 7

Taioroniote, Sose, 51, 58–59, 65

Tawehiakenra, Rowi. *See* Jackson, Louis
Tawennaronkwas, Tewen. *See* Antoine,
Herbert
Tehorakaron, Rowi, 60
Teka[r]ihoken, Dominic. *See* Two-Axe,
Dominic
Tekanasontie, Martin, 56
Tenihatie, Joseph, 56
Thaiaiake, Sawatis. *See* Rice, Baptiste
thanksgiving ceremonies, 7, 17, 155
Therrien, Alexander, 25
Thomas, George, 141, 143
Thunderwater Movement, 118–35, 147–
48, 177–79, 185, 212n11. *See also*
Council of the Tribes
Ticonderoga, 2
Tiohatekwen, Thomas, 56
Tionnontoguen, 2
Tonawanda reserve, 17
trade: assimilation and, 4. *See also* subsis-
tence economy
traditionalist movement, xviii, 90–102,
170–79, 183–84
treaty rights, 150
tribal government, 38–39, 50–69. *See
also* band council system; council of
chiefs; politics
tribes. *See* clans
Tsawennoseriio, Kateri, 25
Turtle clan: Chief Karaienton and, 137–
40; clan mother of, 149; clan system
and, 55–56; council of chiefs, 169;
and Kahnawà:ke Longhouse, 146–47,
165–66, 180
Tuscaroras, 57, 131
Two-Axe, Dominic ("Chief Tamenk"),
137–41, 150–51, 179, 215n42
Two-Axe, Martin, 138
Two-Axe, Mary, 138, 158
Tynedinaga reserve: band council system, 84; council of chiefs, 57; and
Council of the Tribes, 123, 127–28;
establishment of, 16; and traditionalist movement, 93

United Church of Canada, 164
U.S. government, 135, 149–56, 163–64

values, traditional, 6, 8–9. *See also* cultural values; Longhouse
Vankoughnet, Lawrence, 34–35, 37, 39, 69, 73–74
Vignaut, Olivier, 25
visions, Skaniatariio, 17

Walbank, William McLea, 39, 75
Walbank Survey, 36–49, 168–69, 193n9, 195n43, 196n52
wampum, 131, 141–45, 161, 166, 211n6, 214n25
warfare, 4, 6
War of 1812, 16–17, 150
white population. *See* Canadians; Métis
Wikwemikong Industrial School, 108
Williams, Joseph (Sose Skatsienhati), 53, 58–59, 64, 67–68

Williams, Peter, 109
Wolf clan: clan system and, 55–56, 138; and council of chiefs, 169; and Kahnawà:ke Longhouse, 146–47, 154–55, 165–66, 180
women: and allotment claims, 40–41, 44–45; appointment of chiefs by, 57; band council system and, 103; band membership of, 28; and division of labor, 9, 15; and land ownership, 87; and marriage and family, 14; and political power, 90–92, 197n55; school teachers, 109. *See also* clan mothers
Woodrow, Mike, 157, 160

"young warriors." *See* Progressive faction